## Praise for *Salsa, Soul, and Spirit*

"What a remarkable contribution *Salsa, Soul, and Spirit* makes to leaders in all three sectors as they work to provide rich diversity, powerful inclusion, and equal access within their organizations and in society."
—**Frances Hesselbein, CEO, Leader to Leader Institute, and former CEO, Girls Scouts of America**

"This wonderful book made me want to dance with joy. In Western society, we suffer from a loss of community and spirit because we're so disconnected. American Indian, Latino, and African American cultures have never forgotten that we need to be together and that diversity is not a problem but a blessing. May this book lead you to discover what we've been missing—each other."
—**Margaret J. Wheatley, author of *Leadership and the New Science***

"Juana Bordas has broken new ground. She has documented and analyzed the effective and unique practices of Latino, Black, and American Indian leaders. *Salsa, Soul, and Spirit* is a fascinating read that shows us the road to leadership for a multicultural America."
—**John Echohawk, Pawnee, Executive Director, Native American Rights Fund**

"To be relevant—let alone thrive—in the 21st century, business leaders need a new awareness of our interdependency and a new leadership paradigm like that described in *Salsa, Soul, and Spirit*."
—**Jack Lowe, Board Chair, TDIndustries**

"The politics of inclusion is not just some politically correct idea. It's essential to the adaptability of any organization or society that must rely on new ideas and synthesis in a changing world. Juana Bordas has given us a firsthand inspirational primer, full of wisdom and insight, for anyone practicing leadership that challenges people to thrive anew."
—**Dr. Ron Heifetz, cofounder, Center for Public Leadership, John F. Kennedy School of Government, Harvard University**

"*Salsa, Soul, and Spirit* is a refreshing and inspiring vision of a new form of leadership for the 21st century. Bordas captures the unique but successful models of leadership developed by racial and ethnic minorities. Our nation would greatly benefit from leaders who embody these traits."
—**Honorable Federico Peña, former Mayor of Denver, former US Secretary of Transportation, and former US Secretary of Energy**

"Frequently, people say it is too hard to have both excellence and diversity. *Salsa, Soul, and Spirit* shows not only why it doesn't have to be that hard but also why it is critically important at this moment in history to develop organizational leadership that is both excellent and diverse. People need to read this book."
—**John Hickenlooper, Governor of Colorado**

"Bordas has taken the philosophy and spirit as espoused by Martin Luther King Jr. and other civil rights leaders and fashioned leadership principles that further the dream of an equal and just society."
—**Ambassador Andrew Young, civil rights leader, former Mayor of Atlanta, and former Congressman from Georgia**

"*Salsa, Soul, and Spirit* is a compelling, vibrant, and engaging exploration of the deep roots of multicultural leadership. It will challenge your view on leadership. Bordas's personal journey to integrate her Hispanic culture into her own leadership witnesses the great benefits of blending cultures rather than assimilating them."

—**John Izzo, author of *The Five Secrets You Must Discover Before You Die* and *Stepping Up***

"Reflecting the traditions of Black, Latino, and Native American cultures, *Salsa Soul, and Spirit* fashions a leadership model based on community, generosity, and a commitment to work for the common good. These proven leadership practices that sustained communities of color for generations are a source of strength, hope, and wisdom that will guide us through the turbulence of the 21st century."

—**LaDonna Harris, Comanche, President and founder, Americans for Indian Opportunity**

"*Salsa, Soul, and Spirit* fills a necessary void in the study of leadership with its integration of the common elements of spiritual and programmatic leadership that are typical of minority approaches to social problems and also build the basis for coalition politics."

—**Dr. Ronald W. Walters, coauthor of *African American Leadership***

"It is empowerment time in America—a time to live up to the basic values of equality and justice. Empowerment means closing the racial divide and opening the doors to leadership at all levels, so it represents our great and dynamic diversity. *Salsa, Soul, and Spirit* is a road map to guide us on this journey and invites us to work together to create an America that benefits from the beauty and potential of all its people."

—**Marc H. Morial, President and CEO, National Urban League, and former Mayor of New Orleans**

"Juana Bordas clearly understands that building an inclusive America requires leadership forms that respect and resonate with our growing diversity. *Salsa, Soul, and Spirit* provides an excellent road map that can transform and energize leadership into an authentic multicultural form that is truly representative of our great nation and its unifying ideals."

—**Honorable Anna Escobedo Cabral, former Treasurer of the United States**

"The new America is a web of myriad cultures and traditions. In this new era, we must enlarge our vision of what it means to be an American as well as embrace our identity as world citizens. This inspirational book can guide us to this multicultural future and sets forth a visionary leadership model that is founded on both our democratic traditions and our great diversity."

—**Dr. James Joseph, former Ambassador to South Africa and author of *Remaking America***

"Juana Bordas is one of our nation's most effective facilitators of leadership development. *Salsa, Soul, and Spirit* brings together her years of experience and insights. Her book is unique because it offers principles for leading in an increasingly diverse America. A must-read for those interested in becoming leaders of our multicultural society."

—**Raul Yzaguirre, President Emeritus, National Council of La Raza**

# Salsa, Soul, and Spirit

# Salsa, Soul, and Spirit

## Leadership
## for a
## Multicultural Age

**Second Edition**

**Juana Bordas**

**BK**

Berrett–Koehler Publishers, Inc.
San Francisco
*a BK Business book*

Berrett-Koehler Publishers, Inc.
235 Montgomery Street, Suite 650
San Francisco, CA 94104-2916
Tel: (415) 288-0260
Fax: (415) 362-2512
www.bkconnection.com

**Ordering Information**

**Quantity sales.** Special discounts are available on quantity purchases by corporations, associations, and others. For details, contact the "Special Sales Department" at the Berrett-Koehler address above.

**Individual sales.** Berrett-Koehler publications are available through most bookstores. They can also be ordered directly from Berrett-Koehler: Tel: (800) 929-2929; Fax: (802) 864-7626; www.bkconnection.com

**Orders for college textbook/course adoption use.** Please contact Berrett-Koehler: Tel: (800) 929-2929; Fax: (802) 864-7626.

**Orders by U.S. trade bookstores and wholesalers.** Please contact Ingram Publisher Services, Tel: (800) 509-4887; Fax: (800) 838-1149; E-mail: customer.service@ingrampublisherservices.com; or visit www.ingrampublisherservices.com/Ordering for details about electronic ordering.

Berrett-Koehler and the BK logo are registered trademarks of Berrett-Koehler Publishers, Inc.

Printed in the United States of America

Berrett-Koehler books are printed on long-lasting acid-free paper. When it is available, we choose paper that has been manufactured by environmentally responsible processes. These may include using trees grown in sustainable forests, incorporating recycled paper, minimizing chlorine in bleaching, or recycling the energy produced at the paper mill.

Library of Congress Cataloging-in-Publication Data

Bordas, Juana.
Salsa, soul, and spirit : leadership for a multicultural age / Juana Bordas.
— 2nd ed.
p. cm.
Includes bibliographical references and index.
ISBN 978-1-60994-117-8 (pbk.)
1. Community leadership--United States. 2. African Americans.
3. Hispanic Americans. 4. Indians of North America. I. Title.
HM781.B67 2012
305.800973--dc23
2011053361

Second Edition
17 16 15 14 13           10 9 8 7 6 5 4 3 2

cover designer: Barbara Haines
interior design and composition: Seventeenth Street Studios
developmental editor: Kristi Hein
copyeditor: Laurie Dunne
indexer: Richard Evans

*Para mi Madre, mis Hermanas, mis Hijas, y mis Comadres*

You have been the cradle and the substance of my life.

*For the Millennial Generation, born at the dawn of this century:*

You will lead us back home.

# Contents

# Preface

T HE RAPIDLY INCREASING cultural and racial diversity of the U.S. workforce, consumer base, and citizenry is challenging leadership to better reflect the values and worldviews inherent in our multicultural society. As the world becomes flatter and globalization creates a world village, leaders must have the cultural flexibility and adaptability to inspire and guide people who represent the whole rainbow of humanity. The central purpose of *Salsa, Soul, and Spirit: Leadership for a Multicultural Age* is to put forth a leadership model, based on the practices and principles of communities of color, that will move us toward a more pluralistic and equitable society. Authentic diversity will be realized only when the voices, values, and contributions of all Americans are integrated into mainstream leadership.

Since the first edition of this book, a number of transformative events have made multicultural leadership even more crucial. First, the historic election of Barack Obama was not just the symbolic fulfillment of the civil rights dream; it meant that the country's highest leadership position was no longer reserved only for White men. Second, the 2010 Census provided an updated snapshot of the American people and documented that within the next four decades minorities will constitute over 50 percent of the population. Third, the new demographics predict the advent of not only a rainbow nation but also a more youthful one. In just one decade, a majority of Americans under age eighteen will be non-White.[1] A new generation is emerging: the Millennials, who reflect and embrace our great diversity. And fourth, globalization and the growing interdependence of our world community are making the ability to lead and build community with people from very distinct cultures, nationalities, and ethnic groups fundamental to effective leadership.

Finally, along with these four changes, technology—both wired and wireless connectivity and social media—has become ubiquitous. Technology and social networking connect people instantly and allow them to easily share information and ideas. Cell phones, texting, Facebook, Twitter, YouTube, and other social networking tools have changed the face of political and social organizing, expanding our ability to share common concerns and take collective action.

These transformative changes underscore the urgency of using leadership principles that respond to our ever-expanding cultural mosaic and changing world. Despite this urgency, however, there are still far too few leadership principles or practices that draw on multicultural approaches. Today's leadership models, although they may differ from person to person and method to method, generally have a common bias toward Western- or European-influenced approaches. Contemporary leadership theories center on the dominant or mainstream culture and exclude the enormous contributions, potential learning, and valuable insights of leaders in diverse communities. Thus, the need for this updated and expanded edition is all too clear.

This new edition responds to these dynamic changes, updates demographics to include 2010 Census data, considers the impact of Obama's leadership, and includes a new principle: the Seventh-Generation Rule: Intergenerational Leadership. It is based on the great law of the Iroquois, which impelled leaders to always consider the impact of their decisions on their children, their children's children, and unto seven generations.[2] In the past this implied one generation shepherding and guiding the next. Today, for the first time in history, four generations are working side-by-side, requiring an intergenerational approach in which different ages work together compatibly to create a viable future.[3]

Within this intergenerational context, we will take a closer look at the Millennials, born between 1980 and 2000. The largest generation in the history of our nation, they are becoming the architects of the twenty-first century. Millennials have a predilection for the inclusive, relationship-based, and activist leadership of communities of color.[4] I hope that they will fulfill the promise of civil rights, infuse American leadership with multicultural practices, and lead our nation to higher ground.

People continue to ask why I, as a Latina, wrote a book on multicultural leadership rather than leadership that springs from the community of my heritage. Although it is informative to look at Latino, or Black, or American Indian leadership separately, such a focus implies that leadership in each of these communities is pertinent only to that one group and is not relevant or generic enough for widespread application. Latino leadership is commonly seen to be of interest only to people who are involved or work with this population. Black leadership is not regarded as applicable to mainstream organizations. Likewise, American Indian spirituality is not understood as the very essence of their leadership that can enrich all cultures.

Multicultural leadership has broad relevance and application to our diverse world. This culturally integrated leadership model has *greater impact, influence, and scope.* Delving into leadership models from specific communities will certainly enhance a person's ability to relate more effectively with that population, but it will not necessarily be applicable to other groups. A multicultural leadership approach, on the other hand, offers practices and tools that will be effective with many populations.

Furthermore, even though Blacks, Latinos, and American Indians have distinct ways of leading, there are key *points of convergence*—they share a number of core cultural dynamics. Their history as colonized people is a common denominator in engendering leadership that is people-centered, community-focused, and advocacy-oriented. All three cultures center on collective or group welfare, and all three value generosity and reciprocity. By identifying such points of convergence, multicultural leadership that integrates Black, Latino, and American Indian strengths can be brought forth.

These unifying factors lay the foundation for the nine principles presented in this book, which I believe have a universality across many cultures. I have distilled the nine principles from our Black, Latino, and American Indian communities. Voicing these commonalities will cultivate a greater sense of unity among communities of color and encourage them to actively disseminate more culturally inclusive leadership. Focusing on the cultural convergence points that shape multicultural leadership in no way denies the power or importance of leadership within the Black, Latino, or American Indian communities. Recognizing common abilities and celebrating differences are two of the touchstones of diverse leadership.

My own background is multicultural: Central American Indian, Spanish, and French. My grandmother was indigenous—her long braids hung down her back, as she never cut her hair. Coming from the Caribbean coast of Nicaragua, I have Black and Latino relatives. Through marriage, my daughters are of Hispanic, Irish, and Norwegian ancestry.

My adopted daughter is African American and Anglo. I have had the enriching experience of living in an integrated neighborhood for over thirty years. The multicultural zenith of our family is my grandson; the rich diversity of his heritage—Black, Latino, Irish, Blackfoot Indian, French, and English heritage—represents our global future.

I also feel uniquely qualified to discuss leadership in Black, Latino, and American Indian communities. I was the first president and CEO of the National Hispana Leadership Institute and have directed Latino organizations for over twenty-five years. Through the Chevron Management Institute, I designed a leadership program that trained ninety Urban League presidents. Spellman College's Center for Leadership and Civic Engagement honored me with their Legacy Award. I was initiated into the Colorado Women's Hall of Fame and presented the Wise Woman Award by the Center for Women's Policy Studies. I also taught at the Center for Creative Leadership in the Leadership Development Program, the most highly utilized corporate training program in the world. The U.S. Peace Corps acknowledged me with the Franklin Williams Award for my lifelong commitment to advancing communities of color. Most important, I have listened to the voices of diverse leaders, many of whom I have worked with closely. This book reflects the composite of our experiences and ways of leading.

In this book, my use of the term *communities of color* refers to African Americans, Latinos, and American Indians. These communities' own preferred terms for themselves have changed over time. I use *Hispanic* as well as *Latino*. For African Americans, *Black* is a descriptor in usages such as Black History Month or the Black community. I refer to *American Indians* in general and indicate tribal membership whenever appropriate; I also use the term *Indian*, a short form accepted within that community, and *Native American*. These terms distinguish people, honor their identity, and highlight their cultural characteristics.

Other groups, such as Asian Americans, may wonder why they are not included here. There are several reasons. Asian Americans, for instance, come from many countries with numerous languages, customs, and nationalities: Chinese, Japanese, Korean, Pacific Islanders, Cambodians, and East Indians and other South Asians—groups with such distinct histories, philosophies, and cultural attributes that it would be difficult to integrate their leadership approaches into the model proposed in this book. This complexity and scope merits separate volumes on Asian leadership experiences and styles. It is also beyond the capacity and length of this book to do justice to their rich contributions, and my limited experience with these cultures would not allow me to be an authentic voice.

My hope is that this book will start a dialogue on multicultural leadership with the Asian American community and others who will widen the conversation. Creating authentic multicultural leadership is an ongoing and organic process. The principles articulated in this book provide a solid foundation from which other writers can expand and develop additional work on diverse leadership practices.

Finally, I want to speak of our elders. In communities of color, age is venerated and respected. The leaders interviewed for this book are largely elders and stand as beacons who have guided their communities. Most grew up in the civil rights era and thus incorporate a social responsibility aimed at building the good and just society. Studies on the Millennials indicate that they look to older generations for guidance.[5] I hope that this new edition will promote intergenerational leadership, a timeless tradition in communities of color that ensures continuity.

Each principle section starts with a story from my life, adding my voice to those of the other leaders who have graciously shared their wisdom. The first part of my life, for instance, mirrors many of the experiences that shaped leaders of the civil rights movement. Each section ends with suggestions and exercises for practical uses of the principle. These have been particularly useful in classrooms and leadership programs and offer a creative way to learn collectively and to put multicultural leadership into practice.

## Acknowledgments—*Gracias*

IN THE LEADERSHIP FIELD, there are practitioners and scholars. Practitioners design, implement, and teach in leadership programs, as I have done for the past twenty-five years. Scholars research and formulate leadership theories and models, then write books on their findings. As an author with many years of practical experience, I am a crossover. However, I had not thought about writing until Dr. Larraine Matusak, the past director of the Kellogg National Fellows Program, invited me to become a Leadership Scholar. Exchanging ideas with authors such as Bernie Bass, James

MacGregor Burns, Ron Heifetz, Barbara Kellerman, Dick Cuoto, and Gill Hickman gave me a new perspective on how influential leadership books could be. They encouraged me to write about my experiences and perspectives in communities of color, as a needed addition to the leadership field.

It is impossible to thank all the people who have helped me with this venture. However, a few folks warrant special appreciation. Let me start with my *familia*, who have supported me in being a Latina maverick who strayed from traditional roles, and my multitude of *comadres* across the country with whom I have shared my life's path. This second edition is possible only because of the many people who have used my book in classrooms, leadership programs, and community work. Thank you for honoring the leadership practices in communities of color.

A special *gracias* to David Perkins, Arnie Langberg, Lynette Murphy, Eric Fransen, and Rich Chavez for guidance on the manuscript. To Lillian Jimenez, director of the Latino Educational Media Center, thank you for helping me capture the wisdom of Dr. Antonia Pantoja. To Steve Piersanti, the best editor in the world, and to the staff at Berrett-Koehler, thank you for your brilliance in shaping this work.

All of you have been my muses. I am blessed with an extended family like this and am forever grateful. In starting this second edition, the inspiration of President Obama reenergized my work: "We will need to remind ourselves, despite all our differences, just how much we share: common hope, common dreams, a bond that will not break."[6]

Juana Bordas

Denver, Colorado

January 2012

# Special Contributions: Profiles of Leaders

SINCE THE CIVIL RIGHTS MOVEMENT, there has been a virtual renaissance in the leadership of communities of color. Leaders have stepped forward in unprecedented numbers and answered the call to serve, and they are guiding their communities with a deep sense of purpose. Yet these leaders, their incredible leadership journeys, and the many lessons they offer are relatively unknown outside of their communities, particularly in mainstream America. I believe these leaders hold up a lantern of hope that can guide us over the troubled waters of the twenty-first century. Their integrity and deep compassion for humanity can help to shape a more caring and responsible world.

It has been my privilege to interview the outstanding and visionary leaders profiled here and to draw from their wisdom and experience in writing this book. I hope that this book brings their inspiring stories to a wider audience and integrates their contributions into a new direction for leadership. (Unless otherwise noted, all the quotations from these special contributors that appear in this book come from personal interviews conducted with them, which were transcribed verbatim and then coded for common themes and patterns.)

## African American Leaders

**Dr. Jim Joseph** has served four U.S. presidents. President Clinton appointed him chairman of the Corporation for National Service and U.S. ambassador to South Africa. He was the only American ambassador to present his credentials to President Nelson Mandela. In 1999, President Thabo Mbeki awarded him the Order of Good Hope, the highest honor the Republic of South Africa bestows on a citizen of another country. Dr. Joseph was formerly president and CEO of the Council on Foundations, and currently he is Emeritus Professor of the Practice of Public Policy as well as Director, United States–Southern Africa Center for Leadership and Public Values, both at Duke University. An ordained minister, he taught at Yale Divinity School and the Claremont Colleges. His writings include "Promoting Peace and Diplomacy" in *Nelson Mandela: From Freedom to the Future;* and *Remaking America: How the Benevolent Traditions of Many Cultures Are Transforming Our National Life.*

**Dr. Lea E. Williams** currently serves as the associate vice chancellor of academic affairs at North Carolina A&T State University. She is the former executive director of the National African-American Women's Leadership Institute, Inc. (NAAWLI), a leadership program for women that helps them discover their leadership talents and use these in community service. Dr. Williams began her career in higher education at the United Negro College Fund. She authored *Servants of the People: The 1960s Legacy of African American Leadership,* documenting the tradition of Black Americans as dedicated servant leaders.

**Andrew Young** was a top aide to Martin Luther King Jr. and a frontrunner in the civil rights movement. As vice president of the Southern Christian Leadership Conference, he was instrumental in crafting the historic Civil Rights Act of 1964 and Voting Rights Act of 1965. Young was elected to the U.S. House of Representatives and later served as the U.S. ambassador to the United Nations under President Carter. As a two-term mayor of Atlanta, he led an economic rebirth. An ordained minister, Young was the head of the National Council of Churches and was awarded the Presidential Medal of Freedom. He has authored two books, *A Way Out of No Way* and *An Easy Burden.*

# American Indian Leaders

**Ada Deer** was the first woman to head the U.S. Bureau of Indian Affairs. Under her leadership, tribal sovereignty was advanced to 180 additional tribes. As the first woman elected chair of the Menominee Nation, she led the movement for federal recognition of her tribe. Deer directed the American Indian Studies Program in the School of Social Work at the University of Wisconsin, Madison. During her tenure, she cofounded Milwaukee's Indian Community School and created the first program to provide social work training on Native American reservations. Deer was the first Indian woman to run for the U.S. Congress in Wisconsin.

**John Echohawk** is a cofounder and executive director of the Native American Rights Fund (NARF) and has been with the organization since its founding in 1977. A member of the Pawnee Nation of Oklahoma, he was one of the first graduates of the University of New Mexico's special program to train Indian lawyers and a founding member of the American Indian Law Students Association. Echohawk has worked to correct centuries-old injustices for Indian tribes for over forty years. Since 1988 he has been recognized by the *National Law Journal* as one of the one hundred most influential lawyers in America and has received numerous service awards for his leadership in the field of Indian law.

**LaDonna Harris**, Comanche, is one of the most influential, inspired, and determined Native Americans in politics. Since 1970, she has served as president of Americans for Indian Opportunity, which catalyzes and facilitates culturally appropriate initiatives that enrich the lives of indigenous peoples. Harris was instrumental in helping the Taos Pueblo regain control of Blue Lake, and helped the Menominee gain federal recognition after their tribe had been terminated by the U.S. federal government. Her publications include *To Govern or Be Governed: Indian Tribes at a Crossroads* and her autobiography, *LaDonna Harris: A Comanche Life.*

**Benny Shendo Jr.**, a native of the Jemez Pueblo, was appointed by Governor Bill Richardson as cabinet secretary of the New Mexico Indian Affairs Department. Secretary Shendo was the senior manager of Native American Programs for the University of New Mexico and director of the American Indian and Alaskan Native program at Stanford University. He serves on the National Institute for Native Leadership in Higher Education and cofounded the Riverside School in Jemez Pueblo—the first charter school on an Indian reservation. In 2008 he made a bid for the third congressional district seat in New Mexico.

## Latino Leaders

**Anna Escobedo Cabral** held the office of Treasurer of the United States until 2008. Previously, she directed the Smithsonian Institution's Center for Latino Initiatives. Cabral also served as president and CEO of the Hispanic Association on Corporate Responsibility, a coalition of the sixteen largest Hispanic nonprofits that advance Hispanic representation in corporate America. From 1993 to 1999, she was deputy staff director for the U.S. Senate Judiciary Committee under Chairman Orrin G. Hatch and executive staff director of the Senate Republican Task Force on Hispanic Affairs. Currently Anna holds a leadership position at the Inter-America Development Bank that supports economic development throughout South America and the Caribbean.

**Dr. Antonia Pantoja**, the first lady of the Puerto Rican civil rights movement, described herself as an "institution builder." Though she passed away in 2002, her profound legacy continues shaping Puerto Rican youth through ASPIRA (to aspire), which instills cultural pride, leadership, and motivation. Dr. Pantoja was the first Puerto Rican woman to receive the Presidential Medal of Freedom and the John W. Gardner Leadership Award. It was my honor to work with her on the curriculum for the National Hispana Leadership Institute and to review interviews for a film on her life—*Antonia Pantoja: Abriendo Caminos* (Opening Pathways, 2006). Her autobiography, *Memoir of a Visionary*, was published by Arte Publico Press in 2002.

**Federico Peña** served as cochair of the historic 2008 Barack Obama campaign, assisting with the phenomenal increase in voting by communities of color. He was elected mayor of Denver in 1983 and 1987, the first Latino mayor of a city with a minority Hispanic population. He revitalized Denver's economic health by initiating projects such as the Denver International Airport, a new convention center, and the Coors Baseball Stadium. A civil rights lawyer, Peña served in the Colorado House of Representatives and as U.S. Secretary of Transportation and U.S. Secretary of Energy during the Clinton administration. Peña is currently the managing director for Vestar Capital Partners.

**Raul Yzaguirre** served as cochair of Hillary Clinton's valiant bid for the presidency in 2008. He was president of the National Council of La Raza for more than thirty years, building it into the largest national Hispanic civil rights and advocacy organization in America. He is a founder of the Hispanic Association for Corporate Responsibility, the New American Alliance, and the National Hispanic Leadership Agenda. Recognized as one of the most influential Hispanic leaders of the twentieth century, Yzaguirre was the first Hispanic to receive a Rockefeller Award for Outstanding Public Service from the trustees of Princeton University and the John W. Gardner Leadership Award. He was appointed the ambassador to the Dominican Republic by President Obama in 2010.

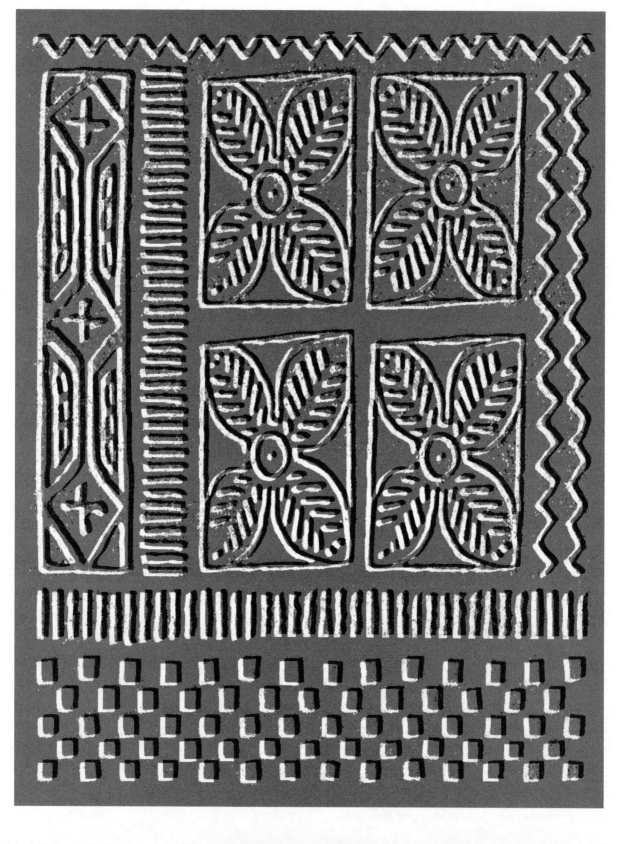

# INTRODUCTION

# Diversity is Transforming Leadership

**M**Y MOTHER, FOUR BROTHERS, MY SISTER, AND I stood at the ship's rail watching the image of our beloved Nicaragua become smaller and smaller and then finally disappear into the Caribbean Sea. In the hull of a banana boat, we rocked and swayed, across *El Golfo de Mexico*. The voyage was as endless as the torrential rains of the hurricanes that had erased the coastline of *Cabo Gracias a Dios* where my family had lived for generations. We docked in Tampa, Florida, and fell into the welcoming arms of *mi Papa*. He had arrived earlier, earning money to bring his *familia* to America so his children could have a better life.

This immigrant dream has been the promise of America and the wellsprings of its greatness. "You should always be thankful you are here," my father would remind me.

My parents were relentless about unlocking the doors of opportunity for their children. The key, they knew, was education. Like the majority of Hispanics, we were devout Catholics. My mother knew just where to look for help. With her soulful eyes and broken English, she approached the parish priest: "I can cook, clean, and take care of children. Can you give me a job to help my family?" How could he refuse a pure and selfless soul like that? Cooking and cleaning in the school cafeteria, she got her children tuition scholarships so they could get *una buena educación*.

When I became a teenager, there was no Catholic school on the outskirts of Tampa where we lived, but this did not deter my parents. My mother boarded a bus with me in tow and journeyed across town. Humbly, she entreated the nuns at the Academy of Holy Names to give her daughter a scholarship. Every Sunday we would go together to babysit children during services at Christ the King Church so I could earn the remaining part of my tuition. It took me a while to realize that many of my school classmates were going to college. I would never have thought of that, but, hey, my parents told me we came here so I could get a good education. College sounded like a great idea to me.

I could hardly speak, I was so excited. "*Mama y Papá*, I got accepted to college!" Their response shook my world. "Where did this idea come from?" My mother, with her fifth-grade education, thought a high school diploma was *una buena educación*. The University of Florida was 120 miles away—to my parents, this was as far as their distant homeland. And how could I travel there—a girl, alone? In the old country, I would have been chaperoned or lived with family. My father lamented, "Shouldn't it be your brothers who go to college?" But seeing my determination, my parents in their loving and humble way gave me their blessing.

I worked my way through college, and the land of opportunity made good on its promise. My parents' vision, faith, perseverance, and selfless service were an endless source of inspiration and strength. They were the greatest leaders any young person could hope to emulate and the source of all the goodness in my life.

During my forty-five years of working in communities of color, I have listened to thousands of such life stories, and I know mine is not unique. Our stories are a collective journey, small streams forming a powerful river, a dynamic force that is restructuring our country into a multicultural society—and transforming American leadership.

## The Movements of Our Time

O N A HOT, HUMID DAY IN MAY 1963, I was sitting outside my dormitory when I saw my political science professor, Dr. Kantor, in a long line of people walking toward the administration building. I ran up and asked, "What are you doing?" He responded solemnly, "We are marching to integrate the University of Florida." I jumped into the line and joined a whole generation of people who believed that America should live up to its founding values.

Just as I was the first in my family to go to college, young people from communities of color across the country did likewise. Universities were being desegregated, and attaining a college degree was finally a possibility for us. For the first time in history, we could become educated at universities and learn how to operate effectively in dominant cultural systems. A great illustration is John Echohawk; the long-time director of the Native American Rights Fund was part of the first cadre of Indian lawyers who interpreted the old treaties and won sovereign rights for their people.

The civil rights movement was a training ground for leaders, empowering communities of color to establish their identity and to seek their birthright as full and equal citizens. Black, Latino, and American Indian organizations flourished and developed culturally effective leadership models based on the values embedded in these communities—models that can inform and inspire multicultural leadership today.

As an immigrant Latina, I am also part of the demographic revolution that has altered our nation's complexion. Population growth in minority communities is so rapid that the 2010 Census revealed they composed 35 percent of the U.S. population.[1] The first wave of American immigrants was Euro-American; today, immigrants look more like my family and represent the diverse spectrum of the world's people. In the spirit of ensuring that history is accurately depicted, we must remember that American Indians are indigenous to this land and that most of the ancestors of African Americans arrived shackled on slave ships.

The movements of the last half of the twentieth century—continued immigration, civil rights, demographic shifts, and educational opportunity—made their mark on my early life and the lives of a whole generation in communities of color. These movements spawned a diverse leadership core that reflected the history, challenges, and cultural values of their communities. This book provides practical insights that incorporate these dynamics into an inclusive leadership model for effectively leading our diverse society.

## Diversity Is Destiny

The realization of full democracy includes the vision of a pluralistic society. Our democracy is fashioned on the principle of inclusive governance originally used by the Iroquois Indians. Yet when the Constitution was written, only free men were allowed to vote. Black men, as slaves, were counted as only *three-fifths of a person*, and women were not allowed to vote until the passage of the nineteenth amendment in 1920.[2] The discrepancy between the vision of democracy and the reality of racial and cultural segregation has caused a continuing tension in U.S. society. These inconsistencies are most apparent in leadership that is not reflective of our multicultural nation.

 *The realization of full democracy contains within it the vision of a pluralistic society. Our democracy is fashioned on the principle of inclusive governance originally used by the Iroquois Indians.*

Dr. Martin Luther King Jr. believed that America had a date with destiny. America's destiny was to fulfill the democratic principles inherent in our country's founding and become a society that established equality and domestic tranquility for all people and for generations to come. Leadership in communities of color reflects democratic values such as justice and promoting the common welfare, and it uses practical approaches that engage and empower people. This participatory form of leadership can replenish American democracy right at a time when there is an urgent need for civic engagement.

There is also an economic engine driving the need for inclusive leadership. Businesses today desire access to the fast-paced growth and lucrative markets in communities of color. According to Jeff Humphreys, author of "The Multicultural Economy: Minority Buying Power in the New Century," in 2010, the combined buying power of African Americans, Asian Americans and Native Americans exceeded $1.6 trillion, more than triple the 1990 level of $454 billion.[3]

Women today comprise the majority of the labor force and a quarter of all managers. By the middle of this century, Latinos will be the majority of workers.[4] As the fastest growing demographic group, one whose members are on average thirteen years younger than the Anglo population, Latinos have accounted for half the U.S. labor market growth since 2004.[5] To be viable, businesses must tap the potential of the changing American workforce and this requires diverse approaches.

As noted, globalization is also fueling diversity. The world is fast becoming a virtual community, where a technological network connects us like next-door neighbors. In today's global environment, in which people from widely varying backgrounds live and work side by side, leaders need cultural flexibility and adaptability. Frances Hesselbein, former president and CEO of the National Girl Scouts, speaks to this urgency: "Perhaps the biggest question in today's world is 'How do we help people deal with their deepest differences?' Governance amid diversity is the world's greatest challenge."[6] Similar to King's vision, it is time for America to embrace her great diversity and to fulfill her destiny as a democratic nation.

The dynamics shaping leadership into a multicultural form are both historic and current. Historic events consist of

- America's democratic traditions.

- Immigration.

- The legacy of the civil rights movement.

    Current dynamics influencing leadership include

- Demographic changes leading to a diversified workforce, consumer markets, and citizenry.

- Globalization and the emerging interdependent world community.

- The education of leaders from diverse communities.

- The development of leadership models in communities of color.

All together, these dynamics have transformed our nation from a White homogeneous society to one in which our growing diversity is represented by the TV anchors on our nightly news, football players, students on college campuses, film stars and performers, and an increasing number of political and business leaders. One additional dynamic has evolved over fifty years of social change in America: a mandate (sometimes disparaged as "political correctness") that inclusion and fostering of diversity be seen as a social responsibility, a key function of leadership, and culturally desirable. Today, young people in particular are embracing an interracial and global culture. They are in tune with the creativity, excitement, and learning that cultural interchange offers. For them, mixed cultural groups and activities are hip or *sweet* —the *in thing*.

Promoting social and economic equity is in tune with our values, religious traditions, and historical foundation. As a result, leadership is challenged to be culturally relevant and incorporate inclusive values and principles. The multicultural model for evolving leadership offered here invites leaders to be in step with the dynamic changes that are transforming our country.

## The Global Connection

Although my emphasis is on Black, Latino, and American Indian communities in the United States, the multicultural principles apply to other communities such as Asian Americans, and the many countries in which leaders address the challenges of a diverse society. Even in countries such as the former Soviet Union, whose populations are distinct from those in the United States, the process used for identifying multicultural principles can be a model for fashioning their own diverse forms of leadership. Furthermore, Black, Latino, and American Indians have historical antecedents and current-day connections across the globe.

Latinos, for instance, are linked to twenty-three countries where Spanish is the primary language and are related to the Portuguese and the Italians, who share their Mediterranean ancestry. These cultures center on the extended family, have traditionally espoused the Catholic faith, and value the emotional or feeling aspects of human nature. In addition, the Moors, who occupied Spain for over eight hundred years, left their cultural imprint on music, architecture, and philosophy, and this cultural cross-pollination with Northern Africa is still evident; for example, fully one-quarter of all Spanish words are of Arab origin.[7]

It is estimated that during the African diaspora twelve million people were taken to the western hemisphere.[8] African culture was embedded in many countries, including Barbados, Haiti, Jamaica, Trinidad, Cuba, Puerto Rico, and, of course, Brazil. The racial heterogeneity in Brazil birthed a diverse, rhythmic, and unique culture whose population is 39 percent mixed race and 45 percent Black. Brazil—the fifth largest country in the world, with the fifth largest population—is one of the best examples of a multicultural nation combining Black, indigenous, and European influences. The principles presented here offer a rich resource for countries like Brazil that are addressing their own multicultural challenges, as well as others across Latin America for which population statistics indicate 27 percent mixed African ancestry.[9]

Through the dark night of slavery, African slaves fashioned a unique culture that sang of their tribal ancestry and the collective values of their homeland. Not only did their spirit of community survive, but new forms and meanings evolved from their African heritage. The leadership forms cultivated by Blacks in America are rooted in the African soil and offer contemporary models on leading from an Afro perspective. Certainly, the South African movement that ended apartheid grew out of King's and Gandhi's work and is indicative of how leadership in one country can flow from another's freedom movement. When the Berlin Wall fell, the Germans were singing "We Shall Overcome."

American Indians are kin to indigenous people in the western hemisphere and on every continent. They often share similar worldviews, a nature-based spirituality, and communal values whereby the good of the tribe supersedes the individual. The pre-Columbian western hemisphere, as will be explored, was resplendent with thousands of unique indigenous cultures. Mexico today is still 30 percent indigenous, and 60 percent identify as mestizo or mixtures of European, predominately Spanish, and Indian.[10] Across Latin America, the native or indigenous population is estimated at 12 percent, with 23 percent mestizos.[11]

The western hemisphere, then, is a rich jambalaya of African, Spanish, and indigenous cultures. The nine multicultural leadership principles apply directly to the many countries with multicultural populations, where leading diversity is a critical issue. For example, England, which historically was predominately Anglo-Saxon, now has significant Black and East Indian populations and could benefit from using inclusive leadership principles.

*The western hemisphere is a rich jambalaya of African, Spanish, and indigenous cultures. The nine multicultural leadership principles apply directly to the many countries with multicultural populations, where leading diversity is a critical issue.*

The migration, expansion, and settlement of societies is a phenomenon as old as human history; it has led to the intertwining of many cultures. Going way back, all of us have indigenous antecedents. The principles gleaned from Black, Latino, and American Indian cultures come from these ancient traditions that emphasized humanity's common bonds and counsel us to look out for one another. Multicultural leadership principles are rooted in these traditions and offer the potential to cultivate a strong sense of world community that transcends ethnocentric biases.

## Crafting a Multicultural Leadership Model

ETHNOCENTRICITY IS SEEING THE WORLD FROM ONE CULTURAL orientation and believing it to be the universal standard—or even superior to all others. American leadership, which has been culled largely from White male perspectives, centers on mainstream cultural values and thus reflects an ethnocentric orientation.

A multicultural leadership orientation, on the other hand, incorporates many cultural perspectives, appreciates differences, values unique contributions of diverse groups, and promotes learning from many orientations. People are encouraged to maintain their cultural identity while at the same time participating in the diversity of the larger society.

Multicultural leadership is uniquely suited to our mosaic world because it incorporates the influences, practices, and values of a variety of cultures in a respectful and productive manner. It encourages an inclusive and adaptable style that cultivates the ability to bring out the best in our diverse workforce and to fashion a sense of community with people from many parts of the globe. This inclusive form of leadership

### Multicultural Leadership is . . .

An inclusive approach and philosophy that incorporates the influences, practices, and values of diverse cultures in a respectful and productive manner. Multicultural leadership resonates with many cultures and encourages diverse people to actively engage, contribute, and tap their potential.

enables a wide spectrum of people to actively engage and contribute. Multicultural leadership is a commitment to advance people who reflect the vitality, values, and voices of our diversity to all levels of organizations and society.

When people respect each other and value differences, they can work together more amicably—and more productively. Multicultural leadership encourages synergy, innovation, and resourcefulness. Our future depends on our ability to develop the potential of our culturally diverse world. To that end, the nine principles described here integrate the practices of communities of color into an inclusive and democratic leadership model—a knowledge base to inspire a core of multicultural leaders who recognize that diversity and inclusiveness are intrinsic to an authentic and equitable democracy. These principles apply particularly to the Millennial Generation, as more than 40 percent of them are Black, Latino, Asian, or American Indian, and many identify as mixed race.[12]

Some readers may be wondering why we need to develop a multicultural leadership model. Didn't we just point out that diversity is politically correct and culturally desirable? Isn't America already a multicultural nation? On any given day, a person might have enchiladas for lunch, listen to jazz or hip hop, wear exquisite Navajo jewelry, watch *Oprah* reruns on TV, and cap the evening off with a margarita. It is true that culturally, communities of color have greatly enriched America and that many gains were achieved by the civil rights movement. Today, we live in a smorgasbord society in which many enjoy the fruits of a cultural cornucopia. Despite this kaleidoscope of diversity, mainstream American leadership has not integrated the rich practices of communities of color. Until a more inclusive form of leadership embodies our diverse society, we will not be a truly multicultural society.

## Infusing Salsa, Soul, and Spirit into American Leadership

THE CHALLENGE NOW IS TO SPARK PEOPLE'S INTEREST in transforming leadership into an inclusive and multicultural form. We can ignite this by recognizing the vibrant flavors and gifts that American Indians, Latinos, and African Americans bring to leadership and by emphasizing multicultural leadership as a strategic advantage in our global community.

In the Hispanic tradition, someone embarking on a journey, a new venture, or a new stage of life asks for a *bendición* or blessing from her grandmother or other respected person. American Indians burn sage to purify the person with smoke. African Americans might sing a traditional hymn, followed by a communal prayer, and a collective, heartfelt *amen!* A coach's motivational talk to players, which gets them psyched up and ready to perform at their optimum, is intended, in a similar way, to prepare them for a good outcome. Let our journey begin in an inspirational way by highlighting the energy, spiritual insights, experience, and leadership that American Indians, Blacks, and Latinos bring to America.

## Pass the Salsa

As far back as I can remember, I would be lifted in my father's arms dancing to the salsa beats of quick, quick, pause; quick, quick, pause. Seven beats in all, because when it is repeated there is an empty space, like the zero that my Indian ancestors from Central America discovered. The salsa beat was a magnet. I could never resist the fusion music that blends African drums, American Indian rattles (maracas), Spanish guitars, Moorish sounds, and Caribbean rhythms. It is no coincidence that salsa is also the spicy, hot condiment giving food flavor and bringing zing to the palate. Salsa adds a little variety to the rice and beans that are an everyday staple in Latino cuisine.

Salsa is a great metaphor for diversity. Just as no two individuals are alike, every batch of salsa is *unico*. Each cook makes salsa in a particular way, with a little of this and a little of that. Traditional Latino cookbooks include in their recipes a guideline called *a gusto* (to your liking or taste), reflecting that you must be flexible and adaptable to tend to people's needs and preferences. This is one of diversity's golden rules.

 *Salsa is a great metaphor for diversity. Just like no two individuals are alike, every batch of salsa is* unico.

Besides the fact that every salsa maker has a personal recipe, the size of the tomatoes and the strength of the onion, herbs, and spices change the taste. But the real wild card is the jalapeño peppers. Latinos know you approach jalapeños with *respeto.* You take a teensy little bite to determine whether it is mild, hot, or "*Ay Chihuahua!*" Just as no jalapeños are the same, each individual is unique, a one-of-a-kind design.

Salsa is now one of America's favorite condiments, having passed the more homogenized and sugar-laced ketchup in the early nineties. Salsa dance has swept the nation in the twenty-first century, as young and old discover the pleasure of moving to the Latin beat. But salsa is more than a dance or a racy condiment. Salsa is a way of life. *Tener salsa en la vida* is to fully enjoy life, by treasuring family, relationships, work, and community. Salsa is the spice of life—the, energy, vitality, and *gusto! Salsa en la vida* has been a key ingredient enabling Latinos to sustain themselves through the past five hundred years since the conquest of this hemisphere.

## Putting the Gusto into Leadership

Latinos are invigorating American leadership. They have the highest participation in the labor market of any group tracked by the U.S. Census and are the fastest growing small business sector.[13] Their core values include faith, family, hard work, honesty, sharing, inclusion, and cooperation. It could well be that Latinos will make their most significant contribution in the realignment of America's values. As Raul Yzaguirre surmises, "Latinos live America's core values of family and hard work. Instead of asking us to change our name and culture and to assimilate, Latinos should be saying, 'You should become more like us.' We espouse an America that lives up to its values. America is the best country in the world—but it cannot become a true world leader unless it embraces all people. *America will become more American* when Latinos are fully integrated at all levels of our country."[14]

*Latinos live America's core values of family and hard work. Instead of asking us to change our name and culture and to assimilate, Latinos should be saying "you should become more like us."*

—Raul Yzaguirre

In Thomas Friedman's book *The World Is Flat,* he surmises that the twenty-first century will be "more and more driven by a more diverse—non-Western, non-white—group of individuals . . . You are going to see every color of the human rainbow take part."[15] As a fusion culture and not a race, Latinos are a rainbow people: white, red, black, brown, yellow, and all the mixtures in between. Almost 80 percent speak some Spanish at home (Spanish is the language spoken in the greatest number of countries in the world). Connected by language to twenty-three countries, they are a springboard to our global community.[16]

Within the U.S. the Latino landscape is also varied, containing a wealth of histories, backgrounds, and counties of origin. Sixty-three percent of Latinos are of Mexican descent. Puerto Ricans form the second largest group, comprising 9 percent. Cuban Americans are 4 percent. Latino diversity continues to expand. In the 2010 Census, 10 percent were of Central and South American descent.[17] Interestingly, almost four million people living in mainland Puerto Rico are not included in the Census, even though they are U.S. citizens. Puerto Rico was invaded by the United States during the Spanish-American War in 1898 and has remained a commonwealth. Despite over one hundred years of strong U.S. influence, Puerto Ricans are proud of their distinct culture, history, and language, enriched by the mixture of aboriginal, Spanish, and African peoples. Today, there are more Puerto Ricans in the continental United States than on their beloved island.[18]

As shown in the sections on the nine principles, Latino values and worldview align with those of cultures emphasizing collectivism, generosity, mutual help, extended family, and the common good. Latino leadership reflects a social and celebratory nature, a community-oriented approach, and a people-centered process that are becoming valued traits of twenty-first-century leadership. Latinos only emerged as an identifiable group in the last forty years. As a budding force their influence and flavor have just begun putting the salsa into American leadership.

## The African American Soul Sings

SOUL HAS BEEN DEPICTED AS THE IMMATERIAL ESSENCE or substance, the animating principle or actuating cause of life. Soul represents the immortal and permanent, the spirit, life, and vitality. The atrocities and dehumanization of slavery were rationalized, in part, by propagating the belief that Africans did not have a soul and were therefore less than human. This was reinforced by the Constitution's designation of the Black man as three-fifths of a person.[19] Nevertheless, the African soul was resilient, rooted in a spiritual tradition birthed in ancient times on the continent where humans first evolved. Like the tradition of the indigenous people of the Americas, it is nature based and sustained by community ritual, song, and dance. *The struggle of African slaves is the struggle of a people who were literally fighting for the recognition of their souls.*

W. E. B. Du Bois, the first African American awarded a Ph.D. from Harvard, explored the philosophical, spiritual, and cultural dimensions of Black people's religion in his classic book, *The Souls of Black Folk*, written in 1903. Du Bois wove the sacred and the secular together, setting the stage for the advent of African American leadership, which would spring out of a spiritual foundation and address social injustice.[20]

The Black church had become the social, intellectual, and economic anchor of community life. A distinctive religion developed in which emotional release, communal refuge, and wailing against injustice were found. Out of the pain of slavery a unique spiritual music was born, which Du Bois called the "sorrow songs," designating them as "the greatest gift of the Negro people" and the only distinct "American music" form. Sorrow songs were the voice of an oppressed people, and yet they are prayers that breathe hope, faith, and renewal. This vigorous spiritual musical tradition incorporated African aesthetics through call and response, melodic riffs, repetition and revision, and the integration of song and dance through foot stomping and clapping. It would evolve into a new gospel sound, eventually become rhythm and blues, and then be transmuted into soul music. These sounds are the lifeblood of much popular music today—jazz, rock and roll, and rap all spring from the gospel tradition.

Soul, which some attempted to deny to Black people, bloomed into one of their essential cultural features. Soul reflects a deep well of resilient hope, a spiritual family bonded by common hardship, and an emotional connection that forges community consciousness. Even physical

 *Soul, which some attempted to deny to Black people, bloomed into one of their essential cultural features. Soul reflects a deep well of resilient hope, a spiritual family bonded by common hardship, and an emotional connection that forges community consciousness.*

sustenance became soul food—a delicious masterpiece born of adversity. Scraps from the slave master's table became tasty dishes of black-eyed peas, cornbread, sweet potato pie, catfish, or turnip greens seasoned with pigs' feet or ham hocks. The resilient and creative impulse that engendered soul food fed the spirit, not just the body.

Soul music, soul food, soul brother—the concept of *soul* permeates African American culture. Soul represents a deep understanding that their spiritual wellspring sustained Black people through the trials and tribulations of slavery, racism, and oppression. When gospel music sang out about freedom, it was about liberty not only in heaven but also on the earth. The infusion of soul into all facets of life brought forth a unique form of spiritual activism in which leadership was ignited from the pulpits in the sermons of ministers. This tradition blossomed during the civil rights movement, infusing American leadership with a new moral fiber.

Furthermore, the African American adage "if it doesn't kill you, it will make you stronger" reflects a biological reality. Those who made it across the Atlantic and withstood the hardship of slavery had a vitality, resilience, and spiritual strength. Combined with the mutual support of the slave quarters community, this strength enabled people to survive the traumas of their history and evolved into an unshakable sense of community, which continues to be the basis for African American progress and leadership.

## The Soul of Leadership

Dr. Jim Joseph, former U.S. ambassador to South Africa, explains the power of this form of leadership: "The initial group of African American leaders in the fifties and sixties were ministers. They were totally independent and had the freedom to act on the basis of their social conscience, without the threat of being terminated by some white-controlled structure. Their source of livelihood came from Black people and Black churches." The most prophetic voice to arise from the Black churches in the last century was that of Martin Luther King Jr. He poignantly challenged the materialistic and racist bent of the American culture: "We are prone to judge success by the index of our salaries or the size of our automobiles, rather than by the quality of our service and relationship to humanity."[21]

King believed that Black spirituality and faith would bring a moral reawakening that would restore economic justice and social responsibility, and affirm the sacredness of life.

He built on a pervasive spiritual tradition that had nourished Black people for generations, allowing them to shed the residues of slavery and oppression without destructive bitterness or anger. King cultivated a scope of leadership that had, at its core, redemption and forgiveness. These may be said to represent the higher qualities of human consciousness or soul. It is ironic that the very soul qualities once denied Black people constitute one of the great legacies they bring to American leadership.

## American Indian Leadership— Being in Right Relationship

AS THE SUN COMES UP EACH MORNING AND as it sets in its resting place in the evening, the native peoples of the Americas give praise to the Great Spirit. They believe that all life flows from this one source—*the unifying life force*—that is present everywhere. The rivers, rocks, earth, plants, animals, and all people are made of this same spiritual essence. All life is related and sacred. Benny Shendo Jr., a young Jemez Pueblo leader who was also New Mexico's Secretary for Indian Affairs, reflects on this way of life: "I was taught we are spiritual people living in a spiritual world, walking the spiritual path, and there is a higher power."

This core spiritual belief defines the nature of relationships: human beings belong to one spiritual family. In the Lakota tradition, when people meet, they say *mitakuye oyasin* or "all my relatives." This ancient way of acknowledging each other, which is also followed by the Cherokee or Tsalagi people, contains the idea of kinship—of being family and thereby being responsible for one another.[22] The Mayan golden rule "I am another yourself" represents another universal way of reflecting the oneness of humanity. Within these traditions, everyone must be treated with the respect due a family member.

Seeing human relations in this way is based on a circular view of the universe. Giving and sharing provide a way to nourish and regenerate oneself. In many tribes, people are respected not for how much they have, but for their generosity, how much they share and give away. This extends to sharing ideas, stories, and life experience, giving of one's time, and contributing one's talents to the well-being of individuals and the community.

*The belief in the pervasiveness and continuity of spirit unfolds a way of life that is collectively rather than individually oriented. Even the names of many tribes translate into the people—meaning that everyone belongs.*

The belief in the pervasiveness and continuity of spirit also unfolds a way of life that is collectively rather than individually oriented. Even the names of many tribes translate into *the people*—meaning that everyone belongs.[23] Central to Indian culture is the collective welfare and the need to ensure that the tribe continues for posterity. Their leadership forms, which have been on the earth for many generations, flow from this orientation.

## The Spirit of Leadership

An eagle feather lifts the sweet grass smoke into the sky. A prayer of gratitude is offered. People ask for guidance and good outcomes. First, there is silence as people gather themselves and connect with the spiritual force that unites them. Then the meeting begins. Prayers, rituals, celebrations, and ceremonies are ways that Indian leaders make the *spirit visible in everyday life* and bring a higher dimension to community endeavors. By acknowledging that everything comes from and is unified by the one life source, leaders remind people of their responsibility to one another. Offering a prayer to begin any endeavor, and expressing gratitude for all that has been given, reinforces this bond.

American Indian culture impels a leadership form that centers on communal responsibility, a concern for the welfare of the tribe, and stewardship for all life. As Benny Shendo describes, "In the other society, when a person is elected to office, he is responsible in a sense to the people who voted for him. But the eagles don't vote, the trees don't vote, the buffalo don't vote, the waters don't vote, the stars don't vote, so in the other society people don't understand the broader concept of what our overall responsibility in this world means. The only responsibility is to you as a voter, because you can vote me out tomorrow. The Jemez leader has to be responsible for the community, for the future, and for the natural world in which all people live." John Echohawk emphasizes this responsibility: "Native American leadership is based on time-honored traditions, cultures, and religious beliefs, including an understanding of the relationships between human beings and the larger world. Tribes have a long-term view of things."

Many authors today emphasize the spiritual dimension of leadership. Often, this refers to "working on oneself," developing better habits, or becoming a better person. This reflects the individualist orientation of the dominant culture in which spirituality is a personal focus and endeavor. In the Indian tradition, spirituality is the unifying factor infusing all aspects of one's life—one's relationships, responsibilities, community obligations, and connection to the natural world. American Indian spirituality demonstrates how centering on *collective* rather than *individual* advancement can lay the foundation for a society that places the community's welfare above individual gain. Like the Great Spirit—which is pervasive, life-generating, and timeless—American Indian leadership brings a spiritual foundation, which respects and benefits all life and ensures the continuity of future generations.

 *Native American leadership is based on time-honored traditions, cultures, and religious beliefs, including an understanding of the relationships between human beings and the larger world. Tribes have a long-term view of things.*

*—John Echohawk*

Clearly, Latinos, Blacks, and Native Americans are bringing wisdom, vitality, and vision to American leadership. So let us begin our journey to infuse American leadership with *salsa, soul, and spirit*. The next section offers an overview of the nine principles that can be used as guideposts for leading from a multicultural orientation.

## Nine Principles of Multicultural Leadership—An Overview

THE FIRST STEP IN INTEGRATING THE LEADERSHIP PRACTICES of communities of color into an inclusive and multicultural form is exploring a number of core values that are keystones for these cultures. Values, explains Burt Nanus in *Visionary Leadership*, shape our assumptions about the future, provide the context within which issues and goals are identified, and set standards for people's behavior and actions.[24] Values also define the range of people's choices, identify what is good and desirable, and give definition to a society's culture. Leadership, therefore, reflects cultural values and societal norms.

Part One, A New Social Covenant, describes the value changes that are necessary to create an environment in which inclusive and multicultural leadership can thrive. These three principles are:

- Principle 1: *Sankofa*—Learn from the past
- Principle 2: *I* to *We*—From individualism to collective identity
- Principle 3: *Mi Casa es su Casa*—Developing a spirit of generosity

Many African Americans honor the symbol of *Sankofa,* a mythical bird with its feet firmly planted forward and its head turned to look backward. Coming from their West African ancestors, *Sankofa* means "Return, go back, seek, and retrieve." *Sankofa* urges us to reflect on and learn from the past.[25] To expand leadership into a multicultural form, we must understand how Eurocentric and hierarchical leadership became dominant in the first place. We must look beyond the traditional version of the settling of America, which denies the historical contributions of communities of color, to discover the leadership practices of the diverse groups that shaped our country—some of which existed before Columbus landed in this hemisphere.

Building a pluralistic and equitable society requires a shift from today's emphasis on individualism to one in which people's mutual welfare and the social good come first. This change from an *I* to a *We* reference alters our orientation: the collective welfare becomes central to each of us. Blacks, Latinos, and American Indians consider the family, tribe, or community before individual advancement. Today, many young people are following this tradition through a collective identity and a commitment to the greater good over individual gain.[26]

A *We* perspective nourishes the spirit of generosity as people understand that a collective approach is the foundation of a society that takes care of its people. *Mi casa es su casa*—"my house is your house"—denotes the generosity found in communities of color, which is reciprocal, circular, and a way to nurture oneself and others. Generosity and sharing enabled these communities to survive when faced with scarcity and oppression. Generosity is an expected leadership trait that is equated with integrity and garners respect.

Part Two, Leadership Styles in Communities of Color, speaks to three primary roles and functions that American Indian, Latino, and African American leaders assume:

- Principle 4: *A Leader Among Equals*—Community-conferred leadership

- Principle 5: *Leaders as Guardians of Public Values*—A tradition of activism

- Principle 6: *Leaders as Community Steward*—Working for the common good

A *leader among equals* comes from the Indian tradition in which leadership was rotated and shared. This principle levels the playing field and supports a distributed and circular form of leadership, which topples hierarchy and privilege. In these communities, leaders' influence and authority come from being part of and sanctioned by their people. Conversely, being perceived as someone who puts oneself above others will destroy one's credibility.

Because leaders from communities of color represent people with unequal access to opportunities and benefit, they are responsible for addressing issues and institutions that bar full participation. By articulating values such as pluralism, justice, and equality, leaders beckon our society to live up to the *public values* on which our democracy was founded. During the civil rights movement, Black Americans brought leaders as guardians of the equitable society to the foreground and inspired people to collective action.

As builders and guardians of community progress, *leaders as community stewards* nurture a network or legacy that continues to advance people. Community stewards foster group consensus, create a shared community vision, weave partnerships, and use culturally effective communication. Community Servanthood redefines servant leadership as social responsibility and addressing the common welfare.

Part Three, Creating the Circle of Leadership, reflects the expansive view of people's relationships that is integral to Black, Latino, and Indian cultures. They understand that the community's continued growth and development can be accomplished only if subsequent generations are prepared to lead. Three principles embody these tendencies:

- Principle 7: *The Seventh-Generation Rule*—Intergenerational leadership

- Principle 8: *All My Relatives*—*La familia*, the village, the tribe

- Principle 9: *Gracias*—Gratitude, hope, and forgiveness

Intergenerational leadership is founded on the seventh-generation rule of the Iroquois Indians, which directed leaders to always be cognizant of the impact of their actions on subsequent generations. Preparing young people to assume leadership is essential to sustainability and to building a circle of leadership. Because of the phenomenal age shift in the U.S.—the Millennial Generation, born after 1980, is poised to become the dominant age group—we consider how leadership principles in communities of color and an intergenerational approach can prepare this diverse and socially responsible group to assume the leadership of this century. By 2030 their ages will span from twenty to fifty and they will be in key positions of influence.

The eighth principle, the Lakota tribe's traditional greeting "All my relatives," conveys the concept of kinship and responsibility towards one another. The belief that we are all connected leads to a collective way of life and repositions a leader's relationship with people as ongoing and reciprocal. Regardless of position, social class, or ranking, people should be treated equally and as valued family members.

Leadership in communities of color is grounded in spiritual responsibility: leaders attend to people's material and social needs, as well as provide inspiration and hope. Spirituality has flourished, despite oppression and economic need, because of several cherished attributes expressed in the ninth and final principle, *Gracias*, which signifies thankfulness, a deep-seated optimism, and the ability to forgive regardless of past transgressions or difficulties. The tradition of *gracias* has very old roots in America, going back to the first multicultural celebration, in which native people joined with settlers to express thanks for their survival. This feast day is a beautiful model that illuminates the benefits of integrating practices from communities of color into mainstream society.

Part Four, Leadership for a Multicultural Age, sounds a call to action: an invitation to join the growing cadre of leaders who are crafting our global future. Like world music, which reflects the melodic creations and the upbeat sounds of our expansive globe, this part invites the reader to make a commitment to become a multicultural leader and to join in the dance of our kaleidoscope world.

Multicultural leadership entails changing organizational structures so that diversity becomes part of the standard way of operating. This requires a transition from *hierarchical pluralism*, which expects people to conform to dominant cultural norms, to *egalitarian pluralism*, which embraces the values and norms of many cultures. We review practices that promote egalitarian pluralism, comparing acculturation—the process through which people learn how to expand their repertoire and adapt to different cultural perspectives—with assimilation, which negated the cultures, languages, and histories of America's great diversity.

In a democracy, voting holds the key to a truly representative government. This section discusses both the steps needed to bring about public leadership that mirrors our pluralistic society and the challenges we face in achieving this.

# PART ONE

# A New Social Covenant

T HE UNITED STATES WAS FOUNDED on the values of rugged individual-ism and competition. In our review of the first three principles we see how these qualities fashioned a society in which people have a greater orientation toward their individual needs and desires than to the collective good. In the spirit of *Sankofa,* which beckons us to reconcile our past with our present, we question the historical belief that human nature is only driven by self-interest, competi-tion, and acquisition. This notion of individualism replaced early collective and coop-erative cultures and established a social covenant in which government or society was a safeguard against man's competitive and aggressive nature. In this worldview, leadership was the domain of the enlightened few, was competitively oriented, and focused on power and control.

This view is no longer suited to our world village, in which advances in technology and communication link us intricately together. Lance Secretan, in his book *One: The Art and Practice of Conscious Leadership,* reflects, "We have become aware that the world is smaller, more interdependent, and integrated. Community is growing in importance. The new reality is that we are one."[1]

In response to this new environment, the old individualist form of leadership has been shape-shifting from a self-centered orientation to a *We* or *other-centered* orientation, a cooperative, collaborative, and people-oriented form. This shift is in alignment with leadership in communities of color, which must be other centered because leaders derive their authority from the people they serve. Leaders are sanctioned by their communities by putting the collective welfare above self-interest.

Putting the common good first goes against the grain of individualism—*We* takes precedence over *I* and sustains a deep sense of generosity, sharing, and reciprocity. Leadership in this context is not a vehicle for individual advancement, but instead is based on social responsibility.

Principle 3, *Mi Casa Es Su Casa*, expresses the profuse generosity common in communities of color, in which wealth traditionally meant giving to others and assuming responsibility for community needs. To take more than one's share and to accumulate excessive wealth was a cultural anathema. Generosity encompasses a long-term perspective that includes the sustainability of future generations and the natural environment.

Today's interdependent and fragile world calls for a new social covenant centered not on every man for himself, but on caring for each other. This covenant was envisioned by Martin Luther King Jr., who believed that other-centered men could build a society that would restore "dignity, equality, and freedom for people's spirit"; a society in which "people everywhere can have three meals a day for their bodies, education and culture for their minds." King appealed to our morality and conscience: "What self-centered men have torn down, other-centered men can build up."[2]

An other-centered society would incorporate the core values of collectivism and generosity that emanate from communities of color. These values are the touchstones for multicultural leadership principles dedicated to building a benevolent and just society that upholds the well-being of all people and nurtures future generations.

## In Search of Multicultural Excellence

**M**AINSTREAM BOOKS ON LEADERSHIP routinely emphasize organizations and companies that represent "the ideal." Books such as *Good to Great*, *Built to Last*, and *In Search of Excellence* put forth models that illuminate the possibilities when visionary leaders take the helm. Authors do not spend much time on topics such as "In Search of Mediocrity" or "From Bad to Worse," although there are plenty of examples of middle-of-the-road organizations and leaders who falter in their commitments. By stressing the ideal—the best of the best—and by having positive models to emulate, leaders and organizations expect to improve and move toward that vision.

Likewise, when Anglo values and cultural norms are discussed, the positive attributes are usually highlighted and even revered. Individualism is rarely discussed as a value that may lead to social isolation and personal discontent as one is constantly comparing oneself to others. Competition is seen as a positive force that brings out the best in people and organizations, not as a stance that sometimes rends the fabric of support in which everyone is valued. Youth is venerated and in alignment with the new and improved mentality of today's marketplace; the youth cult is not presented as a dead-end street leading to a society with a short-term memory that disregards the wisdom of age and the lessons from the past.

Accordingly, in this book I present African American, Indian, and Latino cultures in light of the *highest standards* of these communities. This is not to deny the inconsistencies and undesirable aspects present in all cultures. In communities of color, however, oppression, slavery, and colonization are historical traumas. Remnants of these difficult circumstances endure in higher rates of poverty, low self-esteem, and low educational levels. We must strive to separate the gifts and positive attributes in these communities from the residues of discrimination and oppression that manifest today as lower economic, educational, and social status.

The leaders whose voices resonate on these pages are some of the most talented and committed people who have guided communities of color in the past decades. They represent the ideal. Their values, approaches, and dedication have laid the foundation for multicultural leadership. Concentrating on the ideal is intended to call forth the best in communities of color and construct a mental model of a desirable future state. As these communities step forward, embracing the leadership principles described in this book, they will embark on a bold and worthy journey to build a world that honors our human potential and celebrates our great diversity.

For mainstream leaders, recognizing this ideal is an opportunity to incorporate the best practices from communities of color into their repertoire and to acknowledge their promise and potential. Young and emerging leaders of color will expand their understanding of the tremendous contribution our communities bring to America. I hope this inspires them to stay true to the values that have shaped their communities and to realize that their greatest contribution comes from being the architects of our multicultural future.

In 2008, young people voted in droves to elect the first Black U.S. president—an electrifying social transformation and the culmination of a long and arduous civil rights journey. The principle of *Sankofa* can instill in the younger generation an understanding of the historical struggles that led to this watershed event—and the wisdom and experience of the elders profiled in this book can inspire and guide them as they tackle the many social and political challenges of their times.

**PRINCIPLE I**

*Sankofa—*
# Learn from the Past

FILLING OUT MY FIRST U.S. Census form in 1970, I searched for a category that acknowledged my Latino roots. I felt a loud thud in my heart as I finally checked the Caucasian box. Latinos were not recognized as a group by the U.S. government until the 1980 Census. We all have a deep need to be accepted for who we are, but this is particularly so in communities of color, whose members have been relegated to a minority status and measured by a White ideal. As I filled out the form, I heard my grandmother's sweet voice, "*Aye mi jita, nunca olvides quien eres y de donde venistes*" ("Oh, my dearest little daughter, never forget who you are and where you came from").

This notion of remembering your roots and staying connected to your ancestry is of biblical import in Black, Latino, and Indian communities. Forgetting where you came from is known as *selling out*, becoming an Uncle Tom or an Oreo or a coconut (Black or Brown on the outside, but White on the inside). Staying connected to one's roots includes being in tune with the history and struggles of one's people. Communities of color relate to the past as the "wisdom teacher," the source from which culture flows.

*Sankofa,* the mythical bird who looks backward, symbolizes African Americans' respect for insight and knowledge acquired from the past. A legacy of their West African ancestors, *Sankofa* reminds us that our roots ground and nourish us, hold us firm when the winds of change howl, and offer perspective about what is lasting and significant. Although *Sankofa* rests on the foundation of the past, its feet face forward. This ancient symbol counsels us that the past is a pathway to understanding the present and creating a strong future. *Sankofa* invites us to bring forward the meaningful and useful—including the values and spiritual traditions passed from previous generations—to learn from experience and to avoid the dead ends and pitfalls of history. The song that is considered the Black national anthem, "Lift Every Voice and Sing," proclaims: "Sing a song full of the faith that the dark past has taught us."[1] The song also inspires hope, because despite past trials and tribulations, people survived and are now thriving.

Latinos connect to the past during *El Dia de los Muertos* by recognizing the gifts inherited from their *antepasados* (those who came before) and the wisdom their ancestors have passed on. On this day, many Latinos compose an altar with pictures of their family members who have passed on. Surrounded by marigold flowers, flickering candles, and perhaps a mantle embroidered by their grandmother, they play old songs and tell stories about these relatives. Fried plantains, *arroz y frijoles,* rice pudding, or other special foods are made. Brandy, chocolate, strong coffee, and other treats are left on altars so that those who came before know they are welcome, loved, and remembered. Latinos also take flowers and food to family burial plots, and thus the roots of the past are affirmed and strengthened.

 *Sankofa is a mythical bird with its feet firmly planted forward and its head turned to look backward. Sankofa means return, go back, seek, and retrieve. Sankofa urges us to reflect on and learn from the past.*

American Indians believe their ancestors, the venerable ones, walk right alongside them and are accessible even though they have passed on to the spirit world. They pray to the grandfathers and grandmothers, asking for their blessings and good counsel. The Navajos honor this connection each time they introduce themselves: "I am the grandson of . . . and the great grandson of . . . " Indian history, culture, morals, and values are passed on through the oral tradition in stories and fables that often enumerate the feats of ancestors. "Learn from the past," a former slogan for the Native American College Fund, encapsulates the belief that by under-standing history people will not repeat past mistakes and will create a better future.

Thus, these cultures keep the past alive and accessible so it feeds the present. Because their history is a tale of conquest, cultural oppression, and racism, reclaiming and reme-dying the past is crucial to recovering power and wholeness. For many, this is not about times gone by but about their recent family history. Ana Escobedo Cabral, former secre-tary of the U.S. Treasury, grew up in a migrant family in the Santa Clara Valley, listening to the stories of her grandparents and great grandparents. She says, "I feel very fortunate that I lived with several generations. I learned about the struggles they endured—losing children to disease and hunger, coming across the Rio Grande, and walking all the way from Texas to California with no money and then working in the fields." Cabral believes this motivates her to improve the lives of others. "One thing that will always be cultur-ally important is the connection to your own family history. Through that you'll under-stand people's pain, suffering, and struggle."

## Healing the Past

MANY PEOPLE MAY HAVE difficulty understanding why we need to reconcile the past in order to build a pluralistic society and fashion multicultural leadership. Yet the vestiges of the past and the inequities that existed for centuries continue to impede inclusiveness and equity. For example, embedded racism, which has its roots in slavery, is evident in school systems that "push out" Black students, graduating fewer than 70 percent in some urban areas.[2] Inequality has lingered long after emancipation. Similarly, five hundred years after the conquistadores slashed their way through this hemisphere, Latinos still struggle with the legacy of being colonized people. Latino wages are actually falling even as their labor participation increases; they are working more and earning less.[3] Latino high school dropout rates hover at 40 percent, which is attributed to inadequate and poorly funded schools in high-density Latino neighbor-hoods.[4] By understanding the historical systems that entrenched this type of discrimi-nation, Latinos can remain resolute and stay the course.

Indian lands were snatched from them *way back* during pioneer times. After the Indi-ans were rounded up and confined to reservations, Christian ministers baptized them and banned many of their religious practices. Children were sent to boarding schools to learn the White man's ways. Stripped of their spirituality and land, they could have had their heritage wiped out like the bison that once grazed the open range. The movement to reinstate tribal lands took shape only in the 1960s when the first Indian lawyers examined the old treaties. The Indians' battle for tribal sovereignty and cultural preservation persists today.

These examples shed light on how history continues to affect people of color and how reconciliation is needed to create a truly inclusive future. Understanding and healing the past can move people beyond the vestiges of oppression and old transgressions. The South Africa reconciliation movement illuminates the past as a force for new beginnings. Leaders urged people who had suffered under apartheid to come forward and publicly acknowledge their grievances and transgressions so that the past could be healed and a new country could be born.

In practicing *Sankofa,* our starting point will be the genesis of America. The convergence of certain European philosophies drove the exodus across the Atlantic and made the settling of the western hemisphere a de facto conquest based on the oppression of indigenous people. This set in motion an exclusionary leadership form that denied the history and contributions of diverse people. For mainstream leaders, understanding the history that gave rise to ethnocentricity is perhaps the most difficult step in transforming leadership to an inclusive, multicultural form.

 *The convergence of certain European philosophies drove the exodus across the Atlantic and made the settling of the western hemisphere a de facto conquest based on the oppression of indigenous people.*

History recounts the events of the past, but not from an objective frame of reference. Depending on the particular view of the author, a certain perspective is espoused. Women in the last century, for example, realized that history was written by men, which affected women's current self-concept and collective empowerment. *His*-story and not *her*-story revealed a past in which men were the great heroes and women's contributions were lost like etchings in the sand. Likewise, people of color know the prevailing history also is not *our-story* but instead reflects an Anglo and European philosophy and worldview; they see history in a different light. Sharing these perspectives can level the historical playing field. Constructing a future that integrates the perspectives of all Americans must start with an inclusive historical foundation.

*Sankofa* beckons us to look at the past courageously and to learn from history, and it assures us that this will give us the clarity and power to construct a better future.

## Whitewashing the Settling of America

OKAY, I'LL ADMIT IT. I am "old school." I was raised in the 1950s, when the settling of America was presented as a romantic adventure. "In fourteen-hundred-ninety-two," my classmates chorused, "Columbus sailed the ocean blue." I envisioned the first Pilgrims in their crisp white collars stepping off their boats, amazed at this vast and beautiful land, unspoiled and untamed. The first Thanksgiving was a wondrous feast, with helpful Indians serving up hearty portions of squash and corn. In my vivid child's imagination I saw covered wagons forging across the rugged plains to settle the wild, wild West. American history at that time was written *of, by,* and *for* the people who conquered this land; it described what happened from their viewpoint. And I believed every word of it.

What kind of trauma do persons of color undergo when the reality of what really happened to their ancestors unfolds like a jarring nightmare in the dark night? I remember my grandmother admonishing me, "Don't wear your skirts too short, like I did." As a Central American Indian she blamed herself, and did not understand that the ravishing of young native girls was a tradition carried over from the conquistadores, who took what they wanted. In fact, the mestizo or mixed race throughout Central and South America is the offspring of the forced integration between Indians and Spaniards. For Indian women, it didn't matter how long or short their skirts were.

The traditional story of the settling of America is a cultural construct. What really happened after Christopher Columbus set foot on the coast of San Salvador and the Pilgrims eagerly followed, landing at Plymouth Rock? Was the land free or stolen? The sugar-coating of history is a hard pill to swallow if it was your grandmother who was abused or your native soil that was lost. To build a multicultural nation, we must peer through a different glass. Are we going to refer to this as the *discovery and settling* of America or are we going to call it a *conquest, colonization, attempted genocide*?

Looking at the past from this frame of reference may be disturbing and seen as irrelevant, or, worse, may create resistance. Contemporary American culture lives in the *ahora*—the present. Getting things done now is imperative! The past is tucked away, mythologized, and certainly not seen as the backdrop for the present. Some may complain, "Do we have to revisit the antecedents of racism again? Haven't we done enough of this? Besides, it wasn't me!" The individualist nature of American culture makes it difficult to assume a collective understanding of—or responsibility for—how the past structures our current reality and affects us today. Cultural amnesia results, so people have no memory of the trials and tribulation of the past or how inequality and exclusion continue.

Can we go down a different road? Is it possible that, by getting right up in the face of historical whitewashing, we can heal the social disease that finds justifications for why one group is better than another? Can we uproot the mind-set that proclaimed that this hemisphere was here for the taking and its inhabitants were savages? When the past is reconstructed in the bright light of honesty—or at least when everyone's story is told—we can begin restructuring leadership from a Eurocentric form to one that reflects and respects the history and culture of all Americans.

*Bueno*; to do this, our story must start before the Pilgrims and conquistadores. Estimates of the native population in the Americas in pre-Columbian times range from twelve and a half million to twenty-five million. Central Mexico alone, it is conjectured, contained almost ten times the number of people in England at that time.[5]

So why did Columbus sail the ocean blue in 1492, why did the inhabitants of this hemisphere stay home? The cultures of the western hemisphere, as we will explore, were rooted to their homelands, whereas Columbus's landing in America spurred an exodus that would become one of the greatest in history.

## The European Exodus

BEGINNING IN THE SIXTEENTH century, religion, politics, and economics converged in Europe, spawning a new worldview. It defined man's nature as acquisitive and competitive, supported the advent of capitalism, and provided a strong rationale—even a religious mandate—for conquering the Americas. When Martin Luther, a devout Catholic priest and a purist, nailed his ninety-five theses to the door of the Wittenberg Church, man's very relationship to God was turned upside down. The Protestant reformation took hold, and a central tenet of Protestantism was that the individual did not need an intermediary—a priest, a saint, or even *Santa Maria*, the Holy Mother of God—to communicate directly with God. This was heresy to the Catholic Church, which for centuries had controlled the pipeline to the deity through their black-clad priests and holy saints.

Fueled by Calvinism in Germany, the Protestant ethic promulgated industriousness, duty, hard work, progress, and the accumulation of wealth. This was a 180-degree turn from the partnership-oriented early cultures that had stressed sharing and living in harmony with nature. Furthermore, Protestantism ran a pretty tight ship. Rules, formal regulations, self-control, rationalism, and subduing of the "pleasures of life" reigned. A diligent person would be working too hard to have time for such frivolities.

It was the entrée of economist Adam Smith's idea of capitalism in 1776, however, that spelled doom for the mutually assisting early cultures. Capitalism compelled individuals to go in search of personal wealth. As the free-market economy proliferated, the belief in self-interest superseded public welfare or social good. The individual no longer had to consider the effects of his actions on the collective.[6] The free market economy, competition, and "survival of the fittest" replaced early communalism. Now the operating words were looking out for *numero uno*—every man for himself.

Political theorist and influential thinker Thomas Hobbes capped this off by espousing that the fundamental motivation of human nature was selfishness—a perpetual struggle for individual advantage, power, and gain. Hobbes argued that society was simply a group of selfish individuals united to maximize safety and protect themselves from one another. His social contract was based on human beings wanting a moral authority to safeguard them from their own selfish nature.[7] This is evidenced today in the mushrooming number of laws intended to contain and police human behavior.

One shift that altered humanity's entire cosmology was the Newtonian concept of the natural world as a machine to be engineered for humankind's benefit—a far cry from early

 *The free market economy, competition, and "survival of the fittest" replaced early communalism. Now the operating words were looking out for* numero uno— *every man for himself.*

societies' belief that the earth was a living being and humans one part of the intricate web of life. Hobbes and Newton provided a platform on which rugged individualism and materialism formed the matrix of the *individualist* culture. Changing man's relationship to the earth from steward to subjugator also set the stage for an economic system that allowed the using up and abusing of natural and human resources.

Writing in the 1950s, historian Max Weber accurately described the Protestant ethic as the seedbed for the capitalist economy. Its proponents reason that making money is an expression of virtue and one's purpose in life; thus, becoming wealthy is an end in itself—and even a moral imperative![8]

Yet while Adam Smith was writing about the benefits of free market politics, approximately twenty-six million peasants in Europe were unemployed and starving. In France, the widespread famine led to peasant revolts and the destruction of feudalism. People became more autonomous and separate, as the Industrial Revolution lured them to factories in urban areas. There people became, of necessity, more self-reliant. In addition, the means of production were consolidated into fewer hands. Factories were organized hierarchically, with owners at the top, then bosses, managers, supervisors, and workers. This replaced the age-old, more collaborative orientation of agrarian communities, intensified inequality, and laid the foundation of today's social class structure.[9]

## This Land Is My Land

The European exodus spanned almost four centuries. The conquest and colonization of the western hemisphere was fueled by overpopulation and the broken promise of the Industrial Revolution, which left many people in Europe earning meager wages and living in squalor. Armed with a strong Protestant work ethic, a competitive drive, and an individualist spirit, thousands crossed the Atlantic seeking land, wealth, and prosperity. In the expanse of the American frontier and its wealth of natural resources, the Europeans saw a bonanza that fulfilled and sanctioned their thirst for material gain, ordained by the Protestant God.

While their northern European counterparts came to homestead and profit, the Spanish conquest was couched as a holy crusade. The Catholic Church sent priests to save the souls of the heathen savages—which didn't preclude enslaving them and profiting from their forced labor. Unlike North America—which, despite the extensive inhabitation by thousands of native tribes, was essentially still a natural wilderness—

the city of Tenochtitlán (now Mexico City) was larger than any city in Europe, with more inhabitants than London or Seville. Hernán Cortez found a radiant island metropolis laced with canals, beautiful palaces, and accumulated treasure.[10] A different kind of exploitation followed: mass quantities of gold and silver were plundered and sent to the Spanish crown.

In *The Rediscovery of North America*, Barry Lopez proposes that the conquest was from the outset a series of raids and irresponsible and criminal behavior, a spree whose end was never envisioned. Timber, land, gold, precious ores, as well as indigenous people, were bountiful and there for the taking. He notes that the conquerors' belief in their imperial and unquestionable right, conferred by God, was supported by a belief in racial and cultural supremacy. Sanctioned by the state and the militia, and fueled by the Protestant ethic, the assumption that one is due wealth became justification for exploiting the land, water, and people.[11] This acquisitive mentality meant there would never be a time when one would say *Basta!* ("This is enough"). The new frontier was seen as boundless.

The indigenous cultures in America could not understand or withstand this avaricious and acquisitive behavior. They had no frame of reference for dealing with a worldview so divergent from their own. Pre-Columbian cultures were tightly interwoven. The group took precedence over the individual. People shared what they had and cared for one another. Cooperation, not competition, nurtured the collective and group harmony. Many tribes had creation myths in which their homeland was bestowed by the Creator. Everyday life was punctuated with rituals and celebrations to mark the passing of the seasons. People strove to live in harmony with nature, which they regarded as sacred. These cultures honored the wisdom of their ancestors. The idea of getting on boats and crossing to another continent to find more land or resources was as foreign to them as the conquistadores on their large, swift, and powerful animals. The native peoples felt blessed to live in a place that was both beautiful and rich in the resources needed to sustain life. Why would anyone leave one's family, tribe, the comfort of community, and the sacred land that contained the bones and stories of one's ancestors?

The clash between these two worldviews is illustrated by the story of the Aztec emperor Montezuma. Knowing the Spanish wanted gold, Montezuma took Hernándo Cortez to his palace, where mounds of the precious substance were kept. He told Cortez, "Take what you want," thinking Cortez would be satisfied. The emperor did not realize that the lust for gold was endless and this would only whet the Spanish appetite. Similarly, the Indians who taught the Pilgrims to survive their first winter and shared Thanksgiving dinner with them could not fathom that their new neighbors would soon declare them savages, devastate them with war and diseases, and gradually herd them onto reservations.

Out of over a thousand distinct pre-Columbian cultures in the western hemisphere, only three can be described as acquisitive—the Aztecs, Mayans, and Incas. Although these cultures built empires that might be considered akin to the European model of expansion, they were also decentralized and, historical studies suggest, often preserved the cultures and languages of subjugated people. It is safe to suggest, then, that the cultures in the western hemisphere were overwhelmingly collective, lived in harmony with nature, and valued cooperation.

Perhaps it is fitting that this hemisphere bears the name of Amerigo Vespucci, the Florentine explorer, because he saw the western hemisphere as a utopian world: "The people live in agreement with nature. They have no property; instead all things are held in common." Without the concept of private property, there was no need for the strong tethers of the individualist culture. "They live without a king and without any form of authority. Each one is his own master."[12]

# Work and Individualism Become an American Ethos

WHEN I SHARE the preceding perspective on the "settling" of America with young students of all races, they are usually captivated by the fact that although they learned about the discovery of America and may have studied Thomas Hobbes, Adam Smith, and the Protestant Reformation, they never connected these to current issues of racism or exclusion in America. Other readers may be discomfited by these revelations. Yet the recent designation of months to honor women's contributions, Black history, Hispanic heritage, Asian American and Pacific Islanders culture, American Indian traditions, and lesbian, gay, bisexual, and transgender pride underscore the need to broaden the ethnocentric funnel of American history.

Looking at history from different cultural perspectives is quite relevant for young people as they prepare to craft the future. How can they ensure that the past is not repeated without understanding how history frames the present? How can they partake of the cultural gifts of the myriad peoples that built America if they are ignorant of their history and contributions?

Another incentive for examining the past is "fast forwarding" to today and taking into account how unfettered individualism, the Protestant work ethic, and capitalism may be impairing our quality of life. One benefit of multicultural perspectives is that they allow us to tap a wider range of choices and potential benefits. The next section, Principle 2, looks at the societal downsides of the Protestant ethic and individualist values and discusses the benefits of balancing these values with more communal ones from communities of color.

The Frenchman Alexis de Tocqueville, in his astute observations of our young country in 1835, noted that the characteristic he most admired was our individualism. He clearly warned, however, that if not continually balanced by other habits that would reinforce the social context and fabric of community, it would inevitably lead to separation and division.[13] Sociologist Robert Bellah and his colleagues, in their book *Habits of the Heart,* argue that the time warned of by de Tocqueville has come—unchecked individualism has led to emotional isolation and fragmentation.[14]

In his acclaimed book *Bowling Alone: The Collapse and Revival of American Community,* Harvard professor Robert Putnam identifies the phenomenon of withdrawal from community as both the cause and the result of larger social changes. The title reflects his research showing that although the number of people bowling increased in the last twenty years, bowling leagues have declined. As Americans become more isolated, civic engagement, social involvement, and volunteerism are declining. Even entertaining at home has dropped 45 percent since the mid-1970s.

 *Alexis de Tocqueville clearly warned that if individualism was not continuously balanced by other habits that would reinforce the social context and fabric of community, it would inevitably lead to separation and division.*

Putnam ascertains that mobility has also contributed: nearly one in five Americans moves each year. It's been demonstrated that these new arrivals are less likely to vote, join civic organizations, or build lasting ties with neighbors. He surmises, "For people as for plants, frequent repotting disrupts roots systems."

Putnam also notes the increase in commuter time, estimating that every ten minutes spent in the car cuts civic engagement by 10 percent.[15]

As suburban sprawl widens the distances between people, we are losing familiar community meeting grounds and a sense of place. Community connection points have been replaced by festively decorated shopping malls and bustling airports where our lives intersect in transit. People buzz around, shopping, drinking lattés, but the crowd is made up of strangers. These mass commercial spaces are designed not to connect us but to move us from place to place or from store to store. We are among others, but the sense of belonging, community, and relatedness that was once the core of human identity is not being nurtured.

Researchers skeptical of Putnam's conclusions conducted a major national survey, only to find that although people are networking on MySpace, text messaging on cell phones, and blogging at all hours, they are less up close and personal than they used to be. One-quarter of those responding indicated that they have no one with whom to discuss the most important personal issues of their lives. The researchers reported that in the past two decades, based on comparison data from national surveys conducted in 1985, the average number of close friends of an individual has dropped from three to two. This powerful evidence supports Putnam's research, indicating that we are becoming increasingly isolated even as cell phones, the Internet, and technology make us more interconnected.[16]

The good news is that the trend toward community disintegration and social isolation is being reversed by younger generations who use technology to build community, act collectively, and stay connected (almost constantly).

## Balancing Individualism with Community Good

THE PROTESTANT ETHIC, which equated wealth with virtue coupled with capitalist economics, forged a country with once-unimaginable wealth. Through their industriousness, Americans became some of the richest people on the planet, boasting the ninth highest per-capita income in the world. However, has the drive for materialism mutated into obsessive consumerism? The drive for more and more material consumption is apparent when we note that in 2009 the world's average per-capita income was $8,732[17]—and the average credit-card debt in the United States was $8,329.[18]

The emphasis on industriousness also instilled a propensity for overworking. Americans are the most workaholic people in the industrial world, working 30 percent more hours each year than their European counterparts. In 2007 43 percent didn't even take a week of vacation, while the British enjoyed six and a half weeks of holidays and the French topped out at almost twelve weeks. The United States, unlike 127 other countries, has no law specifying that workers must have vacations. It is difficult to enjoy the fruits of one's labors when working without respite; this also jeopardizes family life, community involvement, and health. Imagine how fulfilling life could be with a stretch of weeks of vacation each year to enjoy family and travel, to read and learn, and to take up a hobby, exercise, or engage in community service![19]

Does focusing on ourselves and our material acquisitions at least make us happy? Isn't materialism a fulfilling trip to nirvana? In their book *From Me to We: Turning Self-Help on Its Head*, Craig Kielburger and Marc Kielburger, two Millennial brothers who are Canadian altruists, dispute the assumption that "mo money equals mo happiness." Citing a Roper Organization poll of 1,500 Americans, they concluded that unless you are desperately poor and do not have basic necessities, money has little bearing on how happy you are. Seventy-four percent of those earning less than $25,000 a year reported that they were somewhat or very happy with their lives. Interestingly, among those with incomes of $50,000 or more, this dropped to 10 percent.[20]

*The emphasis on industriousness instilled a propensity for overworking. Americans are the most workaholic people in the industrial world, working 30 percent more hours each year than their European counterparts.*

How does the "American happy quotient" compare to the rest of the world? According to the 2009 Happy Planet Index, the country with the highest number of happy citizens was Costa Rica, followed by the Dominican Republic, Jamaica, and Guatemala. America ranked 114![21] Even worse, happiness levels have been declining in the U.S. for decades, having peaked in 1957. Even though Americans consume twice as much as we did in the 1950s, it has not made us happier.[22] *Apparently, we were happier when we had less stuff to worry about.*

Obsessive U.S. consumption is well documented in *The Story of Stuff*, a book that inspires people to change their keep-on-buying-and-accumulating pattern. Author Annie Leonard laments that the U.S. makes up 5 percent of the world's people but consumes 30 percent of the world's resources and generates 30 percent of the world's waste. Meanwhile, almost half the world lives on less than two dollars a day. Unchecked and rampant expansion of production, consumption, and disposal is jeopardizing our happiness, health, and communities, and the very survival of our planet and upcoming generations.[23]

## Returning to a *We* Culture

The next section, Principle 2, continues in the tradition of *Sankofa* by reviewing the change from first cultures that centered on *We* to the individualist or *I* culture. *Sankofa* reminds us that for most of human history, people lived in *We* or collective cultures, in which the collective superseded individual gain. The strong hold of the *I* culture in America has weakened the support systems and relationships that once existed in extended families and communities. It's telling that more than one out of four Americans now lives alone.

Author M. Scott Peck, after searching for the keys to human fulfillment in his classic best seller *The Road Less Traveled*, turned his attention to the role community plays in people's well-being. Peck found that people thirst for a sense of place and belonging. He envisioned a world in which a "soft individualism" acknowledges our *interdependence*. Rugged individualism demands that we always put our best foot forward, hide our weaknesses and insecurities, and don a mask of self-sufficiency. This leaves people feeling inadequate, exhausted, and alone. Peck believed that humanity stands on the brink of annihilation if community and interdependence are not rewoven, stating, "In and through community lies the salvation of the world."[24]

This longing for community reflects the collectivism of early *We* cultures, which remains the essence of African American, Latino, and Indian people. *We* satisfies our need to belong and have meaning in our lives. *We* values generosity and taking care of one another. As collective cultures were the cradles of humankind, *We* is an intersection and connecting point that can bring people together. *We* means remembering that our mutuality ensured our survival, and it holds the promise to our future existence.

Developing a collective *We* orientation can heal much of the social malaise that unbridled individualism, overwork, and materialism have spawned. Thus, in the spirit of *Sankofa* in which we learn from the past, we can heed the good counsel given by de Tocqueville almost 175 years ago: balancing individualism with the collective good will reinforce the social context and fabric of community.[25]

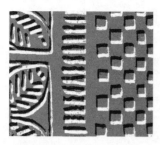

**NEXT STEPS**

**Reflecting On
and Applying
Principle One**

# *Sankofa*—Learn from the Past

## Honor your heritage that you may honor the heritage of others

When people immigrated to America, they were urged to cut ties to their homelands, forget their customs and language, and merge into the melting pot. Thus, homogeneity and a monocultural approach emerged. A multicultural perspective requires honoring the history and culture of all people. *To do this we must first honor our own heritage so we may appreciate the heritage of others.*

This exercise lays the foundation for leading from a multicultural perspective. It is a reflective piece that participants may want to later think about and research. I have found that sharing in pairs followed by a group summary works best.

- What is the story of how your family "got here"?

- Who in your family might shed light on your heritage and family traditions?

- What characteristics, strengths, values, and family traits have you inherited?

- How have they helped shape who you are today?

- What else would you like to know about your heritage, and how can you find this out?

## Connect to your collective history, extended family, and "tribe"

This exercise illustrates the American Indian connection with their ancestors and their understanding that a person's lineage provides wisdom, guidance, and energy. Introduce yourself, using the Navajo greeting that follows to delineate your lineage. Groups can share this and talk about the unique qualities of their ancestry. People who do not know their grandparents' names and histories often decide subsequently to seek out their history and reconnect to their cultural roots.

I am _____, the daughter/son of _____,

the great grandson/granddaughter of_____,

the great-great grandson/granddaughter of_____.

Participants discuss their feelings about connecting with their past and their roots. Did they experience the power of ancestry? Those who do not know their history may decide to talk to older people in their families and find out more about their ancestry.

## Seek out and learn from people with a different perspective on history

To create our multicultural future, all people's voices and perspectives must be welcome. History is not an objective narrative. Many people from communities of color have a different slant on historical events but have not shared this openly. A genuine dialogue on these perspectives can be the first step in creating open communication and learning from one another.

The following guidelines for dialogue can assist with this process:

- Listen and speak without judgment.

- Respect differences.

- Reexamine all positions.

 (NEXT STEPS I CONTINUED)

- Search for strengths and values in the way others see things.

- Explore common ground.

- Focus on learning.

- Release the need for outcomes.

- Seek to walk in another's moccasins.

## Participate in the historical celebrations of diverse groups

Seek out information on the designated celebrations (days, weeks, or months) for Women's History, Black History, Hispanic Heritage, Native American Heritage, Asian-Pacific American Heritage, GLBT, and so on. Attend these events and learn about the contributions of these and other groups to America.

## Recommended readings and resources

### Books

- *1491: New Revelations of the Americas Before Columbus* by Charles C. Mann (Knopf, 2005).

- *Guns, Germs, and Steel* by Jared Diamond (W.W. Norton and Company, 1999.)

- *On Dialogue* by David Bohm (Routledge Classics, 1996).

- *The Rediscovery of North America* by Barry Lopez (Vintage Books, 1990).

- *The Story of Stuff: How Our Obsession with Stuff Is Trashing Our Planet, Our Communities and Our Health and a Vision for Change* by Annie Leonard (Free Press, 2010).

- *The Story of Stuff Reading Guide.* Story of Stuff Project, 1442 A Walnut St., #242, Berkeley, CA 94747; 510.883.1055; info@storyofstuff.org; www.storyofstuff.org.

## Films

- *Dances with Wolves* (produced by Tig Productions, Majestic Films International, 1990). The film depicts the fate of the Lakota Sioux Indians who lose their lands as European migration spreads westward.

- *Guns, Germs, and Steel* (produced by Lion Television for PBS Specials and National Geographic Television and Film, 2005), http://www.shoppbs.org/home/index.jsp. Based on Jared Diamond's Pulitzer Prize winning book, the series answers the question: Why were the Europeans the ones to conquer so much of our planet?

## Video

- *Guns, Germs, and Steel*, (YouTube), available in 18 sections, http://www.youtube.com/user/bfq3000.

## PRINCIPLE 2

# *I* to *We*—From Individualism to Collective Identity

I WAS BORN INTO a *We* culture in which seven people lived in a tiny house with one bathroom. There was no concept of private space—a person never went to his or her room; the whole house was common ground. A *We* culture meant my mother, Maria, dressed us up on Sundays and marched us to church, where we took up the whole pew. She watched over us like an eagle circling the morning sky. She only had to give us that look to scare us into perfect piety. *We cultures have a strong sense of belonging and sticking together.*

A *We* culture meant my mother hurried home from church, took off her black mantilla, and then cooked the Sunday chicken, which was carefully divided so that every other Sunday, for example, I got a leg. *We cultures share everything.* A *We* culture meant that on Saturday mornings everyone scrubbed doors, walls, and windows, shook rugs, took out the mattresses for a good airing, and washed down the sidewalks. *We cultures work together so everyone benefits.*

The preparation for a *We* orientation starts early in life. Latino babies are never left at home with a babysitter. At Sunday gatherings or *fiestas*, babies are passed around like precious treasures. People anxiously wait their turn to sing to the baby, pinch its cheeks, and make it laugh. Babies are called *preciosa* and told over and over how *linda* (pretty) they are! At parties, they are bounced from lap to lap. When the music starts, they are sashayed onto the dance floor and rocked to a ranchero or salsa beat. Latino babies get accustomed to people at an early age; that is how they become *We*. **We cultures center on people.**

One time when I had a bad tooth, my mother took me to the dentist and then we went to see the movie *The African Queen*. It is a vivid memory, because it is the only time I remember one-on-one time with my mother. *We* meant I was almost never alone or with just one other person. **We cultures are collective and relish togetherness.**

No one gets left out of a *We* culture. Uncle Huey showed up on a sweltering August day to the warm embrace of my father. He would spit brown tobacco off the front porch and aggravatingly clear his throat ten times a minute. His trousers hung off him like the laundry on my mother's clothesline. We pleaded with our Papí, "He is embarrassing, *pleeeze* send him back home." This was to no avail. No matter how obnoxious he was, he was part of the *We*—he was my uncle. **We cultures are impeccably inclusive.**

For Latino Catholics, first Holy Communion is a solemn and festive day, one's first encounter with the heavenly host—a baby step into spiritual maturity. As the big day approached, I was worried. We didn't have any money and all the young girls would be kneeling before the holy altar in fancy white dresses. From an old trunk, my mother took out the precious cotton brought from Nicaragua that she had been saving for herself. She measured me here and poked me there. After working all day, cooking the family dinner, and putting her children to bed, she would sew late into the night. A week later she proudly held up a simple white dress with lace stitched around the collar, on which she had pinned a cotton flower from Woolworth. The other girls had store-bought dresses with lace and taffeta, but my dress was the most beautiful because no one else's mom had sacrificed so much. **We cultures put benefiting the whole before the individual.**

I still can't imagine how my mother, with her broken English and limited resources, figured all this out! It was her total dedication to the *We*, that unbroken promise that her family and children came first. *We* was all she knew. She passed on that sense of a family and culture of togetherness to me. *We* was embedded deep in my soul. I didn't understand it then, but it sustained me when I left my family to go to college and live in the strange land of the *I*'s. *In **We** cultures the I exists only in relationship to others, not as a separate entity.*

# *I* and Individualism or *We* and Collectivism

ANTHROPOLOGISTS WHO STUDY and categorize cultures make broad distinctions between collectivist or *We* cultures, such as American Indians, Latinos, and African Americans, and those that are more individualistically or *I* oriented, such as modern North Americans and western Europeans that are considered individualist. In *Managing Diversity: People Skills for a Multicultural Workplace,* Norma Carr-Ruffino comments that most of the world's cultures, as well as women in all societies, are collectivist.[1] This is understandable, as individualism is a historically new phenomenon that grew out of the Protestant ethic and European intellectualism. Of course, these cultures are not rigidly separate; in today's rapidly changing and interdependent world, cultures are blending aspects of both. For instance, to function successfully in dominant culture organizations, people of color have learned the individualist orientation.

In our discussion of the previous principle, *Sankofa,* we reviewed the roots of the individualism that dominates in the United States today; we will now take a closer look at collectivist or *We* cultures To integrate the best of each viewpoint into a multicultural leadership model, we must understand the nuances of both orientations and how these have influenced leadership.

It is important to clarify that the term *collectivist* refers not to today's political concept of socialism, but rather to an ancient, tried-and-true form of social organization. Collectivist *We* cultures have been on the earth for a very long time; their traditions and histories go back many millennia. These are stable cultures with highly defined rules, and they change more slowly than individualist cultures. Collectivist cultures are usually tightly woven and integrated. As noted previously, these cultures cherish group welfare, unity, and harmony. To maintain these, people behave politely, act in a socially desirable manner, and respect others. The family, community, or tribe takes precedence over the individual, whose identity flows from the collective. People work for group success before personal credit or gain.

Individualist cultures, on the other hand, appeared relatively recently in history, and they are more loosely integrated. Change and risk taking are embraced. Individuals are *highly differentiated* from others. Self-identity and self-interest are keystones. To grow up means to become independent, autonomous, and responsible for one's own life. Individual freedom and choice are highly valued. In these cultures, individual needs supersede collective ones. This is not considered selfish. The individual serves society by living up to her or his potential. Achievement and getting things done take priority.

Whether a culture is individualist or collectivist depends on the degree to which individuals' beliefs and actions are independent of those of the group. *We* cultures emphasize group opinions and actions, and they stress psychological closeness. Individual goals are integrated with those of the collective. Individualist cultures, on the other hand, emphasize personal opinions. Being able to think for yourself signifies intelligence and competency. Competition with others is considered healthy, motivating, and beneficial. One advances by calling attention to oneself or standing out from the group.

 *Of course, these cultures are not rigidly separate; in today's rapidly changing and interdependent world, cultures are blending aspects of both.*

The extent of one's individualist or collectivist orientation determines how much control one assumes in life. The individualist focus says, "To a very great extent, I control my life, determine my reality, choose my experiences, and shape my destiny. I am the captain of my own ship." Collectivist cultures are more in tune with natural cycles and believe in a life power that is external to them. These forces influence their lives. They also take into account what other people think, want, and need. These lessen individual freedom of choice.

People from collectivist cultures, therefore, have a greater belief that things happen to them. The Spanish language contains a passive tense in which innate objects or others assume responsibility: "The glass fell"; "The taxi left me"; "It didn't call my attention." Similar verbal constructs, found in languages of African tribes such as the Zulu and

*Culture, the lens through which a group of individuals defines reality, has been described as collective programming. Culture determinism proposes that a person's values, beliefs, and worldview are riveted on this early conditioning.*

Xhosa.[2] signify an external source of control to be consulted and considered—there are many more factors than just "what *I* want."

Culture, the lens through which a group of individuals defines reality, has been described as *collective programming*. Cultural determinism proposes that a person's values, beliefs, and worldview are riveted to this early conditioning. Today's diverse society and global marketplace require leaders to free themselves of this type of conditioning in order to attain a broader cultural perspective and repertoire. Cultural adaptability and flexibility have become essential leadership skills.

The next section reviews early *We* cultures that have existed since prehistoric times. Considering these antecedents provides insights for understanding how leadership in Anglo society is different from leadership in communities of color.

## Our First Culture Was a We Culture

BEFORE THERE WAS an *I* culture, *We* ensured our continued existence. Those who trace man's evolutionary heritage from anthropoids—the great apes—can witness even today their cooperation, strong sense of family, and mutual care. Genomics has confirmed that fully 99.4 percent of our DNA is similar to that of the anthropoids. Much early human behavior was patterned on the great apes and their communal behavior.[3] Obviously, no "lone wolf" survived and evolved alone. (The idea of the lone wolf is actually a misnomer; wolves are wedded to their pack.) Our evolutionary journey has been a collective one. Even today we live through a long, dependent childhood before we can live on our own: someone feeds us, cleans us, and makes sure we are safe, warm, and dry. *We is the reason we are alive.*

Primitive times were brutal and treacherous, with wild terrains, hunger, predatory animals, and exposure to tempestuous weather. Early humans had to be constantly alert—ready to defend themselves or to take rapid flight and flee the threat. Alone, a person would die from the elements and a multitude of dangers. The tribe was the warm bear robe essential for protection. Whether for hunting, taking care of domesticated animals, raising children, planting or harvesting, or preparing medicinal and herbal remedies, the tribe brought people together for preservation, safety, comfort, ritual, and celebration.

Through tribal living, human beings developed complex and mutually beneficial ways of working together, including the differentiation of roles based on one's abilities or lineage—which today is still the basis of organizational development. The herbalist, the potter, the fire keeper, the weaver, the warrior, the chief, the ruling council, and the hunting party, all first came into form when humans lived in tribes. Just as important, the tribe uncovered and explained the meaning of the universe and man's place in it. In times when the mysteries of life were stupefying, humans looked to the medicine man, the chief, or the wise woman to explain events in the natural world and provide guidance.

Tribes were the vehicles for a collective human identity or the sense of *We* to evolve. Even today, many tribes dress in identical clothes, wear their hair the same, adorn themselves similarly, and follow the daily rituals that give meaning to their lives.

Individualist cultures would have us believe that survival of the fittest was an every-man-for-himself instinct in a dog-eat-dog, competitive environment. In actuality, the collective lifted humans to the top of the evolutionary pyramid. In her notable book *Calling the Circle*, visionary author Christina Baldwin uses the term *first culture* to refer to the time when humans lived in tribes or small communities in which everyone was needed and included and everyone belonged. Baldwin points out that human beings survived and thrived because of their ability to care for each other, work together, and help one another. *We* was our "competitive evolutionary edge" over other species. Survival of the fittest was a cooperative and reciprocal experience.[4]

 *Human beings survived and thrived because of their ability to care for each other, work together, and help one another. We was our competitive evolutionary edge over other species. Survival of the fittest was a cooperative and reciprocal experience.*

Riane Eisler's landmark work *The Chalice and the Blade* documents early societies across Europe, Asia, and the Americas in which people worked in partnership, living in harmony with nature. She notes that human survival was largely due to the cultivation of highly sophisticated ways of working together that included collaborative decision-making structures. Eisler describes many Neolithic cultures as ones in which "social relations are primarily based on the principle of linking rather than ranking, [and] may best be described as a partnership model where both men and women worked together for the common good." First cultures by necessity were tight as a drum, and their foundation was *mutual assistance* and *loyalty*.[5]

To understand the deep groove that "the tribe" or collective existence has made in our memory banks, consider that humans first appeared about 195,000 years ago.[6] For over 80 percent of this time span, humans lived in caves, surrounded by a tribe that provided protection, love, warmth, food, family, and a sense of identity.[7] Human beings are social animals; *We* have always lived in groups. Through our long evolutionary journey, our reliance on each other was linked directly with the need for survival—the strongest instinct we have. First cultures, therefore, are humanity's home base.

## We Is the Tribe, Community, and *Familia*

The mutuality of early cultures has survived in its most vibrant forms among indigenous people and in the Indian, Latino, and Black communities, in which sticking together has been a survival tactic. Their collectivism, which centers on group identity and the common good, is still evident today.

American Indian leadership, for instance, is based on a great deal of introspection and work on identity—both individually and collectively, for the two are intertwined. Individuals are like the reeds making up a woven basket that is decorated with traditional designs and colors. The basket is the tribe, holding individuals in place and giving them a sense of unity, identity, and sustenance.

LaDonna Harris, president of Americans for Indian Opportunity, observes how this works: "In Native cultures, *strong personal identity and collective identity stand side by side.* A good tribal person must have self-worth, positive qualities and skills, and be as healthy as possible so they can contribute to the community. The collective is only as strong as the individuals who give it life." Benny Shendo concurs: "The tribe and community are central, then the extended family, the clan, and then perhaps the individual. Yet, people are secure in their personal identity. In the Anglo culture, individualism is stressed. The reality is you can be collective *and* still be an individual. You can be totally yourself, a real character, but you are yourself within this spectrum of community and tribe first."

Shendo reflects on the collective identity: "For Native Americans, who you are depends on what tribe you belong to. Your rights, like the right to live on our lands, for example, come from your tribal membership. It's not about the individual. In all Indian cultures, the tribe is paramount because it's that community, that group of people who create the collective identity, the songs, traditions, and culture . . . When I meet Indian people, the first thing they say is 'what tribe are you?' That's how we establish our initial relationship, and it is a collective identity."

The first premise of the American Indians for Opportunity Ambassadors Program reflects this point of view: "The strength of the Indian peoples, both collectively and individually, is the tribe. It is our culture, family, community, and tribe that define our role in society and our self-identity." Collective identity is in sharp contrast to individualism, which touts personal achievement and competition. There is no concept within each American Indian tribe of winning at the expense of others.[8]

*The reality is you can be collective and still be an individual. You can be totally yourself, a real character, but you are yourself within this spectrum of community and tribe first.*

—Benny Shendo Jr.,
Jemez Pueblo

Similarly, a core belief in Hispanic culture is that other people come first. The Latino tendency toward collectivism is evident in the treasured value of *la familia,* which broadly refers to groups with a special affinity who provide assistance and support. Latinos cherish belonging, group benefit, mutuality, and reciprocity. Interdependency, cooperation, and mutual assistance are the norm. Unlike the Anglo nuclear family, the Latino *familia* is elastic and grows to include *padrinos* or *madrinas*—godparents for baptisms, weddings or confirmations—and *"tías"* or *"tíos"*—honorary aunts or uncles.

A person who is simply walking down the street with a close friend may be suddenly introduced as a *compadre or comadre,* indicating that he or she is now considered family. Even sponsors for *quinceaneras* (the ceremony presenting a young woman to the community), wedding anniversaries, or baptisms become part of the family. Latinos have an open-door policy when it comes to *We. Bienvenido*—welcome, hospitality, and inclusiveness—makes for a dynamic and expanding family much like a tribe.

This tradition has roots in both the indigenous and the Spanish cultures that are the ancestry of Latinos. The large extended families in Spain ensured that a relative or close friend was contacted when a need arose. The Aztec culture was organized in multiple family groups who governed themselves and worked as a unit. The growing of crops, building of homes, trading, and caring for children were all collective *We* endeavors.

African Americans ancestors came from tribal cultures that mirror a similar sense of connectedness, interdependence, and reciprocity. Dr. Jim Joseph, in his insightful book *Remaking America*, termed this the *cosmology of connectedness*. "The idea that a person cannot be fully understood apart from the community which determines his or her personhood was fundamental to the African view of moral duty and social obligation."[9]

African Americans carry on this collectivist tradition. Under slavery, everyone suffered under the same yoke. Black people faced discrimination and racism by "sticking together." The *We* in the song "We Shall Overcome" indicates an understanding that solidarity is their source of strength and salvation. Indeed, since the practice of slavery tore families apart, African Americans don't know if someone is a blood relative or not, so they refer to each other as brother, sister, or cuz (cousin). On a first encounter, although Black people may not know each other, they feel their common history, faith, and culture.

Dr. Joseph believes the large-family patterns that Black people develop, which include stepparents, peer group members, community leaders, meeting brethren, teachers, and special friends, is also a legacy from the African world: "While the bonds of the extended family were severed by the massive transcontinental displacements that brought Africans to American shores, the spirit of community not only survived but took on new forms and meaning."[10]

 *Black people faced discrimination and racism by "sticking together." The* We *in the song "We Shall Overcome" indicates an understanding that solidarity is their source of strength and salvation.*

This immutable group identity endures. In 2005, Kanye West, the controversial rap singer, was chosen by news columnist Barbara Walters as one of the most fascinating people of the year. When asked to describe himself, his first word was "*Black!*"[11] Likewise, when I am working on identity with African American youth, I give them a sheet with the question "Who are you?" For almost every teenager "Black" is the first choice. The White culture does not have that kind of centralized identity with people of their race or color.

*The highly developed sense of* We—*community, extended family and tribe—has kept communities of color intact for the past five hundred years. That strong sense of* We *was their survival, hope for tomorrow, and anchor of mutual protection, support, and celebration.*

## *I* Is Contained in *We*

AND *WE* ARE NOT A DICHOTOMY. *I* is intrinsic to the *We* orientation—individuals must be strong for the collective to thrive. *We* do not have to choose one or the other. This concept of *both and* rather than *either or* is a thread that runs through collectivist cultures. Because they are more tightly woven, there is a wholeness in which many things, including differences, can exist at once. Just as the corn stalk grows tall on its own, but only fully matures when many are planted and cross-fertilization occurs, the *I* is nourished in the rich soil that has been cultivated by many generations.

The challenge is to balance communal good with individual gain—to reach the higher ground of interdependence, where personal gain is not achieved at the expense of the common good. Today, the widening gap between the haves and have-nots and the lack of regard for the well-being of our children and our grandchildren's economic security indicate that the pendulum has swung too far in the *I* direction. Balancing individualism with collectivism may sound easy; however, it proposes a new *cultural equilibrium* that runs contrary to the social conditioning and historical antecedents of the dominant culture.

When competitive and acquisitive individualist cultures have clashed with collective ones, the *We* has always been relegated to the underdog position. Individuals from collective cultures may feel exploited or ripped off when they sacrifice for the group or organization and are not recognized for their hard work or are passed up for promotion. The question is: How do we balance the *I* with the *We*? If we can accept that human beings have an innate drive for connectedness and taking care of one another, then returning to a *We* perspective is a natural homecoming.

Einstein once remarked that our sense of separateness was "a kind of optical illusion." To live in a mutually caring world, he continued, we must undertake a deliberate change in perspective. "Our task must be to free ourselves . . . by widening our circle of compassion to embrace all creatures and the whole of nature . . . "[12] Einstein's unified field theory runs contrary to our individualist and autonomy-focused culture; it resonates instead with the holistic worldview of indigenous communities.

## We sustains the Future

THE *WE* ORIENTATION values the common good and safeguards the community's long-term welfare. In *We* cultures it is the solemn responsibility of leaders to ensure that children have the resources and preparation to live a good long life. The *We* identity encompasses ancestors, present-day people, and those who will follow—a vision in sharp contrast to the economic inequality, corporate greed, fiscal irresponsibility, and environmental crisis ravaging our nation today.

Principle 3, *Mi Casa Es Su Casa*, explores how people in communities of color are expected to treat each other with a generosity of spirit and have passed this trait from one generation to another. Almost unanimously, collective cultures understand that the excessive accumulation of wealth or power by a few hinders the well-being of the society as a whole. In collective cultures generosity allows people and the community to thrive. Deep sharing is a cultural touchstone and wealth is defined as being able to give to others.

## NEXT STEPS

**Reflecting On
and Applying
Principle Two**

# *I* to *We*—From Individualism
# to Collective Identity

## Understanding our group or collective heritage
## lays the foundation for appreciating our diversity

People bring the oldest picture they have of their grandparents or *antepasados* and something that represents their culture. Each person shares the story reflected in the picture. (In the oral tradition of communities of color, people embellish imaginatively, using flowery language.) They share the meaning of the object that represents their culture. Pictures and objects are placed on a table draped with a nice cloth and decorated with flowers and even candles. People comment on what they have learned about each other's history and unique backgrounds. This exercise creates a cultural collage of people's backgrounds and family histories.

## Create a collective history for
## your community or organization

Traditionally, people grew up in the same place, knew each other's families, and had a common history and values. In today's mobile society, people from many origins and places live and work together. Building trust is a key leadership challenge when people are diverse, do not know each other, or are newcomers. Creating a community or organizational timeline acknowledges individual experiences, discovers mutual history, and nurtures common ground.

## Step One: Preparing a community or organizational timeline

A long scroll of paper with the words "Our History and Significant Milestones" is placed on the wall. The years are posted across the top in increments of five to ten years, from the organization's founding or other relevant starting point to the present.

## Step Two: Exploring our connections

People reflect on significant global or societal events that impacted their lives: important life decisions, achievements, or events, and milestones or changes in the organization or community. What is each person's history with the organization? Sharing these memories is an opportunity to learn about each other and recognize contributions.

Individual histories are recorded; then small groups discuss the similarities, differences, and unique perspectives and choose three to five significant ones to share with the large group or their community. (Record these on sticky notes so they can be posted on the timeline.)

## Step Three: Integrating our experiences and acknowledging our history

Reflecting on the trends and patterns shown on the timeline, the group discusses what they have learned about each other, the societal influences that have affected them, and the organizational or community changes. Understanding a company's beginnings and founding vision can inspire a sense of purpose and belonging.

# Recommended readings and resources

- *From Me to We: Turning Self-Help on Its Head* by Craig Kielburger and Marc Kielburger (Wiley, 2004).

- For more information on completing a timeline, see *Future Search: An Action Guide to Finding Common Ground in Organizations and Communities* by Marvin Weisbord and Sandra Janoff (Berrett-Koehler, 1995).

# Video:

- You Tube: *If the world was a village of 100.* http://www.youtube.com/watch?v=jNnbO8x4JAY A powerful tool to enhance understanding of our interconnectedness and the dire need to reestablish the conscious sense of *WE*.

## PRINCIPLE 3

# *Mi Casa Es Su Casa—*
# A Spirit of Generosity

MY SISTER MARGARITA was thirteen when we arrived in Tampa, Florida. Since she was raised in Nicaragua, she is culturally more traditional than I am. When I was in my thirties, she was visiting when my next-door neighbor dropped by to meet her. He casually admired a handwoven poncho hanging on the wall. "Thank you," I smiled, remembering its origins. "I got it in Chile." When he left, my sister scolded me: "Have you forgotten everything you were taught? You were supposed to give him that poncho!"

I flashed back to a fiesta I had attended with her a few years previously, when she lived in Guatemala. The hostess had flung open the door and gave me a big *abrazo* (embrace)—even though I had never met her and hadn't "really" been invited. Somewhat stunned at her generous welcome, I managed to gasp, "What beautiful gold earrings!" "Here," she smiled, "you must have them—they're yours." She took them off and handed me the treasured gift without a moment's hesitation.

The Latino saying *Mi casa es su casa* reflects a sprawling sense of inclusiveness and generosity. It encapsulates a joy in sharing and implies "What I have is also yours." In collectivist cultures, possessions are more fluid and communal than in individual ones. This pleasure in giving things away can present a cultural conundrum. As I joked to my sister, unless both cultures value reciprocity, when I say "*Mi casa es su casa*," they will have the deed to my house. Then where would I live? Look at what happened to Montezuma or the Indian tribal lands, or still happens in the U.S. tax system in which some rich people hire lawyers so they don't have to pay their fair share.

*The Latino saying, "Mi Casa es su Casa," reflects a sprawling sense of inclusiveness and generosity. It encapsulates a joy in sharing and implies "What I have is also yours."*

In collectivist *We* cultures, generosity is not a two-way street, but a busy intersection where everybody meets. A good illustration is the way strangers are always made to feel welcome. The host can rest assured that this kindness will be returned. Even though a particular individual many never be able to reciprocate, one day someone else will surely return the kindness. Until people from individualist cultures have experienced this contagious generosity, they may find it difficult to understand or to aspire to this level of sharing. From a *We* perspective, because the self emerges from the collective, generosity toward others is actually giving to oneself. *Cyclical reciprocity means people are continually giving to one another.* This is beautifully captured in the saying of the South African Pedi tribe, "Giving is to dish out for oneself."[1] Generosity is the glue that holds *We* cultures together. The community fiber would be torn if some were to take more than their share or to accumulate great wealth at the expense of others.

## You Are Invited; Please RSVP

INDIGENOUS PEOPLES OF THE Americas had many community celebrations and festivals that honored the changes in nature, rites of passing, or special feats of individuals. Everybody was invited and shared what they had. This strengthened people's bonds and added to their trove of communal memories. In traditional African societies, there were open weddings to which the entire village was welcomed. People did not arrive empty-handed; in the spirit of generosity, they brought gifts, food, and drink. Inclusiveness and sharing are two quintessential values for collective culture. The *We* cannot thrive or continue to exist if people are excluded, take more than their share, or do not replenish the communal treasure chest.

Many years ago, when visiting friends in Spain, I relished their *dias de fiestas*—a one-week community party where all in attendance eat, drink, and dance together. The main streets are closed, and people promenade dressed in the traditional colors of red and white, which adds to their sense of camaraderie. *Dias de fiestas* are like a community vacation in which everyone is off at the same time. Every year a substantial part of the budget or public funds is set aside to pay for bands, parades, fireworks, and special events so that everyone can participate. Bread, sausages, wine, sardines, and coffee are also free on special days. Since each town has its own *dias de fiestas*, some of the folks attending have come from other places. *No importa*— if you are there then you are welcome to share in the food and festivities.

Because of the high value placed on harmonious relationships and inclusiveness in collectivist cultures, its members may find the notion of RSVP—that some people would be invited and others excluded—to be a disconcerting concept. The Latino culture's elastic concept of *familia*, for instance, extends to an open door to special celebrations, meals, and *fiestas*. If Latinos are invited to a party and have friends or family visiting, it is good manners to bring them along. (It is not necessary to call ahead, although it is considered helpful.) The unexpected guests are not a problem, because of collective generosity. At a Latino *fiesta* or event, all who attend bring gifts, flowers, food, wine, special treats, and desserts to share with their hosts. This is something akin to the parable of the loaves and fishes in the New Testament, in which there is more food and drink at the end of the gathering than at the beginning.

Generosity is also evident in one of the Latino golden rules: if everyone contributes and pitches in, no one bears the burden and there will be more than enough to go around. At Mexican weddings, there is the tradition of pinning money on the bride's dress or paying to dance with the bride and groom. People line up, and it is great fun as one guest after another steps onto the dance floor for their short twirl with the honored couple. Sponsors for baptisms, weddings, and *quinceaneras* gladly pay for the dress, photographer, *banda,* cake, or bar. In the Anglo culture, it might be embarrassing to ask people to pay for things in this manner. For Latinos, it is an honor that strengthens ties as well as encourages sharing which is the heartbeat of the culture.

Latino hospitality is effusive. People always reserve the best for their guests, serving special food and treats. The Mexican saying *Hechalé agua al caldo* (put another cup of water in the soup) means that no matter how little a person has, there is always enough to go around. Being generous also means showing a genuine caring and concern for people's needs, listening, and giving of one's time. In traditional families, it is embarrassing to have more or to advance ahead of the group. Success is evidenced by one's ability to take care of others and assume greater financial responsibility, as well as by one's willingness to help with special needs. Having more means being able to give more.

## Giveaways, Throws, and Potlatches

THE ANTECEDENTS OF LATINO GENEROSITY can be found in the indigenous culture of the Americas. In early Indian cultures, people often competed with each other to see who could give away the most. No one wanted to be seen as a person who had more than others. Giving was seen as a way to honor people and to strengthen collective ties. LaDonna Harris illustrates how this generosity is still structured in Indian cultures: "The emphasis is not on accumulation, but on sharing what a person has. Everything is reciprocal, so possessions are more fluid and shared. Things are redistributed. There are many formal mechanisms for redistribution. Giveaways, throws, and the potlatch ceremony are three of the methods that demonstrate how integral these values are to Indian culture."

*In early Indian cultures, people often competed with each other to see who could give away the most. No one wanted to be seen as a person who had more than others. Giving was seen as a way to honor people and to strengthen collective ties.*

A striking difference between a materialistic culture and one based on generosity can be seen in the birthday celebration. In Pueblo cultures, when someone has a birthday, instead of receiving gifts, the celebrator might give back to the community by having a *throw*. After buying food and gifts such as blankets and shawls, the person goes up on the roof and throws the stuff out to the community. The celebrator is recognizing that many of the good things that happened in her or his life are largely due to the care others have provided.

Indian cultures also emphasize achievement as a collective feat rather than just a personal one. In the mainstream culture, when someone graduates from college, people bring gifts to acknowledge this person's achievement. But in the tradition of the Plains tribes, a person might have *giveaways* on such occasions. LaDonna explains, "A young Comanche woman might be recognized by her tribe when she graduates, with song, dance, and a ceremony. However, the young woman understands she didn't accomplish this by herself. Many people contributed. In return, she might have a *giveaway* to thank people. She would give them valuable things, like blankets, household goods, or jewelry."

The potlatch, at which people share prized and beautiful possessions, is another way material goods are redistributed. These offerings are placed in the center of a circle where people can admire them. After a thanksgiving is offered, people talk about what they brought and why they are worthy gifts. Slowly and deliberately, people go to the center and choose an object to take home with them. It is a joyous sharing and celebration; people leave with a treasured item given in generosity—"richer" than when they arrived.

LaDonna sees these forms of redistribution as ways in which communal societies keep different economic and social classes in balance: "There isn't as much ranking. People save up for giveaways for years. Redistribution ensures that no one accumulates so much wealth or material things that it sets that person above others, thereby disrupting the circle of relatedness so pivotal to Native American philosophy."

*Redistribution ensures that no one accumulates so much wealth or material things that it sets that person above others, thereby disrupting the circle of relatedness so pivotal to Native American philosophy.*
—LaDonna Harris, Comanche

Dr. Joseph, describing American Indian tribes in his book *Remaking America*, admired this profuse generosity: "The early Indian tribe was by its very nature a benevolent community in which sharing was a primary virtue and selfishness a primary vice." He observed, "In the Native American tradition, wealth is generated for its distribution, not its accumulation. The good of the community takes precedence over the good of the individual . . . This produced economic as well as social benefits by distributing goods widely throughout the community."[2]

## Sharing Is the Soul of Community

FROM THEIR AFRICAN ROOTS, Black people inherited the concept of *the village*, meaning people regarded themselves as an ancestral group who tended their land and livestock communally, with little regard for individual ownership. The care and nurturing of children was everyone's responsibility. This same sentiment surfaced in the slave quarter communities that functioned as a family. The hardships of slavery necessitated sticking together for mutual protection and survival.

Throughout slavery, African Americans demonstrated a deep sense of taking care of one another and sharing what little they had. Assisting others was a moral obligation that extended beyond the quarter community into a network of mutual aid that encompassed all slaves. Even in the face of need, lack, toil, and trouble, people shared whatever they had with others who were in need. Dr. Joseph believes the benevolent actions of slaves who cared for people who were sick and in need, whether they were White or Black, is reminiscent of tribal society. "The capacity to express sentiments of generosity for those outside the group, the ability to love the enemy is an African American trait . . . there were evidences of a *universal compassion* within the community of Africans in the Americas that embraced both the near and distant relative."[3]

This tendency remains essential to Black culture. When people succeed, they are expected to help others and to give back to the community. Based on their interviews with over a thousand Black leaders in corporate America, Ancella Livers and Keith Carver found a deep sense of responsibility—a *moral obligation* to help other African Americans succeed—reported by 95 percent of the people surveyed.[4]

Moreover, the African American community trumps other groups in its generosity. A Northern Trust 2010 study showed that affluent Blacks were more charitable and felt a greater responsibility to contribute to people in need than non-Blacks. This confirms a 2003 study by the *Chronicle of Philanthropy* that found African Americans who give to charity donate 25 percent more of their discretionary income than Whites.[5, 6] Even though their economic rungs are substantially lower, giving to and taking care of others is an enduring practice of the Black community. Their deep faith and Christian tradition, observes Joseph, reinforces this tradition. "There is an overriding belief among African Americans that service to God is linked to service to humanity. Thus, feeding the hungry, housing the homeless, and providing educational opportunities, social liberation and economic empowerment are viewed as part of the *moral imperative* of religious faith."

## Community Celebrations: Generosity in Action

IN ALL *WE* CULTURES, generosity strengthens social bonds. Sharing is not limited to material possessions alone; it includes listening, visiting, and spending time with people; storytelling, singing, and dancing; participating in rituals and celebrations; and working for community advancement. *We* cultures create a collective spirit in which sharing and generosity permeate the social fabric.

The African American adage "Make sure people are *singing from the same hymnal*" expresses the need for unity and like-mindedness before taking action. Singing is a spiritual tradition that reinforces Black people's emotional connections and often describes their common journey. Singing lifted people up during hard times and strengthened resolve during demonstrations or political tribulations. Singing energized the civil rights movement.

This tradition reaches back to the African soil, for which Dr. Joseph identifies a quality he calls *homo festivus*: "The idea that individuals and communities have both a capacity and the need to celebrate life even in the midst of tragedy."[7] In Nelson Mandela's autobiography, *Long Walk to Freedom*, he speaks to this quality as sustaining the South African freedom movement. He recounts the difficult years on Robbin Island doing physical labor in the limestone quarry: "Singing succeeded in turning our suffering into happiness. We sang revolutionary songs as we worked and we deliberated matters of national importance. Singing made us overcome the pain of the work we were doing."[8] Singing builds the collective sense of *We*, allowing people to support and share with one another even under dire need.

The many ceremonies, celebrations, and community traditions in Indian tribes provide opportunities for deep sharing. Everyone brings food and gifts to share and offers to house people. At annual celebrations such as the powwow, dancers wear bright jingle dresses or fringed shawls passed down from their grandmothers. Drummers hammer out a primal beat and sing traditional songs. Each tribe has unique ways of gathering. In September, when autumn floats its cool air, the Comanche come from the four corners of the country to their land in Oklahoma for a Comanche Fair. Through prayer, storytelling, recounting of tribal history, horseracing, games, and special ceremonies that recognize community achievements, the strands of the collective tribal basket are tightly woven.

For generations, the Jemez Pueblo have run over the blue sage hills where the river ambles by on the way to the plains. Benny Shendo explains how running is part of their ceremonial way of life and brings people together: "Everybody runs, from the young boys to the old men. It's not about competition or winning. You are racing for the people and everybody has a place and a responsibility. The literal translation of one of our races is 'praying with the clouds or running with the clouds.' So you are running to bring rain or moisture to the land and to benefit the people."

From both their own indigenous traditions and those of the gregarious Spanish, Latinos have inherited a love of music, dancing, and celebrations. *Gozar la vida* ("enjoy life") is a deep-rooted philosophy: sharing good times with family and friends. Consumer studies show that Latinos spend more money on food, entertainment, and music than other market segments.[9] Regardless of obstacles or limited economic resources, there is a belief that while life may be difficult, it should be enjoyed. "Canta No Llores"—"sing, don't cry"—is a much-loved traditional song reflecting this philosophy. Imagine how this good counsel uplifts people when they are poor, work at menial and backbreaking jobs, or face the social obstacle of racism!

The venerated salsa singer Celia Cruz echoed this in her last popular song: *"Aye, no hay que llorar, porque la vida es un carnival"* ("There is no reason to cry, because life is a carnival"). Latinos will find any excuse to host a fiesta, a celebration given for visiting relatives, births, baptisms, birthdays, anniversaries, Holy Communion day, a young girl's turning fifteen, a new job, moving to a new place, a promotion, or a retirement. Certainly Anglos also celebrate such life events, but for the Latinos' large extended family—not just blood related but more like a tribe—the fiesta is not a small intimate dinner but a community celebration. Furthermore, *bienvenidos* signifies the pervasive hospitality of the Latino culture, an open-door policy that makes people feel at home. Like their American Indian relatives at their celebratory events, everyone contributes; the fiesta is an opportunity to share.

Latinos, with the highest percentage of participation in the U.S. labor market of any subgroup, are great contributors at work and have an admirable work ethic—another reflection of their value of generosity. Work is an opportunity to give of their talents and contribute to the welfare of the group and organization. Latinos strive to balance working, taking time for people, spending time with their families, and enjoying life through fiestas and celebrations. This philosophy is woven into their religious practices and was upheld by César Chávez in the "Farm Workers Prayer": "Bring forth song and celebration, so that the Spirit will be alive among us."[10]

## Generosity Benefits You and Others

By enumerating the benefits of building a benevolent society that values generosity and mutual care, leaders from communities of color can help people remember why it is better to give than to receive. Although many people profess to believe this, the actions of our materialistic culture indicate that they are only paying lip service. But are communities of color who practice generosity onto something? Not only did they survive more than five hundred years of racism and economic oppression, but they kept their values of faith and dedication to the collective good intact—and they are still singing, dancing, and celebrating every chance they get! Perhaps we should look at why generosity is such a healthy prescription for nurturing community, cultivating relationships, and celebrating life.

Let us start by revisiting the "survival of the fittest" theory—the idea that human nature is intrinsically competitive and acquisitive. Earlier, we surmised that our ability to work together and to look out for one another helped humans finish first in the evolutionary ascent. Most people believe (and were taught) that Darwin originated the "survival of the fittest" theory—which fortified the dominant, individualist, and competitive paradigm. But his work on the origin of species presents a more cooperative view.[11] Darwin found in animals admirable examples of reciprocity, cooperation, and even love. In *Darwin's Lost Theory of Love*, author David Loye points out that "love" appears in *The Descent of Man* some ninety-five times, whereas only two entries address the "law of mutual struggle," as Darwin termed it. Darwin argued that the "law of mutual aid" and human solidarity—in other words, *cultural selection*—is more crucial.[12]

 *"Love" appears in* **The Descent of Man** *some ninety-five times, whereas only two entries address the "law of mutual struggle," as Darwin termed it. Darwin argued that more crucial than this is the "law of mutual aid" and human solidarity.*

Over a hundred years after Darwin, Jane Goodall, the renowned primatologist, observed similar behavior in chimpanzees, who aided the weak, shared their resources, showed great affection, and comforted those in need. Like these evolutionary predecessors, human beings are social by nature and have a profound longing for connection and community. Can love, reciprocity, cooperation and mutual aid, and generosity be the core of our true nature? Can it be that the individualist and self-centered view of human nature proposed by our society has overshadowed that generous and communal spirit? The underpinning of any society is its concept of human nature; modify this and, like toppling dominos, other concepts begin to fall.

Again, the early *We* cultures were based on people take caring of and looking out for each other. *Being able to share and be generous was, indeed, a survival tactic.* When a hunter brought back game, the entire tribe partook. When another had good fortune, everyone would eat again. The tribal fire gave warmth to all its members. In a crisis, the tribe would come together to provide for those in need. Traditional African societies followed in this tradition, and Indian tribes have never swerved from this communal pathway. Latino values of mutuality, cooperation, and generosity also mirror the collective values of early cultures.

Communities of color offer rich examples of the benefits of generosity and mutual aid, which are in alignment with the biblical example of the Good Samaritan and the counsel to "love your neighbor." The New Testament warns against being greedy and cautions that wealth can damage one's soul (Matthew, Mark, and Luke all recorded Jesus' words: "It is easier for a camel to go through the eye of a needle than for a rich man to enter the kingdom of God"). The Bible encourages us to be generous and to assume social responsibility for others. "The American way," discerns Benedictine monk Thomas Keating, "is to first feel good about yourself and then feel good about others. But spiritual traditions say it's the other way around—that you develop a sense of goodness by *giving of yourself*."[13] Perhaps it is better to give than to receive because we bring forth our higher self, connect with others, and infuse our communities with generosity.

## The Generosity Gap

Y ET DESPITE all the religious mandates, much of mainstream America today is more concerned about personal accumulation than the welfare of their neighbors. The gap between the rich and the poor has become a chasm. Catastrophic events like Hurricane Katrina in 2005 shockingly remind us of a growing poverty normally hidden from us by the major media. The number of people in the United States living below the poverty line recently hit forty-six million, or 15.1 percent of the population—*an increase of more than 2.6 million in a single year.*[14] America's poverty rate is the highest in the developed world and more than twice as high as those of most other industrialized countries.[15]

There is also a direct correlation between poverty and race: only 9.9 percent of Whites are poor, compared with 26.6 percent of Hispanics and 27.4 percent of African Americans.[16] Many experts report that the primary economic reason for the increase in poverty is low wages for workers of all races. The value of the minimum wage has eroded, despite increases. Adjusted for inflation and the cost of living, the $7.25 minimum wage of 2011 has less buying power than the $4.25 minimum wage of 1995.[17] The one place wages are soaring is at the top. In 1980, CEO earnings were only 45 times higher than that of the average worker. By 2000 CEO wages had skyrocketed to 525 times that of the average worker. At least by 2011 that factor had fallen to "only" 343 times.[18]

However, the Institute for Policy Studies listed twenty-five U.S. corporations whose CEOs earned more in compensation in 2010 than their firms paid in taxes![19] This included General Electric, Capital One Financials, Verizon, Coca-Cola, Honeywell, Boeing, and eBay.[20] Many of these companies have taken federal tax dollars through subsidies, contracts, and even bailouts!

Greed at the top has led to high unemployment, depressed salaries, slashing of worker benefits, loss of jobs, and the end of secure retirement. The income gap shows no sign of closing. A healthy workforce is the wellspring of a healthy economy and vibrant nation, but in this, the only developed country without the basic security of government-sponsored medical care, 50.7 million Americans, or 16.7 percent of the population, were uninsured in 2010, including 8.3 million (about 6.5 percent) of children.[21] Finally, even the American dream of owning a home is evaporating. In the overheated real estate market of the 2000s, speculation and predatory lending practices led to runaway housing prices, subprime interest rates, and cash-out financing incentives, culminating in 2008 in the biggest housing meltdown since the Great Depression. Foreclosures rose 63 percent that year, and in 2010 one million Americans were still in jeopardy of losing their homes.[22]

America's rich resources, entrepreneurial approach, and business and capitalist acumen have unfortunately led to a national crisis. The individual greed of many of our leaders has overcome concern for the common good and for supporting a society in which people can meet their basic economic needs. A safe and sustainable society is not possible with our resources so unequally distributed. *Dealing with the social structures and revitalizing public morality so that an equitable and compassionate society can thrive is a critical leadership issue of our times.* Raul Yzaguirre urges us to follow a new course: "Embracing the Latino values of generosity and helping one another would heal many of the divisions in America. Latinos are taught not to take more than their share. Many of the social ills facing this country today are the result of an unequal distribution of resources. Perhaps the solution is for the rest of Americans to become more courteous, community-minded, and generous."

# Connecting to the Purpose of Leadership

**A**S A PIVOTAL VALUE, *generosity* is a key leadership trait in communities of color. On a personal level, leaders give to community causes, help those in need, share their time and resources, recognize the contributions of others, and empower people. At the community level, these leaders focus on *collective sustainability* rather than individual gain or personal advancement. As we will explore more deeply in the next section, leadership committed to creating a more compassionate and equitable society implies generosity and working for a more equitable distribution of resources.

This brings us to a critical juncture. Before looking at the next three leadership principles in communities of color, let's consider the purpose of leadership. Renowned leadership expert James MacGregor Burns aligned closely with communities of color when he defined leadership as a *collective process* linked to *social change* with the purpose of enhancing the *well-being of human existence*. He noted that leadership implies the ability to *mobilize people* and engage them in a process in which both leader and followers raise one another to *higher levels of motivation and morality*.[23]

Leaders in communities of color receive their legitimacy from the people they serve, by exhibiting a high level of morality, including being honest and humble, and by serving. As they model these behaviors, they lift up the morality of their followers and community as well. With limited resources, leaders must be adept at mobilizing people to address critical issues, including an examination of the social structures that limit equal participation. The purpose of leadership in communities of color is in step with Burns' description—to promote the collective well-being by creating positive social change through a collaborative process; leaders secure opportunities that develop and uplift people. Dr. Antonia Pantoja, the great Puerto Rican activist, stated this well: "I want to live a life of commitment to the human community for the betterment of all people."

The crisis in American leadership today is a failure to provide the high moral ground and morality that Burns describes as critical. If leaders are to enhance people's well-being, then surely they must nurture a social, political, and economic environment in which people can get their basic needs met, including decent housing, work, education, and health care. Inspired leadership implies societal guardianship. The emphasis on wealth accumulation by many corporate leaders and the lack of socially responsible action by government leaders contradicts the fundamental purpose of society: to take care of our own and to ensure that our children have a fair chance to prosper.

Leaders are also guardians of the social contract whereby people willingly follow the rules, laws, and structure of society in return for the benefits received. When these benefits begin to unravel, there is social disengagement, alienation, and increasing economic need, as well as more violence and crime. Statistics presented in the previous section indicated that civic participation is on the decline; people feel overworked and are withdrawing from community. Furthermore, America has more people in prison as a percentage of the population than any other country, the greatest number of laws to follow, and the most lawyers. It appears that the social contract is withering and people no longer see our society as ensuring the means to satisfy their basic needs. We are losing the spirit of generosity whereby leaders are stewards and responsible for tending to people's well-being.

Leadership in communities of color, as described in the section that follows, offers a number of remedies that can heal these ills and reengage people in society. This is not to imply that all leaders in communities of color follow these high standards. Some may have swerved from traditional ways. However, as previously noted, the leaders interviewed for this book represent the ideal, offering the best practices from communities of color—practices we can emulate to create our multicultural future.

## Leadership That Reflects the Spirit of Generosity

T HE IROQUOIS TRIBE'S GREAT leadership rule—considering the impact of their decisions unto seven generations—compelled them to work for tribal sustainability, including nurturing future leaders. To ensure this, *one generation could not take more than their share*. (This commitment to continuity is explored in our 7th principle on Intergenerational Leadership. Safeguarding the prosperity of the community implies an expansive generosity that reaches into the unforeseen future.

Adhering to the seventh-generation rule creates a different leadership perspective. Our *now*-oriented society and results-driven leadership consumes resources and uses people without considering the ramifications. American Indian leadership, on the other hand, is based on ancient traditions that include continuity and stewardship. John Echohawk explains, "Tribal leaders don't see land as a piece of real estate to be bought or sold, but as their homeland where their people will remain for all time. The land has to sustain the people. Leaders are stewards of the land for their tribe."

 *Tribal leaders think long-term, considering the impact on future generations ...Tribal philosophy puts things into a holistic and visionary perspective.*

—John Echohawk

Echohawk sees a sharp contrast with the way Anglo leaders think. "In the American way, land is bought and sold and its value is monetary. We look at our earth as our homeland. We need to take care of it so it will sustain us in perpetuity. Tribal leaders think long-term, considering the impact on future generations. This view oftentimes gets lost in a busy America that thinks in short-term profit and gain. Tribal philosophy puts things into a holistic and visionary perspective." On most reservations, for example, one rarely finds rich individuals or entrepreneurs. There the purpose of economic development is creating *community wealth*, not wealthy individuals.

Generosity, mutuality, and helping one another held Blacks, Latinos, and Indians together through oppression and economic scarcity. These qualities continue nourishing and sustaining these communities today. Generosity runs contrary to a few accumulating so much excess wealth that the well-being of society is threatened. Generosity is the antidote to the rampant materialism that reinforces individualist gain over the common welfare. It is the basis for a more compassionate and caring society—the rich soil from which a benevolent community can grow.

The three leadership principles that we'll explore in Part Two build on the tradition of *Sankofa*. They have emerged from a historical context that was fueled by the civil rights movement. Principle 4, A Leader Among Equals, reflects the *We* or collective orientation in which leadership is shared, rotated, and reciprocal. Principle 5, Leaders as Guardians of Public Values, defines leaders as those who safeguard the values our country was founded on: justice, equality, and the common welfare. Leadership in this context has a moral imperative to exhibit social responsibility. Principle 6, Leaders as Community Stewards, builds people's capacity and ensures continued progress. As leaders serve people by encouraging their participation and nurturing empowerment, they foster a community of leaders and build the critical mass needed to create positive social change. These principles lay the foundation for a leadership model in which generosity and serving the common welfare is the bedrock of an equitable democracy.

## NEXT STEPS

**Reflecting On
and Applying
Principle Three**

# *Mi Casa Es Su Casa—*
# Developing a Spirit
# of Generosity

## Practice sharing and developing a spirit of generosity

Imagine a culture in which people compete to give things away, leaders are respected because of their generosity, and material things are more fluid and shared! Think about giving as reciprocal and circular, with generosity meaning actually giving to oneself. The following exercises will infuse a spirit of generosity and giving.

Sponsor a *potlatch* in your organization, group, or family in which people each give away a treasured item. Place these gifts in the middle of the room and have people gather in a circle to admire them. Each person talks about why his or her gift is special and valuable. People reflect on the gifts, and each chooses one to take home. This works well during the holidays or as an organizational celebration or team-building experience. Discussing the meaning and lessons from the potlatch can instill a new sense of sharing and mutual assistance in the organization and in teams.

On your next birthday or milestone (a promotion or graduation), announce that you are having a *giveaway* to recognize that your achievements have been possible only because of your family, coworkers, and friends who support (and put up with) you. Then be deliberate about buying gifts or finding mementos that are meaningful. Emphasize that this is not about them doing anything for you, but about you acknowledging the support they have given you.

Has someone admired something you own? The next time this happens, think about giving it to him or her. It might really *belong* to them. By so doing, you may put into motion the reciprocity that exists in communities of color, in which sharing of material things and giving gift are woven into the fabric of relationships.

How much of your income or the company's profits is set aside to benefit others? Following the example set by the Black community, do a generosity audit and make sharing a priority. Set a giving goal. This can infuse people and the organization with a higher purpose and sense of success. We have more than enough and can share our good fortune!

## Conduct a life balance audit that includes looking at priorities and key values

At the Center for Creative Leadership, we would end programs with a goal-setting exercise. Before doing this, we asked them to consider the following areas of their lives—career, family, self, and community—and to discern where they were spending their time and which needed tending. Mainstream culture emphasizes work, often at the expense of other areas in life. Communities of color have different priorities. One benefit of a multicultural society is having more choices. Having a balanced life means being generous with yourself and others. Using a total of 100 points that represent how you spend your life energy and time, allocate them among the following six areas.

_____    _____    _____    _____    _____    _____

Personal      Family        Career        Community    Nonfamily     Spiritual
                                                        relationships  sustenance

Based on your analysis, what did you learn about your life balance? What areas of your life need tending and where would you like to spend more of your energy? What is consuming too much of time and energy? What specific and measurable goals would you like set that will balance your life? What compromises or adjustments will you have to make? Who can support you in making these changes?

## Recommended reading

- *The Giving Tree* by Shel Silverstein (HarperCollins, 1964, 1992). A controversial book some believe portrays a one-side relationship between a tree that is a selfless giver and a young boy who is greedy and insatiable. Others argue that the tree gives everything to the boy because it loves him, and its feelings are reciprocated when the boy returns to the tree as an old man.

  Looking at the story from the generosity values of a *We* perspective, what lessons can be learned about societies that use up resources and take more than their share and those that are more giving? What does it say about sustainability and relationships?

  What are the positives and negatives of unbridled (not reciprocal) generosity? Name some possible parallels between slavery, conquest, and colonialism and taking advantage of people, much as the boy took advantage of the kindness and generosity of the tree.

# PART TWO

# Leadership Styles in Communities of Color

**W**HETHER I OR WE is central to a society contours the shape of its leadership. A We identity promotes a collective and people-centered leadership that espouses the well-being of people as a whole, not just individuals.

Anna Escobedo Cabral, who has led a number of national Hispanic initiatives, describes this commitment: "What motivates people in our community who are doing great work and leading efforts is that they are looking out for the collective. *The collective good drives them*." Latino leadership therefore has a particularly people-helping flavor: leaders tend to emerge from their community by addressing critical needs.

Shared leadership is a time-honored practice for Americans Indians, who use a circular approach and rotate leaders so no one is elevated above others. *We* is the fountainhead from which their reciprocal and dispersed leadership flows. Just as identity is collective the source of leadership is collective as well. A leader serves and is responsible to her community, tribe, and people.

*African American Leadership*, by Ron Walters and Robert Smith, defines Black leadership as proceeding from the collective interests and concerns of people focusing on overcoming social, political, and economic impediments. To achieve this, leadership has relied on social rather than economic resources; this requires bringing people together and building coalitions. Walters and Smith speak to this *We* reference point: "Leadership derives its authority and legitimacy from the community from which it emerges."[1]

## The Shift to Collaborative Leadership

MAINSTREAM LEADERSHIP TODAY IS moving toward a *We* or collaborative form that resonates with communities of color—a form in which many people are prepared to participate and share responsibility. Looking at this shift to collaboration is a good starting point for examining the leadership principles in these communities and the connection with the growing emphasis on teamwork, partnerships, and shared responsibility.

For generations, the centerpiece of mainstream American leadership was the *individual leader*. This fashioned a hierarchical leadership form, which was very effective in an assembly-line economy in which people followed orders and looked to the boss or supervisor for direction. However, in the last half of the twentieth century, the same dynamics that we discussed in the section on Principle 1—civil rights, globalization, changing demographics, democratic values, higher educational levels, and political awareness—that are transforming leadership into a multicultural form are also dismantling the hierarchical approach. These powerful social changes are redefining leadership, from the domain of a few individuals to a more participatory and collaborative process that engages many people.

Collaborative leadership has evolved as our economy has changed from an industrial base to one driven by information, mass communications, technology, innovation, and the service industry. Now people must be able to think on their feet, solve problems quickly, and find innovative solutions. Society needs people's active participation and shared responsibility for outcomes. In the complex and rapidly changing society of the twenty-first century, individual leaders simply will not have the best answers or solutions. They must be able to encourage collaboration, so that people generate creative solutions and ideas.

Collaborative leadership transforms the *I* orientation of hierarchal leadership to a group-centered or *We* orientation. Instead of supplying all the answers, the collaborative leader creates an environment that promotes teamwork and learning together. Effective leaders cultivate creative space in which the younger, better educated, and tech-savvy workforce can function more autonomously. To achieve this, the leader must hand over the reins and have the confidence that—as Peter Block, author of *Stewardship: Choosing Service over Self-Interest,* states—"people have the knowledge and answers."[2] This again shifts the locus of control to the *We* or people served by the leader.

Our changing demographics create a pressing leadership challenge: to foster collaborative environments in which people of many backgrounds and many ages can work together creatively and productively. Communities of color offer a rich foundation for building inclusive environments and respecting differences, which increases collaboration by *encouraging equal access* and *urging the involvement of all the diverse segments.*

## Collective and Collaborative Leadership

IN COMMUNITIES OF COLOR, leadership is both *collectivist* and *collaborative.* Collectivist leadership springs from the *We* orientation, centering on what is good for the community, group, or organization. Because leaders identify with, arise from, and depend on their community for power and authority, leadership is also collectivist. To be sanctioned by their community, leaders must be responsive and responsible to the people they serve. By identifying critical needs and interests and then working to address them, leaders stay connected to their people.

Walters and Smith comment on how pivotal this approach is: "The primacy of the community or the Black collective is the basis of the internal democratic system of the Black community and the ultimate basis too of the unity and accountability that are the source of its integrity." Furthermore: "The Black community has had a long history of attempting to fashion collective leadership, the origin of which might have officially begun on a national scale as early as the Negro Convention movement in the 1830s when Black men came together to address the urgent problems facing their people."[3]

*Collaborative leadership* flows naturally from the collective: with this outlook, people readily contribute and work together, particularly as teams, to achieve mutual goals. Leaders in communities of color have traditionally invited participation. By working closely with others, a leader stays in touch with the community pulse and understands people's priorities. Collaboration also nurtures a network of leaders and sustains the web of relationships that forms the *We* identity. Leadership is rotated, distributed, and shared. The process of preparing many people to assume responsibility also increases ownership, nurtures continuity, and develops the critical mass needed to promote social change.[4]

The following discussion of Principles 4, 5, and 6 examines how leadership in communities of color is based on values that support collaboration and emphasize equal access. The first principle—*a leader among equals*—underscores a circular leadership form, in which the leader is not above others but remains part of the group. The principle of *leaders as guardians of public values* speaks to the mandate to transform the social structures that hinder people's full participation and to uphold values such as justice, equity, and the common good—an activist model of leadership.

## Barriers to Participation

Two cultural barriers have long obstructed equal participation: the psychology of oppression and White privilege. The psychology of oppression is a term created by the perceptive Brazilian thinker Paulo Freire to describe the process in which people of color internalize society's negative messages and beliefs about their race and come to believe that they are true.[5] The term White privilege—coined in 1988 by Peggy McIntosh, then a graduate student in women's studies at Wellesley College—describes the unspoken advantages and opportunities bestowed on people by what has long been the dominant culture in the United States.[6] White privilege is not earned; people benefit from it simply because of their race. Both White privilege and the psychology of oppression operate at an unconscious level. Thus, many people are unaware of how these social mechanisms operate by providing advantages to some and denying them to others. On a societal level, these mechanisms reinforce White cultural dominance and institutional control without openly disputing the claim that equality and democratic choice are equally available. The principles of leaders as equal, as guardians of public values, and as community stewards work to dismantle such privilege, replacing it with a respect for all individuals and a belief that many have the capacity to lead. (We will further explore this in the discussion of Principle 5, Leaders as Guardians of Public Values.)

Just as collaboration is a cherished tradition in communities of color, likewise the practice of leadership as *service* is fundamental. The principle of *leaders as community stewards* defines leaders as builders and guardians of community progress who nurture a network or legacy. This expands Robert Greenleaf's work, as described in *The Servant as Leader,* from an individual focus to one that serves communities and society.[7] As Greenleaf's concepts are in close alignment with the leadership in communities of color, a deeper look at his work is included in Principle 6.

The three principles in Part Two offer valuable insights and knowledge for leading from these orientations, restructuring leadership to embrace a higher social responsibility and to better reflect our multicultural nation.

# A Leader Among Equals—
# Community-Conferred Leadership

ARRIVING IN DENVER IN 1971, armed with a master's degree in social work from the University of Wisconsin, I started working in the barrios with low-income Hispanic women. At that time, Brown America was in an Anglo no-man's-land—a group unrecognized by the U.S. Census and barely visible to the mainstream culture.

After a number of years of working there, I was convinced Latinas were on an economic dead-end street and that the way to empowerment was innovative programs, which built on our cultural strengths. As I was mulling this over, the local Mennonite minister called: "There is a group of Hispanic Head Start mothers who want to talk about services for Latina women. They see that their children are learning, and they want to learn too!" Thus began a conversation between a group of community grassroots women and Latina professionals that culminated in our starting a small women's center in the basement of the Mennonite Church. It was christened "Mi Casa" to reflect its role as a place Latinas could call their own and find cultural validation. Mi Casa provided employment and educational services, helping women acquire the skills to become economically self-sufficient.

Although I had no experience leading an organization, I had years of community experience—and a passionate commitment to building the first Latina service organization in Colorado. Anna Escobedo Cabral observes that this has been a traditional pathway: "I think a lot of Latino leaders see a problem, and they work hard to find a solution, and as a result they are put in a position of leadership to make change happen. However, it is not about them seeking that position. Rather it is about addressing some unmet need."

I stayed for the first ten years, during which we developed key programs, bought our own facility, and established a national reputation for empowering Latinas. Key to Mi Casa's success was building a community of supporters and a committed staff as well as designating a group of "founding mothers" who were involved in the formative years. When resources are scarce and people power is critical, collective leadership—in which many contribute and have ownership—is indispensable. Creating a network disperses leadership and shares responsibility. This *la familia* approach was in step with leading from a *We* or collective orientation.

## Leading from a Collective Orientation

THE INDIVIDUALIST-COLLECTIVIST cultural continuum we've considered has had a profound impact on leadership. When people succeed in a collectivist culture, they share their good fortune. Cabral believes this quality is inherent in Latino leadership: "There is this basic value that whatever you do, you do for the community and the family. It is not about you as an individual. Yes, it is important to do well, but because it will enable others to do well. Even in the midst of dire circumstances, people will say 'let me see if I can help.'"

In collectivist cultures, where a leader's authority comes from the group, leaders are expected to listen, integrate the collective wisdom, and reflect the group's behavior and

 *There is this basic value that whatever you do, you do for the community and the family. It is not about you as an individual. Yes, it is important to do well, but because it will enable others to do well. Even in the midst of dire circumstances, people will say "let me see if I can help."*

*—Anna Escobedo Cabral*

values. Leaders charge people up, facilitate their working together, and help them solve problems. As they empower others, a community of leaders evolves. Standing out too far from others or calling too much attention to oneself can damage the group cohesion that is central to collectivist cultures.

In an individualist culture, *I* become a leader because of my personal initiative, accomplishments, and competence as well as my winning personality. *I* have a can-do attitude, a take-action personality. By my calling attention to myself—my accomplishments and skills—people believe *I* am competent and they are comfortable following me. Unanimity or group consensus *follows* the leader's decisions. The leader strives for self-mastery—as *I* become empowered, *I* can empower others. As *I* learn, *I* teach others. Leaders maintain status by remaining youthful, vigorous, attractive, and able. Seniority is secondary to performance. In contrast, a collectivist leader's status increases as he or she becomes older and acquires seniority and experience.[1] In individualist cultures, there is a belief that *I made it on my own.*

*We* cultures acknowledge that the community has nurtured and invested in a person. Bennie Shendo explains the distinction: "In some cultures people believe you achieve alone. I can never think that way." He advises young Indians: "Understand that your success is not yours alone, it's due to your family, tribe, and community, and it's because of the people that have gone before you that have prayed for you to be here."

Ada Deer, a Menominee who directed the Indian programs at the University of Wisconsin at Madison, observes, "When I was growing up it wasn't *Me*—it was *We,* the family and tribe. Later, I understood that we wouldn't have survived as a people if our leaders didn't have that sense of obligation and responsibility to the tribe." Dr. Pantoja saw this as an inherent condition of living in community: "I am interdependent. I was nurtured to be who I am and am responsible and accountable to a community of others."

This brief overview provides a glimpse of how the individualist-collectivist cultural continuum influences leadership. We'll

 *When I was growing up it wasn't Me—it was We, the family and tribe. Later, I understood that we wouldn't have survived as a people if our leaders didn't have that sense of obligation and responsibility to the tribe.*

—Ada Deer, Menominee

now take a deeper look at how the principle of *leaders among equals* empowers people and ensures continuity through the following dynamics:

- Authority comes from the group, which takes precedence over the individual leader.

- Leaders are chosen because of their character, including honesty, humility, and generosity.

- Leaders inspire people to identify with them by setting an example.

- A leader serves something greater than himself—the mission, cause, or well-being of the community.

- A leader plays by the rules.

## Leadership Is Conferred by the Tribe

IN MANY TRIBES, it is considered culturally improper to claim "I am a leader." Leadership is externally conferred by people who recognize a person's abilities, talents, or vision and know how this benefits the community. LaDonna Harris explains how this operates in the Comanche and Iroquois tribes: "A leader was simply someone people followed. The Comanche didn't elect leaders. If a person had admirable qualities—generosity, sharing, responsibility to self and others—people would follow him. In fact, in the Iroquois Nation, a person will not be tapped as a leader if he expresses the desire to be in charge. In a communal society, a person is valued by what they can contribute to their community. Since everyone can contribute, leadership is rotated depending on the task or function at hand, and therefore, is much more distributed."

John Echohawk did not seek out the work, responsibility, or high expectations of leadership. However, as early as junior high, friends and classmates told him "You need to do this. You should do this. You should do this for us [the American Indian community]." Reluctantly, he accepted his election to leadership positions, including senior class president. Similarly, in law school, people wanted him to run for the Student Bar Association. He wasn't ambitious, but he acquiesced and served as president his senior year. Since John was among the first graduates of the Native American Law

Program, when the Native American Rights Fund opened a central-western location in the 1970s, he was asked to become the executive director. "They were saying, 'We need you to do this.' I had to go along with it. If a person is asked to serve the community or tribe, it is his responsibility to comply. Even though it would be easy to say no, you can't, because you would be disappointing people and letting them down."

This sense of leadership as community responsibility is also evident in the Jemez Pueblo, who live on their ancestral lands outside of Albuquerque, New Mexico. The Jemez have been there since before the Spanish arrived, before this was New Mexico, before this was America. Their leadership is based on an ancient heritage. In the Jemez Pueblo, a person does not aspire to be a leader. Their traditional governing body, called the *cacique*, is a group that represents the various clans and religious leaders. Rooted in prehistoric times, it is charged with choosing leaders based on the qualities needed by the tribe and with maintaining tribal spiritual and cultural traditions.[2]

 *For us in Jemez, we are leaders among equals . . . at some point you are called and given certain responsibilities as a leader. People respect that. But, when your time is done, you are among equals again.*

—Benny Shendo,
Jemez Pueblo

Benny Shendo was appointed the council's second lieutenant governor at a fairly young age. "I wasn't trying to be the leader. Since we don't have elections, at some point your name will be called and you won't refuse. When the *cacique* decides you are ready, you are ready! Obviously, certain situations call for a particular type of leadership." After Benny completed his council term, he returned to his role as an ordinary tribal member: "So now I'm among equals. I'm just a common man in the community. Other people will tell me what to do . . . For us in Jemez, we are *leaders among equals* . . . at some point you are called and given certain responsibilities as a leader. People respect that. But, when your time is done, you are among equals again. I can't really say I'm better than you, because in a year or two, I'm going to be an ordinary tribal person again. So leadership rotates and no one is elevated above others." These types of practices promote a leadership in which equity and reciprocity are the norm.

## *Personalismo*—A Leader's Character and Example

L ATINOS IDENTIFY AND WORK with a leader because of *personalismo*—people's respect for the leader as a person. This has deep implications and raises a crucial question: What kind of person are you and how do you treat others? No matter how "important" a leader becomes, she or he must be willing to do the hard work needed for community progress. Leaders are expected to roll up their sleeves, stuff envelopes, clean up, cook, and serve food. Any type of elitism or projection that one is above certain tasks will destroy a leader's credibility. Leaders also earn respect by being accessible and generously giving of their resources and talents. They work hand in hand with people, leading not just by words but also by actions.

*Personalismo* implies that leadership centers on character. The saying *mi palabra es la ley* (my word is law) emphasizes the importance of honesty as a leadership trait. Leaders must do what they say they are going to do. Following through establishes a leader's track record and credibility. In a survey of over three thousand Latinos, the National Community for Latino Leadership (NCLL) found that the quality most valued in Latino leaders was keeping one's word and delivering on one's promises.[3] Yzaguirre further explains: "There is a lot of inconsistency with leaders today who articulate American values but don't live them. Latinos are living them every day. As a culture we believe that you do what you say you are going to do."

In collectivist cultures, a leader must embody his or her community and never forget "where he or she came from." César Chávez, the most revered Latino leader of the last century, was passionate about improving life for farm workers. Latinos saw him living simply, making personal sacrifices, taking risks in demonstrations, and working side by side with people. Because he publicly demonstrated his values and never set himself above others, people followed him and took up the banner of the farm workers' plight. The *New York Times* in 1969 commented on Chávez's dedication to remaining one of the people: "He still lives on the $5.00 a week all union workers receive and he invariably dresses in the same gray work pants and plaid wool shirt."[4]

Federico Peña, the former mayor of Denver, kept his campaign promises. He launched Denver International Airport and the new Convention Center. A major league baseball team, the Rockies, and Coors Field were negotiated under his watch. Denver's downtown was reenergized. Since few minority- and woman-owned businesses could qualify for city contracts, he took the lead in passing an ordinance that required large contractors to subcontract 30 percent of the work to such businesses. Finally, a great city values the arts: Peña started the city's Public Art Council and was a key supporter in the campaign to redesign the Denver Center for the Performing Arts, which today is second only to Lincoln Center in New York for performances, theater space, and attendance. Peña's amazing political follow-through heeds the Hispanic mandate that *leaders keep their word*. He learned this value from his parents: "Consistent with my own upbringing was that your word is your bond."

Peña's mayoral campaign slogan was "Imagine a great city!" One goal was to clean up the city's air. He launched his campaign by riding the city bus to work. Leading by example, Peña got people's attention about air quality for their own health and Denver's future. By actually doing what he asks others to do, Peña led by example. Thus, people identified with him and believed they could do likewise.

## Setting an Inspiring Example

PERSONALISMO RESONATES WITH a valued trait in the Black community—being known as a person who "walks the talk." African Americans value authenticity, genuineness, and being "real." A leader must therefore speak the truth, communicating with sincerity and conviction. The expression "Tell it like it is" puts it well.

In the Black community, although uniqueness and personal style are celebrated, self-expression is a way to enhance collectivism—unlike the usual American individualism that separates one from the group. It's analogous to a jazz group playing different interpretations—each musician has to be in harmony with and contribute to the music of the group. When the piano player takes the lead, he spontaneously adds his own interpretation and style. The other musicians back him up, appreciate his improvisations, and egg him on. Their responses spark greater creativity in his playing. This differs from individualism in which a person sets herself apart, may point out how she is more adept, and may not necessarily enhance the group. To separate oneself, or act as if one is better than or above others, is contrary to nurturing group identity, which is a key function of Black leadership. A Black leader's influence comes from *being part* of the community and having a reputation as one who cares about and serves others. Historically, leadership emerged from the mutual interest and concerns of Black people who were the collective force for getting things done. Attaining the moral authority to lead requires earning the community's trust and respect and modeling the highest qualities of leadership. Then people identify with the leader and sanction his authority.

Anna Escobedo Cabral, who served as the executive staff director for the U.S. Senate Republican Task Force on Hispanic Affairs, observes how this differs for mainstream leaders: "In the Anglo community, it is not necessarily about the community ratifying a leader, but rather, 'I am going to go out and I am going to take this position of congressman or senator; as a result, I'm a leader now . . .' And it's not about whether you can do it well, or not do it well, it's mostly 'this is my personal ambition.'"

In this scenario, somebody from *outside the group* might be promoted or elected to a position or be in charge. The leader, therefore, might not understand the issues people face or know the right solution or direction to take. When leadership is self-directed and self-initiated, the bond with followers may or may not exist. Furthermore, when leadership is robed in status and position, a socioeconomic distance can develop that disconnects leaders from people. Many leaders and politicians in America today are disengaged and insulated from real people's lives because of this phenomenon—particularly by the leaders' wealth.

*In the Anglo community, it is not necessarily about the community ratifying a leader, but rather, "I am going to go out and I am going to take this position of congressman or senator; as a result, I'm a leader now . . ." And it's not about whether you can do it well, or not do it well, it's mostly "this is my personal ambition."*

—Anna Escobedo Cabral

Leadership in communities of color has to be an *inside job.* An outsider would hinder people's identification with their leader, go against the grain of leaders among equals, reinforce people's minority status, and dampen their belief that they have the same potential as the leader. Fortunately, leaders usually come from similar backgrounds, so people can identify with them. Dr. Lea Williams, in her examination of Black leadership, observes this tendency: "Generally, black leaders, even though they tend to come from the black middle class, have experienced the same racial discrimination as working-class blacks, which forms a bond of kinship."[5]

Most people of color have similar stories. Raul Yzaguirre grew up in the poor area of the Rio Grande Valley in South Texas. His grandmother talked about the "race wars," in which the Texas Rangers systemically beat up and killed Mexican-Americans. His grandfather was almost lynched for being on the street after dark. Restaurants had signs in the windows: "No Mexicans and No Dogs!"

Dr. Antonia Pantoja was born in a slum in old San Juan, Puerto Rico, to an unwed mother and was raised in Barrio Obrero, a worker housing community located on the outskirts of the island's capital. When she immigrated to New York, Pantoja worked in factories; she remembers that these jobs, and traveling long hours back and forth, "consumed all my working hours." However, she gained "direct experience with the problems that Puerto Rican immigrants suffered."[6] When one's leader shares experiences such as overcoming discrimination and adversity, a natural bonding and shared empathy occurs.

## Serving Something Greater

FOR THE INDIVIDUAL LEADER, equality in leadership can present a dilemma. On one hand, leadership implies being proactive, assuming responsibility, and taking charge. On the other hand, leaders are expected to remain part of the group and not stand out from others. Cabral's observation that leadership springs from the desire to address an unmet need speaks to this dilemma: "César Chávez was working in the fields and saw people who were being badly mistreated and needed someone to advocate for them. He rose to the occasion, and it was very difficult. He wasn't educated in leadership techniques, he learned these afterwards. But that wasn't his goal—to name himself as the leader of the farm workers and assume a position of power. He was really addressing a tremendous unmet need in a specific population that really needed help."

By putting the issue, the cause, and people's needs *first*, leaders actually serve something greater than they are and lessen their self-importance. Cabral continues, "Latino leaders think about the broader good and are not so focused on individual success, but rather, how do we achieve success for the larger community?" This shifts the focus from the individual leader to the people he or she serves.

Dr. Pantoja believes that to achieve this, leaders must answer a pivotal question. "You have to ask yourself, am I a leader that is going to be accountable to my people, to the community from whence I came? If you decided to be that kind of leader, then your skills, energy, and endurance are for the well-being of your community."[7] Leaders who positively affirm their dedication to serve the collective advancement also treat people equally and with respect.

*Personalismo* refers to the character of the leader and how she treats others; it is the measure of the leader's credibility and effectiveness. Yzaguirre sums up this concept: "Latinos treasure values such as hard work and faith, which can be found in many cultures. But there is also a sense of humility, modesty, and courtesy that means a truly complete human being, a successful person, is one who treats the shoe-shine boy and the maid with the same kind of dignity that he affords the president or CEO."

Federico Peña was noted for this quality. "My parents taught me to treat everyone equally and fairly. The best times I had at City Hall were talking to the janitors and city workers. Today, they come up to me and say, 'I'll never forget, you always talked to me in the elevators. Or you always talked to me when I was sweeping the halls.' The way I looked at it, we were all working together."

## Playing by the Rules

THE ESTABLISHED FORM OF LEADERSHIP today, particularly in corporate America, is associated with fat salaries and megabonuses, the big office, corporate jets, special parking places, and the numerous privileges that come with being in the top echelon. These types of perks contradict the principle of a leader among equals; indeed, they create an economic and social chasm between leaders and followers. There also seems to be an unwritten agreement that leaders are above the rules and can even break the law and get away with it. If, through legal measures or by nature of their position, they can garner more than their share, it's considered part of the entitlement of leadership.

Given that communities of color follow leaders who exhibit good character, taking such privileges would prevent a person from becoming a *leader among equals*. When leaders play by the same rules as their followers, it levels the playing field and boosts their credibility. Raul Yzaguirre observes: "You have to work as hard as [your followers] do, or harder, and *with* them. You've got to be fair. You've got to say 'These are the rules. I will abide by them.' You need to be willing to sacrifice if you are going to ask people to sacrifice. When I was president of the National Council of La Raza, I once mortgaged my house to make the payroll."

Peña believes this is integral to leadership. "Integrity and honesty is not just following up on commitments you made, but there is a way of doing it. There are people who get things done, but the process they use is full of corruption, bribery, and questionable tactics. I never did that. People would suggest it. 'Why don't you give the contract to someone who supported you?' Or they would remind me, 'That person worked against you on your campaign, why on earth are you giving them a contract?' I would say, 'I don't play that way. I represent all the people in Denver. I am not going to have a list of preferred contractors that are just my supporters. That is not right—it is not ethical.'"

Many people believe that politics equals payback and the pork-barrel model "you scratch my back, I'll scratch yours." Peña set a different standard: "I was raised to play by the rules. This means being evenhanded; not having preferences based on color, or friendship, or political support; and not paying people off. When people look at leaders, whether in companies or any field, they want to know if they are going to be treated fairly. If a leader plays favorites, then that person's power is gone. When leaders are consistent and treat everybody the same, when everyone knows what the rules are, and *the leaders follow their own rules*, people will follow the leader to the end of the earth, because they believe and have confidence in him."

 *When leaders are consistent and treat everybody the same, when everyone knows what the rules are, and* the leaders follow their own rules, *people will follow the leader to the end of the earth, because they believe and have confidence in him.*

—Federico Peña

If leaders assume special privileges, a favored status, or make their own rules, they create hierarchy and perpetuate the subservient social status that already exists for people in communities of color. This stance runs contrary to empowering and actively engaging people. When access to resources and influence is limited, people's support and involvement are indispensable. Leaders can bring about social change only if people are willing to walk side by side with them on that long journey to equal opportunity and economic advancement.

Leadership in communities of color has emerged from a long tradition of social activism. According to Principle 5, Leaders as Guardians of Public Values, the leader inspires people to uphold democratic values and to construct a society based on these values. Principle 6, Leaders as Community Stewards, means the power for change and transformation depends on the preparation and involvement of a critical mass of people. Power in communities of color is people power. Walters and Smith describe this approach: "One of the most important resources has been human power and this has required a concentration on the tactics and strategy of mass leadership, designed to effectively target the power of Blacks as a group to certain social objectives."[8]

As a young leader, Antonia Pantoja recognized that power in the Puerto Rican community had its genesis in its people. "I had to find the way to be an agent of change, working in partnership with the community of which I was a member. I had learned that we could work collectively to find solutions to our own problems. I knew we possessed courage and stamina."[9]

*I had to find the way to be an agent of change, working in partnership with the community of which I was a member. I had learned that we could work collectively to find solutions to our own problems. I knew we possessed courage and stamina.*

—Dr. Antonia Pantoja

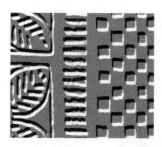

**NEXT STEPS**

**Reflecting On and Applying Principle Four**

# A Leader among Equals

The first part of this book emphasized understanding collective or We cultures and the benefits of incorporating values from communities of color into our society. This part focuses on applying the leadership principles from these communities into your leadership style and organization.

## Collective leadership

What differences have you noticed between leaders from an individualist orientation and those from a collective one?

- How could integrating practices from collective leadership increase your effectiveness?

## A leader among equals

This kind of leadership centers on good character, honesty, humility, generosity, and keeping one's word. *A key responsibility is treating everyone with fairness and consistency and following the rules.*

- Have a discussion about these values—which ones would you like to emulate? How could these enhance the performance of your team or organization? Make individual and group commitments to reflect these values in how you treat one another.

- Have people sign a group values and commitment promise and agree on periodic check-ins.

## Leveling the playing field

Many organizations today practice collaborative leadership yet have hierarchical management structures and reward individual performance. Consider how the practices of a
leader among equals can level the playing field and instill an authentic collective and collaborative spirit.

- What specific steps can your organization take to ensure that leadership is rotated
  and distributed?

## A greater purpose

A leader among equals focuses on the common good. His or her skills, energy, and
endurance are for the well-being of the people they serve. Leaders who serve a greater
purpose lessen their self-importance.

- What is the greater purpose that you serve?

## Recommended readings

- *African American Leadership* by Ronald W. Walters and Robert C. Smith (State
  University of New York Press, 1999).

- *Leadership Without Easy Answers* by Ronald A. Heifetz (Belknap Press, 1994).

# Leaders as Guardians of Public Values— A Tradition of Activism

**M**I CASA WAS A CULTURAL BRIDGE, an oasis, and it worked! Over thirty-five years later, Mi Casa continues to be a buzzing beehive serving thousands of people and their families each year. Service organizations alone, however, cannot stem the tide of the social, economic, and educational disparity that continues to bring women to Mi Casa's doors. Communities of color are caught in a crossfire. Providing services to ameliorate the difficult conditions in which many people live drains the resources needed to tackle the underlying causes of why these conditions exist in the first place.

In my early years with Mi Casa, I realized that breaking through this quandary would require a core of competent and committed leaders that could address these root causes. But leadership development is a Cadillac in a community in which people need bus fare and gas money. Getting a job, finishing high school, and learning English are economic necessities; leadership development, a luxury! Where would the money to train and groom this new cadre of leaders come from?

As I was mulling over this question, the phone rang. It was Frank Solis, community affairs director for the Adolph Coors Company. Coors wanted to initiate a national leadership program for Hispanic women. "Would you be interested in helping us get this program off the ground?" he asked.

I rolled up my eyes upward, thanking Our Lady of Guadalupe. "*Listo!*" I said. "I'm ready! *Vamanos!*" Thus began my long and inspiring journey of learning and teaching leadership.

In designing the curriculum for what became the National Hispanic Leadership Institute (NHLI), I assessed mainstream leadership models and found, not surprisingly, that they did not address or integrate the needs of Hispanics or other communities of color. In these communities, people have to be inspired to work together to solve mutual concerns. This can be difficult, because resources are often scarce and people must be prepared for the long haul. As they gain confidence, they can begin tackling the root causes and social structures that perpetuate the continuing inequitable conditions.

At the same time, leaders in communities of color also must master skills as taught by mainstream programs. The NHLI curriculum combined the good information and savvy approaches of these programs with an emphasis on community leadership, social action, and public policy change. The program was four weeks long. The first two weeks emphasized Latino leadership, critical issues facing our community, and learning how to affect social and public policy change. Next came a week at Harvard's John F. Kennedy Center on Government and another at the prestigious Center for Creative Leadership, where the women learned executive leadership. These mutually beneficial partnerships, which are over twenty-five years old, demonstrate how diversity enriches and benefits organizations.

During this time, I was fortunate to spend time with Dr. Antonia Pantoja and discuss her founding of ASPIRA (to aspire), the first Puerto Rican youth leadership and advancement program started way back in 1961. (For more on ASPIRA, see Principle 7, The Seventh-Generation Rule: Intergenerational Leadership.) "The role of a leader" Pantoja explained, "is the role of advocacy. The purpose of leadership is to exercise one's power, knowledge, and access, to change those aspects of society that are inequitable."[1] Combining services that deal with immediate issues, developing leadership and skills to address long-term solutions, and promoting an intergenerational approach have become the trademarks of effective Latino programs.

# Upholding Public Values

THE EMPHASIS ON LEADERSHIP as community action is in step with the philosophy espoused by Dr. Jim Joseph: "Leadership must address the barriers that perpetuate inequity and economic discrepancy." Joseph believes that to accomplish this, communities of color must assume a macroview of leadership that concerns itself with the public values and institutions that underscore racism and discrimination. He explains, "Even as a young boy, I always wondered why what was wrong and right focused on the rules and behavior of what individuals should do. Yet, as I grew up in the segregated south, where the doors of political institutions and social organizations were closed to Black people, I began to question why ethics concerned itself with individual behavior *but not how institutions acted.* I witnessed how institutions and society mistreated Black people. So, since my childhood, I have been concerned about *public values* rather than just private virtues."

In keeping with the U.S. emphasis on individualism, many people are preoccupied with private virtues—the microethics of personal behavior and morality. Black leaders have had an expanded approach. Dr. Joseph observes, "We had to be concerned with the behavior of systems and institutions, or macroethics that focused on public morality and community values. Because those systems and institutions oppressed the freedom of our citizens, our leaders have focused on *public values* and *institutional ethics.* Historically, an African American leader emerged because he or she was concerned with the macroethics of large systems and institutions as well as the microethics or private virtues of individuals."

Early Black leaders saw the need to realign America with its democratic values and reposition leadership as responsibility for the public good. Joseph sums up: "In a segregated society, there was *intentional underdevelopment* that expressed itself *in* and was held in place *by* social institutions. Black leaders strove to humanize and sensitize these institutions in order to improve the lives of their people . . . incorporate the concept of our common humanity, and open the doors to people of all colors, cultures, and religions."

Because of these efforts, Dr. Joseph designates Black leaders as *guardians of public values.* "Our country's founders talked about justice and forming a more perfect union, so community was a high public value. African Americans are very concerned about community and justice. The Constitution promoted the common good and the general welfare. African Americans aspire to create a better life not only for their own people but to establish a society that cares for all people." Enlightened Black leadership has cultivated social responsibility: "Oppressed people have to be concerned with justice because injustice is what holds them hostage. To change this, they have to reignite the spirit of justice in the general society so that their oppression begins to grate at the community conscience. Martin Luther King Jr. did this. Our founding fathers during our nation's formation did this as well. They rallied people to seek 'justice for all' as a public value."

Leadership development in the Black community incorporates a moral and ethical focus on *what is good for the whole*, not just individual behavior or private virtues. Dr. Joseph explains, "The initial group of Black leaders came from the religious tradition: Martin Luther King Jr., Jesse Jackson, and Hosea Williams were ministers first and then evolved into civil rights leaders. They came with a moral conscience that went beyond the notion of individual salvation to look at institutions that were barring Black people from equal participation here on earth. They appealed to our nation's conscience and tried to exercise power that was moral power . . . a new awareness and commitment to public values—a return to the fundamental principles this country was founded on."

 *The initial group of Black leaders came from the religious tradition. They appealed to our nation's conscience and tried to exercise power that was moral power . . . a new awareness and commitment to public values—a return to the fundamental principles this country was founded on.*

*—Dr. Jim Joseph*

## A Tradition of Activism and Active Citizenship

ACTIVE CITIZENSHIP IS THE lifeblood of a healthy and responsive democracy. The civil rights movement rekindled the flame of citizen involvement as a public value, and a new social activism was born that revitalized America. Joseph explains, "It is not just individuals who have a responsibility to get involved, help change things, and make a difference, but it is also Black churches and organizations. The whole tradition of activism, of 'voting with your feet,' is a legacy that drives the Black community.

Without this, African Americans would have remained economic slaves in the segregated South."

The shaping of leadership as social activism was a natural evolution for collective cultures, in which protecting and sustaining the *We* is the heart of a leader's responsibility. Contrast this with mainstream American leadership, in which there is a strong focus on developing the individual and managing organizations. Addressing the public welfare, societal institutions, or community involvement is not integral to this approach. In fact, public service usually pertains only to those in government or elected office. The need to increase local leadership capacity and citizen participation is usually designated as community leadership. In contrast, *leadership in communities of color is inherently a public responsibility to bring people together to address and change the social and economic conditions that affect their lives.*

This makes sense, considering that people of color are classified as minorities and do not share equitably in the American harvest.  In her book, *Servants of the People: The 1960s Legacy of African American Leadership*, Dr. Lea Williams describes how the lack of political equality, inadequate economic opportunity, racial segregation, and societal violence against the Black community created a leadership form seeking social reform and the redistribution of power and resources. She further explains that because these goals are viewed as antithetical to the status quo, Black leaders must be advocates, battling the resistance of the dominant society.[2]

When African Americans took up the banner of civil rights, American Indians and Latinos followed suit. The next section reviews Indian activism, which targeted tribal preservation to protect their traditions and safeguard their cultural values. The model of American Indian sovereignty has far-reaching implications for rebuilding our sense of community, promoting human coexistence, and supporting global harmony.

## Tribal Sovereignty: A Model for Collective and Tribal Identity

Preserving tribal identities has been a long difficult struggle that required fighting the federal government's assimilation and termination policies. Without this resistance, American Indians would be as extinct as the tall-grass prairies of the midwestern plains. From 1880 until 1934, when the Indian Reorganization Act was passed, minimal efforts were made to help tribes govern themselves. In 1970, the Indian Self-Determination

Act was approved, which strengthened Indian autonomy. The Bureau of Indian Affairs changed direction; it went from managing Indian affairs to helping Indians manage their own affairs.

At the same time, the Indian rights movement began to emerge, with a new breed of activists. Educated and articulate, these leaders were able to navigate the American mainstream while following the drumbeat of their cultural traditions. Depending on the needs of their tribes, they would assume many roles: from warrior to peacemaker, from listener to consensus builder, from the holder of traditional ways to the innovator of new paths. Their ongoing legal battles won back rights that had been guaranteed by the treaties with the federal government, recognizing tribes as nations and self-governing legal entities—and renewing Indian pride and identity.

American Indian sovereignty and tribal identity make a unique contribution to our multicultural nation, demonstrating that different cultural groups can function and retain substantial autonomy within an overarching system or institution. In other parts of the world, different groups exist within one country, yet unlike American Indians they have no legal protection. LaDonna Harris explains, "Tribal governments are pro-tected under the courts and the Constitution and in Congress. This premise anchors our leadership model—*tribal governments are sovereign units of government, and integral parts of the U.S. federal system of government, with the right and power to determine their own futures.*"

Ethnocentric thought and the pull for assimilation raise a question: Can people be Americans *and* still stay connected to their race, culture, country of origin, or ethnic group? Native-Americans, African-Americans, and Hispanic-Americans have been seen as hyphenated people in a cultural no-man's-land. The renowned Chicano colum-nist Ruben Salazar saw that hyphen as a *bridge*, a cultural crossroads that connects two worlds and allows a person to bring forth the best from each one. Ethnocentricity blinds people to the benefits, customs, traditions, and languages of our rich cultural mosaic. This runs contrary to our world economy and the global village in which people with cultural adaptability and flexibility have a competitive advantage.

The task of preserving and honoring cultural traditions and integrating these into a multicultural approach is a key function of leadership in a diverse society. American Indian tribal sovereignty illustrates that people can be loyal and contributing members of more than one group. Just as America is enriched by the over five hundred tribes in our country, our nation can be strengthened by the many colors, races, religions, and cultures that compose our diverse society.

The enduring desire to be part of a "tribe" is a timeless phenomenon dating back to early *We* cultures. Many people today have a heartfelt need for community, to belong and to be valued by others. LaDonna Harris passionately observes, "Perhaps these are the times to '*retribalize*' America. Not in the way politicians talk about—going back to family values—but by rebuilding our sense of community, mutual responsibility, and interdependency." American Indian tribes are a viable model for seeding and sustaining a renewed sense of community.

 *Preserving and honoring cultural traditions and integrating these into a multicultural mosaic is a key function of leadership in a diverse society.*

LaDonna believes there are also global ramifications:

Across the globe, the Kurds, Northern Ireland, the Balkans, Tibet, and parts of the Middle East and Asia are seeking political and cultural autonomy. They want their place in the sun and are saying, "We have a culture and want to keep it." Meanwhile, many Americans and Europeans see this as negative. Tribal sovereignty is five-hundred-year-old model for groups seeking cultural and political autonomy within a national system. As tribal and ethnic strife becomes the focus of unrest on every continent, Tribal America has a unique contribution to offer. We are part of the structure of federalism and coexist within the federal government. Through this system, we have maintained over 500 different cultural groups or tribes. The idea of individual governments within a larger system of government is quite exceptional.

## DISTINGUISHING RACE, ETHNICITY, AND CULTURE

**H**istorically, the debate on race has been an intellectual roller-coaster ride, from race being seen as *the* distinguishing human characteristic to race being seen as essentially a *social construct* and *generally self-defined*. Not that there are no differences based on skin color, facial features, and complexion, but a Black person in America might be classified as *colored* or *mulatto* in other countries. The U.S. Census currently defines six racial categories: Asian, American Indian and Alaskan Natives, White, Black, Hawaiian and Pacific Islanders, and Hispanic (also classified as an ethnic group). Furthermore, the Census identifies sixty-three possible racial combinations. Need I say more about race as a social construct?

Certainly there are genetically determined traits, and scientists can identify a propensity to certain diseases based on such traits. However, most scientists today concur that human beings share a similar genetic profile and that race differences constitute less than 5 percent of genetic variations.[3]

The most significant differences in human beings come from the rich and varied cultural groups that have evolved over centuries. Cultural groups share a common ancestry, language, customs, religion, and historical experiences. Racial groups generally share these characteristics and therefore, in addition to a common race, they have strong cultural ties. In this book, the term *ethnicity* is used interchangeably with *culture*. Ethnic groups have a complex set of distinctive characteristics that set them apart; these are often associated with a geographic region or nationality. (Jewish people and Greeks are examples.) However, as ethnic groups also share a common culture and heritage, they are also cultural groups.

## *La Causa*—The Cause

UNLIKE NATIVE AMERICANS, who have distinct tribal identities and are recognized as sovereign nations, Latinos' identity has emerged only since the 1960s. A fusion culture that spans many nationalities, Latinos are not a race but an ethnic group bound together by the Spanish language, colonization, the Catholic Church, and common values that stem from both their Spanish and indigenous roots. Latino leaders, therefore, are challenged to forge a shared identity, vision, and purpose from a conglomerate of people who are joined together like *pico de gallo*—a Latino condiment that includes bite-size pieces of many spicy ingredients.

To achieve this shared identity, leaders must be consensus builders and community organizers, weaving social and political unity from the diverse Latino subgroups. Like the ancient Incas, who built suspension bridges across mountain canyons by braiding straws into massive ropes, leaders must integrate the many critical issues that touch people's lives and motivate people to work together to address these. In this way, they grow people's capacity to engage in concerted and collective action.

 *In community organizing, when people are asked to take something on, there is no concrete reward. They have to be motivated, not ordered around. It just won't happen without inspired leadership: being able to encourage folks to take on perhaps an impossible task, against what might seem like insurmountable odds, is the ultimate leadership task.* —Raul Yzaguirre

Yzaguirre reflects on this challenge: "In community organizing, when people are asked to take something on, there is no concrete reward. They have to be motivated, not ordered around. It just won't happen without inspired leadership: being able to encourage folks to take on perhaps an impossible task, against what might seem like insurmountable odds, is the ultimate leadership task."

Leaders also have to inspire people to believe in themselves. Yzaguirre has successfully used this technique. "Oppressed people have been taught they can't get things done . . . They have to be convinced they will succeed and *can* do it! So the first step—the ultimate, all-important step—is to build their faith in themselves. Latino leaders' effectiveness depends almost entirely on their ability to work with people and engage them in community issues."

A point of cohesion for Latino leaders is a concept known as *La Causa*—the cause—which recognizes leaders as *advocates* for justice and equal opportunity. La Causa answers the question "Leadership for what?" Leadership is fighting for La Causa—for uplifting people and continuing the movement toward economic and social progress. Like African Americans, Latinos have a tradition of call and response. For Latinos, the call is *"Que viva"* (long live) and the response is the cherished quality. A traditional call for Latino leaders is *"Que viva la Causa!"* César Chávez understood the significance of this connecting point: "In the movement for social justice, our love for one another is sustained by the love of La Causa." La Causa offers an emotional bond that regenerates leaders in the difficult work of social change, which will continue for generations.

When Maria Antonietta Berrizobal served on San Antonio's City Council, she would use the metaphor that she was in the middle of a whole stream of people that began with her ancestors and included the many, many leaders of her time. This stream flowed into the future and would continue when she was gone. "I do my part," she would say, "and others do theirs. Eventually we will make the current so strong that it will sweep away the old and bring in the new." The belief that they are part of a long-term social movement—La Causa—sustains Latino leaders.

Based on their dedication to changing social and economic conditions, Latino leaders emphasize service, community organizing, and giving back to benefit the whole. *Community servanthood* speaks of a collective and collaborative vision of leadership. Anna Escobedo Cabral has seen this tendency in her extended work with Latino leaders. "Our ultimate motivation is a concern for the people we serve."

## Understanding the Barriers of Exclusion

IVIL RIGHTS, La Causa, and American Indian sovereignty are three distinct pathways that leaders in communities can take to tackle the barriers that keep their people from full participation and access. They are challenged by the harsh reality that people of color have been defined as "minorities"—marginalized especially in terms of power and the decision-making structures of society. *Minority* is a recent socioeconomic term and something of a euphemism for people who have historically been in subservient or oppressed positions.

On the periphery of the dominant culture, minorities are always seen in reference to and measured by dominant norms and standards. In the United States, this means White culture is presented as the *ideal*, the standard, innately superior. Anglos are the

*On the periphery of the dominant culture, minorities are always seen in reference to and measured by dominant norms and standards. In the United States, this means White culture is presented as the ideal, the standard, innately superior.*

top dogs; their norms rule. The media, school systems, and society reinforce the message that White is superior. Historically, as this subliminally seeps into the minds of young people in communities of color, it has diminished their self-worth, both individually and collectively. They begin to believe that success requires cloning the behavior and thinking patterns of the White society and distancing themselves from their own group. Yet, no matter how hard they try, they will never totally fit in. This psychological pain of rejecting oneself and one's own group, together with the confused identity that results, is the *psychology of oppression,* so named by Paulo Freire, introduced earlier in this book.[4]

## The Psychology of Oppression

Freire observed that as social mechanisms bombard the oppressed with negative messages and stereotypes about themselves, they begin to believe these to be true and to *internalize* them. Once this occurs, they are held hostage by their own minds. They begin to collude with the system that keeps them "in their place." The ramifications include (1) a lack of confidence in others of their race, (2) the exclusion of those who succeed as "not being like us," and (3) the whitewashing of minority talent, in which people of color disregard their own culture and emulate White people in order to succeed. The psychology of the oppressed is externally reinforced by social stratification, whereby members of White society enjoy greater opportunity, reap disproportionate economic benefits, and have a higher standard of living.

From an individualist orientation, a lack of success or the feelings that one cannot measure up could be attributed to one's personal lack of initiative or abilities. However, when an entire culture or race cannot compete equitably and must battle the obstacles of discrimination, this becomes *systemic oppression.* Dealing with oppression, people's lack of belief in their abilities, and the cold facts of discrimination is a central charge of leadership programs in communities of color.

In the Ambassadors Program, LaDonna Harris defines the psychology of oppression as both a personal and a leadership problem. On the personal level, if none of a young Indian's teachers look like him, the books he reads are written by people of other races, and the doctors and nurses who attend to his health are always Anglos, he may conclude not only that *he* is not smart, but that Indians in general are not smart. The young boy has thereby internalized the stereotype of "dumb Indian," believes it about himself, and projects this onto all Indian people.

Collectively, this can manifest as Indian people putting each other down. If one's reference group is believed to be inferior, then one must separate from them to feel worthwhile and emphasize that one is better than or not like them. Historically, in Indian society this lack of support was not accepted and was considered disrespectful. A person could never be a leader if she was going to put that kind of stigma on her own people. The people who felt offended also had a problem because they believed they were made to feel inferior. However, they allowed that person to put them down and diminish their ability. The Ambassadors Program looks at all these different aspects of internalized oppression to help people let go of negative stereotypes.

Dr. Joseph clarifies how internalized oppression affects Black people: "Because of the inherent nature of racism, whereby African Americans internalized negative stereotypes and were stripped of their identity, they still go through cycles of wanting to escape their history and culture and then recognizing that this is who they are and then coming back. Dealing with these differences—the separation, the internalized oppression, and the healing—continues to be a major challenge African American leaders shoulder today."

*Because of the inherent nature of racism, whereby African Americans internalized negative stereotypes and were stripped of their identity, they still go through cycles of wanting to escape their history and culture and then recognizing that this is who they are and then coming back. Dealing with these differences—the separation, the internalized oppression, and the healing—continues to be a major challenge African American leaders shoulder today.*

—Dr. Jim Joseph

Andrew Young, citing the old blues song, "Been Down So Long, Gettin' Up Don't Cross My Mind," laments, "What many observers have described as apathy is often just a protective attitude that is necessary for survival, like that of the dog who gets kicked all the time and just moves out of the way whenever someone comes along."

The National Hispana Leadership Institute's initial training considered how the psychology of oppression manifests when successful Latina women do not support one another. For a Latina, garnering a good education, learning to maneuver through Anglo institutions, and developing the skills and talents to surface as a leader is a rare feat. As Latinas become successful, the distance between them and their barrio neighbors often widens. In the Latino community, one way in which the psychology of oppression can be detected is by the expression of *envidia* (envy).

*Envidia* attributes negative qualities to successful people; for example, "She thinks she is better than others" or "She has sold out." This isolates and distresses successful people. *Envidia* is, of course, found under different names in other communities of color; it stems from the psychology of oppression in which negative self-worth is exacerbated by other people's successes.

*We* cultures want people to stay with the group, but to achieve in the greater society, a person of color must adapt and learn the success strategies of White culture. Fitting in means

## THE CRAB SYNDROME

**D**ark waves rustled like palm fronds on the coastal inlet. About four feet from shore, the boy in cut-off jeans flashed his spotlight into the black waters. Blinded, the crabs froze; one by one they were thrown into the bucket on the sandy beach. Slowly, the biggest crab began to climb out of the bucket. Strong and resilient, he would be free in a few minutes! Then he felt the sharp claws of the other crabs pulling him back. "Don't leave us. It is dangerous out there, and besides, we need you, and it is dark and cold in here." The big crab fell back, and though he tried to crawl out, he never outwitted the other crabs. So finally he held back, comforting them through the long night. Besides, if he escaped from the bucket he would be all alone, and he did not know what dangers awaited him outside.

learning the dominant culture's language, characteristics, and ways of thinking, and dressing as members of the dominant culture do—opening a psychological gap between oneself and one's family and community. There is also a justifiable fear that the person venturing out may be harmed or rejected and, despite concerted efforts, will not be successful. My parents wanted to protect me; they struggled with my decision to leave home to attend college. They were also afraid that once I left, I would not come back. This tendency to hold onto people for safekeeping, which sometimes prevents them from leaving, is commonly known as the *crab syndrome* by many people in communities of color.

Leaders in communities of color must reveal how the internalization of the psychology of oppression has affected them personally. They must help people become aware of how *envidia*, the crab syndrome, and the lack of support for others can impede community progress. LaDonna sees this as pivotal to American Indian leadership: "To integrate her identity and power, a leader needs to recognize the personal effects of oppression and release the bitterness and anger. *This can only be done through group introspection. Otherwise, the person keeps on internalizing, and believes he is the only one with the problem, or that the problem is inherent to his group.* By letting go of old, ingrained, and limiting concepts, leaders in communities of color can embrace their power. Thus, they can fully contribute to their culture and society at large and help others do likewise."

Yzaguirre concurs; he believes that Latino leaders must work to transform both the internal and external effects of oppression. "These may be more subtle than in the old days when signs in Texas said 'No Mexicans and No Dogs,' but the prejudice and misconceptions are still there. The challenge is to keep reinforcing the positive aspects of the culture so Latinos take pride in their identity and, at the same time, to constantly emphasize to the dominant community the benefits Latinos are bringing to America and the contributions they will make in the future."

*To integrate her identity and power, a leader needs to recognize the personal effects of oppression and release the bitterness and anger. This can only be done through group introspection. Otherwise, the person keeps on internalizing, and believes she or he is the only one with the problem, or that the problem is inherent to the group.*

*— LaDonna Harris*

## The Benefits of White Privilege

Just as people of color must step outside of their social conditioning to understand the psychology of oppression, White people who have benefited from an advantaged position must do likewise. Only by becoming aware of how society is structured to perpetuate the dominance of some groups and to limit access for others will leaders be able to create the framework for the just and equal society in which diversity can flourish. Multicultural leaders must be aware of the ways social institutions have built walls of separation between people of different backgrounds and the mental constructs that have buttressed these walls.

The benefits that White people enjoy just by nature of their color were discussed at length in 1988 by Peggy McIntosh, then a graduate student in women's studies at Wellesley College. McIntosh pondered the fact that men did not recognize that they were at an advantage in society, even though they acknowledged that women were at a disadvantage. She presumed that *this lack of awareness protected male privilege from being full recognized, diminished, or ended.* (If you are unaware of something, or do not recognize that it exists, you cannot address it.) She surmised that if men had an unearned advantage over women, the existence of such a social hierarchy would point to a similar dynamic between the races. Therefore, she determined that White people would have comparable advantages over people who were not of their race. She termed this benefit *White privilege.*

White privilege, similar to the male advantage, is unconscious and invisible. Like the air around us, it cannot be seen or touched, but it is pervasive and always present. Because historically many Whites have not identified as a culture or group, it's understandable that they are unconscious of their advantages or privileges. McIntosh defines White privilege as "an invisible package of unearned assets which I can count on cashing in each day, but about which I was 'meant' to remain oblivious." Being born White gives people "an invisible weightless knapsack of special provisions, assurances, tools, maps, guides, cookbook, passports, visas, clothes, compass, emergency gear and blank checks."[5]

These *societal assets* give White people an unfair advantage over other groups. Furthermore, this advantage is embedded in institutions, creating a society of unearned entitlement in which Whites have favored status. When Whites acknowledge this privilege, they will recognize that many doors have been opened for them through no virtues or special talents of their own. The lack of awareness of White privilege perpetuates the myth that *democratic choice is equally available to all,* which supports the individualist stance of meritocracy—that people make it based on their talent and hard work. Dismantling these myths is fundamental to supporting authentic democracy and to creating a multicultural society that recognizes the value of all people. Our growing diversity challenges White leaders to become aware of their privileged position and actively embrace a new model of social equity that taps the potential of our culturally diverse world.

## Rekindling American Activism

WHITE PRIVILEGE," notes McIntosh, "may confer power, but it does not confer moral strength." In fact, she notes that those who have survived oppression and succeeded despite these obstacles have much to teach others.[6] Her observations ring true when considering the legacy of civil rights. In his autobiography, *An Easy Burden: The Civil Rights Movement and the Transformation of America*, Andrew Young sees the movement's nonviolent approach, exemplified during the Birmingham demonstrations, as a deeply spiritual and rational process that sought to heal rather than defeat the oppressor. The healing process, he noted, went both ways. "The oppressed must be transformed, too. They must learn to value and respect themselves, to understand the ways they support an oppressive system, and they must learn to forgive those who have hurt them. In the process of citizenship schooling, the boycott, and demonstrations, people grew in understanding, and gained a sense of their own worth, power and dignity. In the end, Birmingham and its citizens, black and white, were transformed to the greater good of all involved."[7]

Young believes this focused the country on a specific moral agenda: "The work of Martin Luther King Jr. was to interpret the moral dilemma of America to White America and to the rest of the world. Black people already understood this." [8] America's moral dilemma is that our society speaks the language of equality but does not fully incorporate the founding values of justice, equality, and the common good into our institutions or social structures. The civil rights movement aimed to restore America's public morality. King believed this would redeem the soul of America.

Today, more than fifty years later, the need for moral strength and public morality remains a pressing and urgent leadership issue. Our country flounders, with unethical government officials and greed-driven corporate leaders. The call to serve the greater good and to embrace the public values on which America was founded is the basis of leadership in communities of color. When former Denver mayor Federico Peña stood with millions of people during the "We Are American" march in 2006, which high-

 *The need for moral strength and public morality is a pressing and urgent leadership issue today. Our country flounders with unethical government officials and greed-driven corporate leaders. The call to serve the greater good and to embrace the public values on which America was founded is the basis of leadership in communities of color.*

lighted the plight of immigrants, he urged Americans to embrace our country's higher values. "I believe a great people live by their moral and ethical principles. I believe that a great nation earns respect when it shows compassion and decency."[9]

As leaders in communities of color advocate for an equal and just society, White leaders are challenged to examine the roots of privilege, which sustains inequities in society; to ponder the loss of potential this causes; and to realize how this damages both the privileged and the underprivileged. These reflections will bring leadership to a higher ground—one on which the well-being of all Americans is seen as intricately linked. Martin Luther King Jr. understood these connections: "We are caught in an inescapable network of mutuality. Tied in a single garment of destiny."[10] He also understood the social ramifications of our interrelatedness: "Injustice anywhere is a threat to justice everywhere."[11]

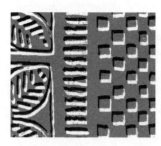

# Leaders as Guardians of Public Values

As guardians of public values, leaders assume a higher level of public responsibility and accountability focused on the common good. This broadens the work of leadership from individuals and organizations to addressing societal values and institutional ethics.

■ Why is a key function of leadership in a democracy safeguarding public values such as justice, equity, and the common good? Do leaders in a democracy have an imperative to promote active citizenship and address the barriers that perpetuate inequity and economic discrepancy?

How would our communities, organizations, and nation benefit if leaders functioned as guardians of the public good?

## The psychology of oppression and White privilege

These social mechanisms function at an unconscious level, providing advantages to some people and limiting access to others. Understanding these reveals how discrimination operates on a personal and institutional level. A group discussion is most effective, as people may be unaware of how these two mechanisms have influenced their lives. This perspective can be gained only by sharing with others.

■ What is White privilege? Have you had any personal experience with how it operates? How does White privilege reinforce cultural dominance and construct barriers to meritocracy and equal access? What are the advantages White people derive from their race and color?

The psychology of oppression describes the internal process whereby people who are not part of the dominant culture collude with the negative stereotypes and limitations placed on them by society. Shedding these requires group introspection so that individuals understand oppression as an external mechanism.

- Using dialogue techniques, have a group discussion on how discrimination is systemic and institutionalized. How this has affected people both in the group and in society as a whole?

- Describe any early experiences you might have had with discrimination. Share any insights or observations about how discrimination has occurred in other people's lives. Listen carefully and allow people to disclose any negative feelings associated with these experiences.

## Preserving and honoring cultural traditions

Leadership in a diverse society must preserve and honor cultural traditions. Tribal sovereignty offers a model for cultural and political autonomy within a national system. (American Indians have over five hundred tribes.) Latinos are a diverse group representing many races and countries of origin. African Americans treasure individuality, yet have an unshakable sense of community and collective identity.

- What lessons do communities of color offer about respecting differences and honoring the cultural integrity of a multiplicity of groups? How can this begin transforming the cultural conformity and ethnocentric tendencies that historically shaped the United States?

## Recommended readings and resources

### Books

- *The Help* by Kathryn Stockett (Penguin Books, 2009).

- *Managing Diversity: People Skills for a Multicultural Workplace* by Norma Carr-Ruffino (International Thomson Publishing, 1996).

### *Films*

- The Help (DreamWorks, 2011). Black and White women in Mississippi during the 1960s form an improbable alliance that gives them the courage to transcend race and class. This is a timeless and universal story about the ability to create change.

## Videos

- "VOCES: Antonia Pantoja ¡Presente!" by Lillian Jimenez (Latino Public Broadcasting, YouTube, September 6, 2009), available at http://www.youtube.com/watch?v=i70BdC_nLpw. The activism of Antonia Pantoja was based on her personal experience with inequities in the United States and Puerto Rico, particularly in educational systems. Her life was spent organizing people to change this.

- "A More Perfect Union" by President Barack Obama (Philadelphia, Pennsylvania, March 18, 2008), NPR transcript, available at http://www.npr.org/templates/story/story.php?storyId=88478467, and video on YouTube, http://www.youtube.com/watch?v=pWe7wTVbLUU. In this speech, Obama addresses issues of racial tension in America, White privilege, and racial inequality. Assuming the role as the leader who promotes public values, he urges Americans to move beyond race and address shared social issues.

# Leaders as Community Stewards—Working for the Common Goal

A S WE LOOK AT leaders as community stewards, I want to begin by emphasizing that nurturing community is very different for Blacks, Latinos, and American Indians from the way it is for Anglos. Our communities have very old roots that have sustained us. They have a purpose—to benefit others and to garner the force for social action and progress.

People of color in the United States, as previously noted, have a heightened collective identity that stems from the tribe, community, and extended *familia*. Black, Latino, and American Indians are intact communities and recognize each other as belonging to the same group even when they don't know each other personally. (We take a deeper look at this in Principle 8, All My Relatives.)

As an immigrant, I didn't always understand this. Unlike those whose families have been here for centuries, my roots and extended *familia* were left in Nicaragua. When

I moved to Denver many decades ago and began working in the Hispanic *barrio*, community events, celebrations, fundraisers, and personal invitations were extended to Latino leaders all the time. I found "all this community stuff" a bit overwhelming.

In my earlier study of social work, there was an emphasis on separating your professional life from your personal one (a White cultural norm). *For Latinos this just ain't gonna happen! No way José!* I began to understand that *my community was my life.* Today when I attend these events I am connecting with my *familia.* It's even more amazing that, because of my national work in most places I travel to, whether I am in Phoenix, Seattle, Washington, DC, San Antonio, or Nueva York, I connect with Latinos in those communities—and I feel at home, like they are part of my tribe and extended *familia.*

One way White privilege surfaces is when Anglo intellectuals talk about *society* as if it includes everyone, when they are really talking about only themselves. For example, Robert Putnam's book *Bowling Alone* does not consider the large extended family gatherings and many events in Black, Latino, and Indian communities. Likewise, Peter Block's book *Community: The Structure of Belonging* laments that our communities are fragmented and that individuals long for connection. He urges us to acknowledge our interdependence, and increase our generosity, personal engagement, and relatedness, to honor our commitments, and put an end to "one up, one down."[1]

*But wait a minute! Communities of color are intact and interdependent.* Block is describing Anglo or White communities, but he never acknowledges this. Thus, the knowledge and contributions of our communities are not validated or adopted. It is my hope that by raising mainstream awareness of the community stewardship practices of Blacks, Latinos, and American Indians they will nourish the connections among all of us and strengthen our resolve to use our collective ability to create vibrant, caring, and equitable communities.

## Leadership as Service

THE CONCEPT OF LEADERSHIP as service was brought to the foreground by Robert Greenleaf in 1979. His modest pamphlet *The Servant as Leader* set the stage for the emergence of the collaborative and participatory process, in which leadership is not the hierarchical domain of the privileged few but entails delegating responsibility, sharing benefits, and developing people. A philosophical and reflective

*Greenleaf tapped into the old forms of indigenous and tribal leadership and then brought it forth into a modern context.*

—Dr. Jim Joseph

man, Greenleaf surmised that the hierarchical leadership approach he had witnessed in his career at AT&T did not nurture other people's leadership skills and, in fact, did not develop the leader's higher capacities.

Greenleaf began reflecting on *why* a person aspired to lead. Unconsciously, he had tapped into an ancient Native American stream of thought in which a person's intention—the *why*—was the central core from which all other actions flowed. In an individualist-oriented society, people are taught that the *why* is generated by self-interest. Leadership, for instance, is a prize people aspire to capture that brings privilege, status, position, glitz, and financial rewards. Greenleaf concluded that these types of leaders did not have a lasting influence on society or the people they led.

If we look at great leaders of the last century who had a substantial impact—Nelson Mandela, Martin Luther King Jr., Susan B. Anthony, and César Chávez—we can agree with Greenleaf that these leaders were not motivated by self-interest or a desire for personal influence or power. In fact, they were sometimes enlisted through the pleas of their followers or drawn to leadership to address the injustices of their time. They accepted the mantle of leadership to serve the people, communities, and ideals they sought to further. This, concluded Greenleaf, was the distinction that set them on the path of what he termed *servant leadership*. They sought to *serve first* and then made the *conscious choice* to lead.

Once a leader was on this path, the litmus test of whether he remained a faithful steward was the effect on followers. Did they become *freer, more autonomous,* and *more capable of serving others*? In other words, did the leader empower people? Greenleaf added another caveat, which was a revolutionary departure from the hierarchical leadership of previous times: What was the effect on the less fortunate members of society? This connection to social good and the well-being of those in need repositioned leadership, bringing it back to the beliefs of indigenous people, and put forth a model closely aligned with communities of color. Dr. Joseph observed, "Greenleaf tapped into the old forms of indigenous and tribal leadership, and then, brought it forth into a modern context."

## Serving Society and the Greater Good

Greenleaf also defined servant leaders as affirmative builders of a better society. At first, he observed this phenomenon as largely person to person. Later, he urged large institutions to assume the responsibility of creating the good society. Greenleaf did not emphasize the social change movements, such as civil rights and women's liberation, that were surfacing during his life. Yet he described the times he lived in as follows: "The late twentieth century will be seen as revolutionary because, in this period, large numbers of influential men and women have come seriously to grips with the issue of power and authority." He saw a clear mandate for these times: "*making power legitimate for the public good . . . as an ethical imperative.*"[2] Greenleaf therefore recognized the underlying power shift that the movements of his time were advocating.

If Greenleaf were alive today, he might note that many people within the dominant culture have not heeded his call to transfer power for the public good. In fact, Dr. Joseph observes a shift in the opposite direction: "Today the dominant society has moved away from communal responsibility and concentrates instead on individual values. This approach blinds people to institutional racism and other social ills. It negates the mutual responsibility leaders have to create institutions that support the good society based on the values this country was founded on."

 *Today the dominant society has moved away from communal responsibility and concentrates instead on individual values. This approach blinds people to institutional racism and other social ills. It negates the mutual responsibility leaders have to create institutions that support the good society based on the values this country was founded on.*

—Dr. Jim Joseph

Fortunately, Greenleaf would be heartened to observe, in communities of color, the blossoming of leadership that is strategically engaged in "making power legitimate for the public good." Servant leadership is deeply anchored in Black, American Indian, and Latino cultures that center on community responsibility, the public welfare, and addressing the social structures that hinder people's progress. Antonia Pantoja was passionate about lifting up the Puerto Rican community. "I felt I was called to do something about the situation of the people I belonged to. That was not an option. I had a responsibility to contribute to my people."[3] Because all leaders, like Pantoja, derive their power from the communities they serve and are accountable to them, they may well be described as community stewards. They are therefore expanding the focus and scope of servant leader to *community servanthood and stewardship.*

# Community Servanthood

OMMUNITY SERVANTHOOD repositions the responsibility of leadership to one of serving people. Federico Peña describes this emphasis: "The way I saw it was that I was a servant. I didn't become mayor because I was great, but because people voted for me. So I was there to serve them and the Denver community." Raul Yzaguirre describes this type of leadership as community empowerment. "Part of what I do is to educate Latinos, help them understand the larger issues, why things are the way they are,

*Part of what I do is to educate Latinos, help them understand the larger issues, why things are the way they are, and what we can do to change that by working together.*

—Raul Yzaguirre

and what we can do to change that by working together." This resonates with the NCLL survey finding that Latinos want *community-centered and community-serving leaders.*[4]

This concept of *community servanthood* is based on involving many people, sharing power, and benefiting others. Such leaders are good stewards who build community capacity and group empowerment. Dr. Pantoja, an early pioneer with Puerto Rican immigrants who came to New York City, reflected on this challenge: "I had to find a way to become an agent of change working in partnership with the community. I learned that we could work collectively to find solutions to our own problems."[5]

John White, in his book *Black Leadership in America,* identifies community progress as a key component. "From colonial times to the present, Black leaders in America have developed and utilized their distinctive personal qualities in attempts to improve (or eliminate) the inferior caste status of African Americans. Their shared concern has been to improve the conditions of blacks through economic, educational, political, and psychological progress."[6] This progress was propelled by the formation of Black organizations in the 1960s.

Dr. Lea Williams documents that organizations such as the Southern Christian Leadership Conference and the Student Nonviolent Coordinating Committee "attempted to absorb the energy of the black masses to further an agenda of Black political and economic power." She goes on to say that these groups "had the potential to create social change through their mutual interaction." They emphasized breaking the chains of segregation and moving the Black community forward. The leaders who shepherded these organizations, she declares in the title of her book, were "*servants of the people*."[7]

Thurgood Marshall, Fannie Lou Hamer, and Fredrick Patterson were part of the cadre of inspired leaders who left their imprints as servants of the people in the 1960s. Dr. Joseph believes they were united by values that led them into community service: "Values such as a concern for fellow human beings, a keen sense of justice, an emphasis on the common good, not just individual attainment, sharing and interdependence are intricate parts of African American leadership and are the public values that shape individual behavior."

These values are also the foundation for authentic servant leadership that goes beyond individuals and institutions to build the just and loving society that Greenleaf envisioned.

Leadership as community servanthood is central to American Indian culture. LaDonna Harris's working definition of leadership is "a communal responsibility with a concern for the welfare of the 'people' or tribe and then sharing the work that needs to be done based on skills and abilities. Leadership is seen as shared responsibility and promoting people's well-being." Similarly, the Jemez Pueblo's first principle of leadership, as described by Benny Shendo, is "responsibility and serving the community." Consequently, he observes, "There is profound trust in our leaders, a deep belief that they will always put people first." Leaders are guided by the question: "What's best for the people, for our community, for our way of life?"

Community stewardship prompts leadership that concentrates on building people's capacity. Leaders grow their communities by engaging

*[Leadership is] a communal responsibility with a concern for the welfare of the "people" or tribe and then sharing the work that needs to be done based on skills and abilities. Leadership is shared responsibility and promoting people's well-being.*

*—LaDonna Harris*

people in the following practices: (1) encouraging participation and building consensus, (2) generating a shared vision, (3) using culturally effective communication, and (4) weaving partnerships and connections.

## Encouraging Participation and Building Consensus

The Native American Council nurtures full participation, promotes consensus building, and fosters respect for each person's contribution. The Council, which in many tribes is their governing body, protects the well-being of its community, honors diverse opinions, and achieves shared ownership.

Only after much listening, interchange, and reflection does a collective answer or solution surface. In the Jemez Pueblo, says Benny Shendo, "Our decision-making is not about majority vote, but around consensus building. Are people comfortable, do they understand enough about it? If this decision is made, will the community move forward? If a decision is not made, how will this affect the community?"

Conflict arose when voting was imposed on tribes that traditionally had made decisions and governed by inclusion, listening, and consensus. The Comanche, for example, have a very flat society in which hierarchical leadership does not exist in a traditional sense. Representative government created elitism and hierarchy: When people were elected, they were elevated above the rest of the tribe.

The American belief that only democratic voting can ensure equal participation is contrary to many indigenous forms and traditional cultures in which *building consensus,*

 *The American belief that only democratic voting can ensure equal participation is contrary to many indige-nous forms and traditional cultures in which* building consensus, integrating people's needs, and strengthening the collective is the goal.

*integrating people's needs, and strengthening the collective is the goal.* In democratic systems, voting signifies that the majority rules. In some instances 49 percent of the group may not agree with the other 51 percent, and rarely is there unanimity. In collectivist cultures, in which relationships are lifelong and ongoing, this would weaken the community fabric. The havoc that can ensue is evident in the political divisions in America today. Building consensus and integrating everyone's opinions takes time and a great deal of patience and dialogue, and it may seem cumbersome! However, it is a surefire way to garner the collective wisdom and to secure the commitment of all involved.

Federico Peña exemplified these qualities: "When I was mayor, I always invited people to participate and to be part of the solution. There was a great deal of community involvement. People would say, 'Why is the mayor putting together another task force?' Well, I understood that you get things done by involving people and working as a community. Now people reflect back and say, 'By having that task force, you saved fifteen years.' When people become part of the effort, they want to support the effort and then they are helping to shape their destiny."

## Embracing a Shared Vision

As community stewards, leaders are dedicated to serving people, a movement, a cause, and a greater purpose. As community stewards, leaders must set a course that represents real progress for their communities. A crucial step is synthesizing a compelling and shared community vision, grounded in people's collective experience, reflecting their mutual concerns, and reaching for a more rewarding future. A shared vision articulates possibilities, opportunities, and people's aspirations. It magnetizes and becomes a focal point for their skills, talents, and resources. A compelling vision helps people believe they can achieve, which encourages them to take risks and make greater sacrifices.

In communities of color, leaders follow the wisdom of *Sankofa* as *keepers of cultural memory*. They integrate history and the lessons of the past with the compelling needs of today. Dr. Lea Williams reviewed Black leadership, beginning with the historical antecedents during reconstruction in the deeply segregated south over 150 years ago. She was able to trace the evolution from a time when Black leaders were controlled and threatened by the White power structure to the activist period of civil rights. Black leaders were able to build on "the proud legacy we inherited" and to reaffirm people's faith and pride in the progress that had been made.[8]

Multicultural leaders must also be *trustees* of their community's future and of younger generations. Yzaguirre notes: "Leaders need to

*In communities of color, leaders follow the wisdom of* Sankofa *as* keepers of cultural memory . . . *they are the* link between the past, present, and future, *promoting a sense of continuity and wholeness.*

think big, but it is the little success that builds people's self-confidence. Having both a long-term vision and building sequential steps, *paso a paso,* keeps people moving and motivated. As people succeed, their vision of what is possible to accomplish becomes wider and more expansive."

Leaders, therefore, are the link between the past, present, and future promoting a sense of continuity and wholeness. Cabral observes: "Leaders in our community have a really good sense of the past and how it relates to the present. However, they know that in the end, they have to address the challenges the community is facing *today,* and be concerned with the impact on the future. Our past guides us. It is important to know the struggles our community has faced, but we cannot live in the past. The challenge is to make sure the community is evolving and creating a better future."

Servant leaders, according to Greenleaf, are guided by an overarching, prophetic, and transforming vision. For community servants, this vision must spring from the people. Cabral sees the leader's gift as being able to carefully conceive and articulate this vision. "Latino leaders take a comprehensive viewpoint. How do I forge a vision? How do I find solutions that respect everyone's contribution and take us in the right direction?" Perhaps the best example of a collective vision is King's "I have a dream" speech, made during the 1963 March on Washington. Starting with the public values of the American creed "that all men are created equal," King mobilized an entire generation to see equality and justice as the fulfillment of our country's greatness.

Just as a midwife guides and sooths the birthing process, community stewards help people craft a shared vision building consensus, clarifying goals, and working together. Integrating a community vision requires listening to different points of view, communicating in an open, give-and-take fashion, and welcoming new ideas. Crafting a shared vision must also include the concerns of multiple generations and communicate in culturally adept styles.[9] (For more on this, see Principle 7, The Seventh-Generation Rule.) Leaders then become spokespersons, communicating the vision with passion and conviction.

## Using Culturally Effective Communication

In collectivist cultures, communication is the heartbeat that nourishes relationships and sustains community. By listening patiently to people's voices and ideas, the leader ensures that everyone is on the same page and ready to lend their resources and energies. This reverberates with the African American adage—to accomplish things together, people must be *singing from the same hymnal.* Although there are similarities in the way Blacks, Latinos, and American Indians communicate, there are also clear distinctions. Leaders from these communities are keenly aware of culturally effective ways of communicating with their people. Three practices warrant special consideration: (1) call and response, (2) it takes as long as it takes, and (3) charisma and *cariño* (fondness or affection). Using these practices can expand a leader's repertoire and enhance his or her ability to communicate in many different contexts.

**Call and Response.** Communities of color have long passed on information through stories rather than in writing, so they cherish the oral tradition. They use animated conversation and gestures not only to pass on information but also to entertain people and nurture relationships. Talking (and listening) reinforces the *We* and strengthens community. There is much more tolerance for lengthy discourse, the use of metaphors, and flowery language. Communities of color relish leaders who are *storytellers* and gifted speakers who can unite people through language.

African American leaders stay connected to their communities through the special language form of call-and-response patterns. The familiar "Do you hear what I am saying?" asks for validation that the leader is on track, and people respond, "I heard that." This creates reciprocity that builds on each other's verbal contributions. As jazz musicians are inspired by each other's contributions, so call and response creates a collective and interactive communication process. Unlike Anglo communication, in which it is considered polite for one person to speak at a time and build ideas sequentially, African American conversation zigzags from person to person. People "piggyback" on each other's contributions, creating a stimulating collective conversation and fusion of ideas.

African Americans have expressive communication patterns that include emotional intensity, colorful language, and an assertive style. There is a high level of comfort with and skill at expressing emotions. Nonverbal language like hugging, the slapping of hands, and nods of the head encourages people to stoke up the conversation.

Traditionally, the prophetic African American pastor used religion to deal with the oppression of everyday life. Dr. Joseph describes how they communicated this: "The ministers were very conceptual, painting pictures with beautiful words and phrases about life as it *could be*, not life as it was. They spoke about what a person had to do to be saved in this life. The slave masters and masters of segregation thought that they were preaching about an afterlife, but they were shaping people to be competitive and to deal with the realities of this life." He continues, "Slaves came together to worship and used the language of religion, whereas allegedly they were sometimes plotting an escape. The Promised Land for the Slave Master was by and by when he got to heaven. The Promised Land for the slaves was the possibility to change their life circumstances. It has always been *both* this life and the hereafter."

From the pulpit to the halls of Congress, Black leaders use inspired oratory to connect with and motivate people. Jesse Jackson, Andrew Young, and Congressman John Lewis used their skills as ordained ministers to follow the tradition of weaving spiritual practice with community activism and service. President Obama, perhaps one of the most moving orators of our times, is bringing this gift to a new generation of Black leaders.

**It Takes as Long as It Takes.** Native leaders spend plenty of time thinking and talking about things. Benny Shendo observes, "Council meetings can last three hours or all night. Time is irrelevant." John Echohawk relates that when people gather to make decisions, "It takes as long as it takes to talk things through. Regular kinds of agendas don't work. There can be a list of discussion items, but exactly how long that will take is secondary. Primary is that everyone has the chance to give their opinion and everyone's opinion is respected. It may take longer for people to agree, but once they come together, there is a melding of different ideas. Through talking, these are refined and the best solutions surface."

This traditional approach follows the tribal consensus form of governing and entails a great deal of listening. John Echohawk observes, "When I am a part of a group that is non-native, I am usually quiet and spend a great amount of time listening and watching. I really want to know what other people think about an issue before I offer my opinion. I have been told that sometimes I am not seen as a leader in these situations. In the Anglo community, a leader takes charge and makes his ideas known first. My natural tendency is to listen first, to reflect on what people are saying, and to discern the meaning behind this. Then I can see the common ground and the unifying themes. Sometimes this makes Anglo people uncomfortable, but *really listening is what I do first.*"

 *My natural tendency is to listen first, to reflect on what people are saying, and to discern the meaning behind this. Then I can see the common ground and the unifying themes. Sometimes this makes Anglo people uncomfortable, but really listening is what I do first.*

—John Echohawk

Deep listening is an ancient tradition that enabled the chief or leader to bring the community consensus together. Nelson Mandela credits the regent or head of his tribe with modeling this form of leadership: "He would open the meeting by thanking everyone for coming and explaining why he had summoned them. From that point on, he would not utter another word until the meeting was nearing its end . . . His purpose was to sum up what had been said and form some consensus among the diverse opinions." Mandela followed this precept: "As a leader, I have always endeavored to listen to what each and every person in a discussion had to say before venturing my own opinion."[10]

Andrew Young notes that King had a similar habit of bringing people together and asking them to discuss an issue. He would not say anything, but would listen intently to everyone. After considering the counsel of others, King would spend time in reflection and prayer before making a decision.

## Cariño and Charisma

Latinos love *charlando*—chatting about ideas, interests, dreams, plans, and possibilities. Being able to keep people engaged is a great asset and part of being *simpático*. When a Latino enters or leaves a room, the polite thing to do is to go around the room talking and "connecting" with each person there. (This can include an *abrazo*, a pat on the back, or a kiss on the cheek.) Before and after any gathering or meeting, a social window must be open to allow people to share and communicate one on one.

Sharing feelings, self-expression, and *cariño* or showing affection are also cherished. The emotional connection between people and their leaders reflects these values. The Latinos surveyed by NCLL wanted their leaders to be *loving and kind and part of the family*.[11] In a world in which many feel isolated and alienated, expressing *cariño* is a special contribution Latino leaders make, demonstrating how truly caring for one's constituents and seeing them as *familia* holds people together during difficult times and makes the long journey more enjoyable.

Leadership experts James M. Kouzes and Barry Z. Posner, in *The Leadership Challenge*, identified leaders as people who "encourage the heart," providing the fuel that inspires and motivates.[12] Latino leaders bring this passion to their work—a fire ignited by their compassion, connection to their people, and commitment to improving the lives of future generations. Because many Latinos have traveled the path of social activism, their sense of urgency can be very different from that of leaders who are more traditional. The many needs and challenges in their community drive Latino leaders to want action *now*—not on a more comfortable timeline! This may lead to the perception that they are too emotional and pushy, and perhaps do not have "good manners" or know protocol.

In her review of key cultural dynamics, Norma Carr-Ruffino comments that Latinos have an idealistic bent. She identifies this with Don Quixote, who tilts at windmills, dreams the impossible dream, and even dies for a noble cause. Idealism is born in the Latino ability to dream and connect with the supernatural, which is intrinsic to their indigenous ancestry. Carr-Ruffino sees this as an integral part of the culture: "The spirit world lives alongside Latino Americans, particularly Mexican Americans, in their everyday lives."[13] The Latino tradition of *flor y canto* (flowers and music) is indicative of the tendency to combine the real with the mystical. Flowers symbolize truth, beauty, and authenticity. Music or song represents the higher ideals and noble aspirations.

In many cultures, flowers are given for special celebrations or as an expression of caring and regard. A Latino custom, *echando flores* (giving flowers) refers to using lavish praise, thanking people profusely, giving recognition, and sharing the credit. Latino events are often characterized by the elaborate recognition of many people. In a people-centered culture, where leaders must have warm personal relations and be seen as never setting themselves above others, *echando flores* is an essential ability. Federico Peña is keenly aware of this valued trait. "A leader recognizes other people—the people who came before you, your parents, and the contributions of others. You don't take the credit. You make sure you recognize everybody else."

Passion, feelings, idealism, and a sense of urgency shed light on why *charisma* is so highly valued. In times of doubt and difficulties, people revere charismatic leaders—those who communicate with passion inspire confidence, and help people weather the storms. Dr. Pantoja, who was charming, courageous, and *charismatic,* urged people to tap into this energy. "One cannot have a lukewarm life. You have to live with passion!"[14] Charisma, when put into service to one's community, channels people's energies toward reaching their shared goals.

> *One cannot have a lukewarm life. You have to live with passion!*
>
> —Dr. Antonia Pantoja

## Weaving Partnerships and Connections

Encouraging participation, generating a shared vision, and using culturally effective communication all help leaders weave partnerships and connections. Leaders must also be shape-shifters, filling multiple roles—consensus builder, listener, and spokesperson. They also represent their community *externally* by cultivating partnerships and accessing needed resources. Weaving these types of community connections requires leaders to be *cultural brokers* and *bridge builders*. One way they accomplish this is to act as *translators* and *interpreters*.

Benny Shendo is a good example of a *cultural broker*. He understands how things operate in the dominant culture and knows how to position himself in this world. At the same time, he is clearly grounded in his family, tradition, and heritage. "People always say to me, you're able to bridge these two worlds very easily, you understand the system and how it works. But you also understand what's important to us as native people and what our sovereign rights are. The charter school is an example of that. Here's my community wanting to have a school that teaches in our language, and here's my understanding of how to get it done in the other world."

A *cultural broker* also identifies external resources, constituents, and institutional supporters. Benny had been the assistant dean of students and rector of the Native American programs at Stanford and held a similar job at the University of New Mexico. These entrées to educational communities provided a natural constituency to support the charter school. As a National Kellogg Fellow, he had connections with resources and contacts that could access funds to keep the Jemez School operational. "So when that moment came when there was a desperate situation in terms of our community, I had to call on just about everybody I knew that could [in] some way help. And they did!"

As *translators* and *interpreters*, leaders ensure that the interests and concerns of their community are represented in mainstream culture. As a community interpreter, Benny Shendo conveyed to the outside world why the school was an important and unique cultural institution: "The Jemez is the only tribe on this whole earth that speaks our language. The school had been there for about one hundred years and educated just about everybody in the tribe. So, this was not just about a school, it was about preserving a community and a way of life. It was about a sense of place and history. It was about one of the few people on earth who know their origins."

In Native American communities, leaders also assume the role of *ambassador*. LaDonna explains, "*Ambassador* is used instead of *leader* because it is more in harmony with the essence of Indian cultures. An ambassador represents his or her community as a messenger or spokesperson. Ambassadors are emissaries sent on 'missions' to voice tribal concerns to the greater society. Because tribes are sovereign nations, [ambassadors] function as diplomats, opening doors of understanding and interchange as well as conducting negotiations between nations—both other tribes and the dominant culture. Native American ambassadors are civil servants, helping their tribal government articulate the concerns of their people."

As *bridge builders*, leaders forge partnerships and coalitions. One very successful example is the Hispanic Association on Corporate Responsibility (HACR), started in 1986 by a group of Latino leaders, including Raul Yzaguirre. Realizing that one organization trying to influence corporate America would be like a voice crying in the wilderness, Latino leaders formed an HACR—a coalition of the largest and most influential national Latino organizations, whose initial mission was to monitor, assist, and prod corporate America to include Latinos on corporate boards, as employees, in their philanthropic practices, and in minority procurement at a level commensurate with Hispanic economic contributions. Over twenty-five years later, HACR has established partnerships with over thirty of the largest American corporations and has made a strong business case for Hispanic inclusion. HACR recognized that preparing the young generation to assume leadership is the only way inclusion and equity will be finally achieved; thus, in 2006 it launched the Young Hispanic Corporate Achievers Program.

As communities of color have developed power and influence, efforts to build partnerships and coalitions have expanded. Just as the Black community took the lead in civil rights, leaders are building bridges across different sectors and using diverse strategies to achieve goals. At a forum of the Congressional Black Caucus, Jesse Jackson suggested that future success would depend on "some combination of registration, legislation, demonstration and litigation."[15] The passing of the national holiday for Martin Luther King Jr.'s birthday is a good example of using multiple strategies and building diverse partnerships. Legislation was proposed for several years. National visibility increased with annual demonstrations. The Congressional Black Caucus mobilized mass support. Stevie Wonder popularized the cause with his rendition of the song "Happy

Birthday to You," celebrating Dr. King's life and contributions. Momentum was built, and the legislation finally passed.[16]

All of these roles enable leaders to function as *community stewards* in the larger society and expand their community's influence. Building partnerships across sectors and with dominant culture organizations lays the groundwork for a multicultural leadership approach. These partnerships showcase the mutual benefits of diverse groups working together. The partnerships that the National Hispana Leadership Institute forged with the Center for Creative Leadership (CCL) and the John F. Kennedy School at Harvard University over twenty-five years ago are prime examples. Harvard has substantially expanded the number of Latinas obtaining master's degrees in public administration in the university's mid-career program. CCL has had over five hundred Latinas attend programs; this diversified their classes and connected it with a new and growing market. Over ten thousand corporate executives have interacted with these high-level Latinas during these classes, learning in a more inclusive and culturally dynamic environment.

## Equality, Community, and Service

Part one of this book looked at three underlying social dynamics that are touchstones for communities of color: the integration of the past, a collectivist orientation, and a highly developed sense of generosity. The three principles we have covered in Part Two flow from those cultural dynamics, fashioning leadership based on equity, strong communal values, and serving one's community. These principles transform the individualist paradigm of leadership to a more collective, collaborative, and people-oriented form and replace the traditional emphasis on hierarchical and power-centered leadership with a circular, shared, and equitable perspective.

The principle of *a leader among equals* adds a new dimension to participatory and team leadership. Leadership is shared and rewards are more equitably distributed. Leaders are expected to set

*The principle of a leader among equals adds a new dimension to participatory and team leadership. Leadership is shared and rewards are more equitably distributed. Leaders are expected to set high standards and adhere to the same rules as followers; they are trusted to not take more than their share.*

high standards and adhere to the same rules as followers; they are trusted to not take more than their share. In this authentic collaborative environment, people work together as equals to attain shared goals. A *We* identity emerges and the spirit of generosity flourishes. When people feel connected, their motivation and commitment increases; this results in high productivity and team attainment, and ultimately transforms organizations.

The values of justice, equality, community, and citizen engagement espoused by *leaders as guardians of public values* are the keystones for building the inclusive society. Today's narrow definition of leadership refers to an individual or group that manages for results or strives to obtain a higher return for corporate investors. Leaders in communities of color embrace a broader perspective, integrating public dimensions and responsibilities. They are actively engaged in creating the just society envisioned in the founding values of our country. The rekindling of active citizenship can infuse our democracy with a new vitality.

*Leaders who function as community stewards* serve the collective, use power for the public good, grow people's capacity, and encourage everyone's participation. This enables many leaders to develop, and the principle of a leader among equals to be real- ized. Martin Luther King Jr. strove to infuse ordinary people with the power of service, declaring, "Everyone can be great because any- one can serve." When many serve, a commu- nity of leaders develops, cultivating the critical mass needed to construct the good and equita- ble society and creating a legacy of leadership.

 Leaders who func- tion as community stewards *serve the collective, use power for the public good, grow people's capacity, and encourage everyone's participation.*

In Part Three, Principle 7, The Seventh- Generation Rule: Intergenerational Leadership prepares younger leaders to continue the work and progress of those who came before them. This intergenerational leadership creates a circle of leaders, nurturing a sense of continuity, wholeness, and hope. Principle 8, All My Relatives, is based on the spiritual belief that we are brothers and sisters. When we see people as belonging to one village, tribe, community, and extended *familia*, serving and sharing are a natural outcome. As this concept extends to the greater society, leaders are called to address inequitable conditions and improve the lives of others.

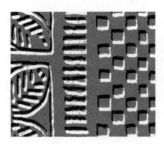

## NEXT STEPS

### Reflecting On and Applying Principle Six

# Leaders as Community Stewards— Working for the Common Goal

## Servant leadership

Reflect on two leaders: one whom you consider a servant leader and another who has attained position, power, and possibly wealth but, in your opinion, did not put people first or serve people's best interests.

- How do these leaders differ?

- What are their personal qualities?

- What do you consider their long-term accomplishments or legacy?

- Which would you follow and why?

## Community stewards

Community stewards derive their power to lead from the people they serve, and they are accountable to them.

- How does this shape leadership in communities of color?

Community stewards build people's capacity and help to empower the group. They are also *trustees* of their community's future and guardians of future generations.

- What are some ways that the leaders described in this book accomplish this?

 (NEXT STEPS 6 CONTINUED)

## A shared community vision

A shared community vision is the collective aspirations of the group or the organization. Community Stewards recognize that a shared vision promotes unity, continuity, and wholeness.

- Discuss the shared aspirations of your community, group, or organization, building on the collective history you shaped in the next steps of Principle 1. Connect this with the group values and commitments already discussed. Based on your history, values, and mutual aspirations, develop a shared vision statement.

## Weaving the collective wisdom

Stephen Covey, in his *Seven Habits of Highly Effective People*, identifies *listening to understand* as a key leadership trait. Many leaders in communities of color take this to a higher level by listening to everyone's ideas before the leader ventures an opinion. Like a weaver, the leader laces together people's ideas and integrates the group consensus so the collective wisdom surfaces.

## The many roles of a leader

Leaders in communities of color assume many roles—cultural broker, translator and interpreter, bridge builder, ambassador, and spokesperson—that require working both in their own communities and in the dominant culture.

- Compile a list of abilities needed in these (diverse) leadership roles. How are these abilities uniquely suited for leadership in our diverse and multicultural world?

## Leadership lesson

What have you learned about leadership in American Indian, Latino, and Black communities that inspires you and that you would like to emulate?

## Recommended readings

- *Memoir of a Visionary* by Antonia Pantoja (Arte Público Press, 2002).

- *Servants of the People: The 1960s Legacy of African American Leadership* by Lea Williams (St. Martin's Press, 1998).

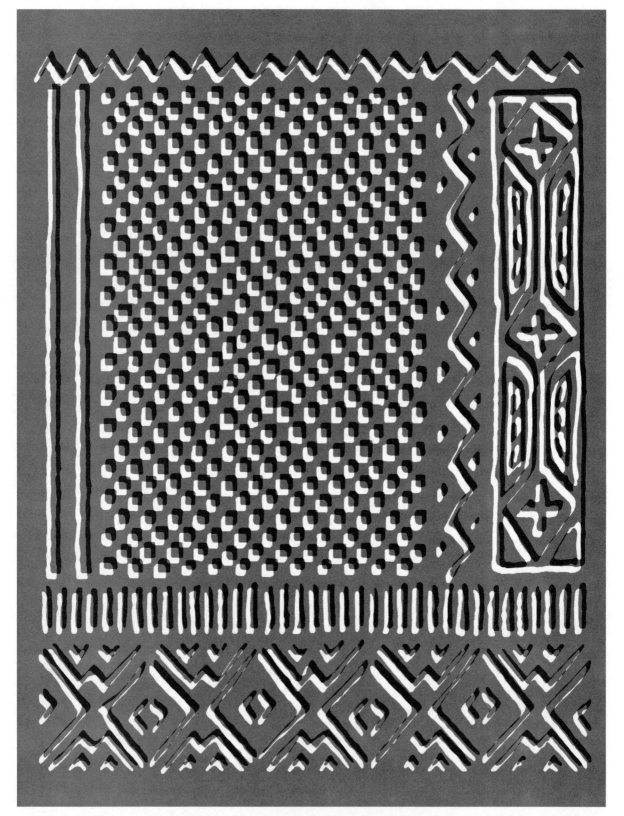

# PART THREE

# Creating the Circle of Leadership

ONG, LONG AGO, when the ancient ones created the magnificent structures of Stonehenge, they placed the monolithic stones in a circular form. Across the Northern Hemisphere, indigenous people built medicine wheels to connect to the power of life. In Africa, where human life first evolved, remnants of very old circles have withstood the ravages of time. And visitors walking the sacred valley of the Incas today can still find round stone formations.

Native Americans have traditionally used a circle for councils and ceremonies. Likewise, people in tribal Africa would sit in a circle in the center of the village to discuss important matters. In early times women would gather in circles to honor the full moon. Historically, in *We* cultures, our tribal ancestors gathered around the fire in a circle for warmth, protection, and the comfort of companionship. *The circle, which has no top or bottom, symbolizes equality.* All can see and hear each other. Everyone is related and equal to everyone else.

The African village, the American Indian tribal council, and the town meeting are examples of cooperative circular structures in which the community considers important decisions. The African saying "One head does not a council make" underlies their old tradition of tapping into the collective wisdom. The Native American "talking stick," passed around a circle, gives everyone a chance to speak from the heart, so that a group perspective surfaces. The core Hispanic values of sharing, mutuality, cooperation, and community certainly imply a circular sense of all members being connected and taking care of one another.

The principle of *Sankofa* also evokes a circular view, one in which the present flows out of the past and the future evolves out of a historical concept. Economic and social struggle in communities of color is centuries old. If people forget how much progress has been made, they may become cynical and think nothing ever changes. If they do not know their history, they will not understand how working together has been their salvation and safety net.

Leadership in communities of color is based on a circular form where responsibility is shared and reciprocal. Building a *circle of leadership* empowers people; creates the critical mass needed for social change; and establishes a legacy for succeeding generations.

## The Continuity of Leadership

AS DESCRIBED PREVIOUSLY, the seventh-generation rule of the Iroquois Indians captures the long-term responsibility and stewardship of leadership.[1] Each generation is entrusted with taking care of those who will follow, with protecting the future, and with continuing the *circle of leadership*. Principle 7, The Seventh-Generation Rule, brings this great rule into a modern context.

In the last century the human life span doubled, and today four generations are working together: the Traditionalists who were shaped by World War II, the workaholic personality-driven boomers, the self-reliant entrepreneurial Generation X, and the technologically wired and collaborative Millennials.[2] The intergenerational leadership of our seventh principle urges us to integrate the knowledge, perspectives, and experiences of these age groups to better address the fierce urgency of our times.

A mammoth demographic change also impels this intergenerational approach. Baby Boomers are turning 65 at a rate of 10,000 per day. The Millennials—at 95 million the largest and most diverse cohort in history—are just beginning their ascent to leadership.[3] They will determine the political and social landscape of the next fifty years, even as our country is transforming into a multicultural nation—which makes the leadership principles of communities of color particularly applicable.

The seventh generation rule directs leaders to ensure the sustainability of subsequent generations. According to the United Nations World Committee on the Environment and Development, "Sustainability is meeting the needs of the current generation without compromising the ability of future generations to meet their own needs."[4] Young people today know this has *not* been the guiding principle of older generations in the last century.[5] Like the people of color who fought a long crusade for justice and equity, younger generations today must get involved and address the inequities that threaten their future.

## All My Relatives Are Part of the Circle

The power of the circle is as old as humankind and centers on the essential belief that held *We* cultures together—the universal connection of the human family. This enduring sense of kinship is reflected in Principle 8, All My Relatives, which has nourished Black, Latino, and American Indian communities through the trials and tribulations of the past centuries. Leaders who see all people as relatives treat every individual with the respect due to a family member—and strive to create a society that does likewise.

# The Seventh-Generation Rule— Intergenerational Leadership

IN 2000, I INVITED a group of established Latina leaders to talk about the need for additional reinforcements—particularly young women—to continue advancing our community. We realized that our hands-on, long-term experience had made us seasoned leaders. We had succeeded through mutual support, networking, working together, and being groomed by more established leaders. Quite frankly, we weren't getting any younger, and we wanted to ensure continued Hispanic progress. We were passionate about passing on the leadership legacy established in our community. Thus was born the Circle of Latina Leadership, a year-and-a-half-long intergenerational program that prepares emerging leaders in their twenties and thirties to guide the future of Denver's Hispanic community.

We didn't realize it, but we were paving a path for Latinas of many ages to learn and lead together. One founder, Lena Archuleta, the first Hispanic principal in the Denver Public Schools, continued mentoring and working with Circle women until she passed away at ninety. The young leaders who participated in the program were mentored by established leaders in their forties and fifties. Participants in turn mentored junior high school girls, helping them succeed in school and embrace their cultural roots. A core tenet of multicultural leadership is ensuring ongoing community progress, which necessitates an intergenerational approach.

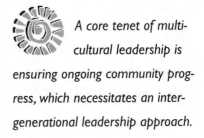

*A core tenet of multicultural leadership is ensuring ongoing community progress, which necessitates an intergenerational leadership approach.*

To date, over 150 young women have completed the Circle of Latina Leadership program. Participants complete a Community Action Project in which they practice and strengthen leadership skills. Vital to our success has been building a circle of leaders, which includes the young women, mentors, board members, community elders, and other influentials. Our mission, "To prepare the next generation of Latina leaders," emphasizes different ages working together to serve the community.

## Creating a Community of Leaders

BUILDING AN INTERGENERATIONAL COMMUNITY of leaders is essential when a group's advancement depends on people power, collaboration, and collective resources. In their book *African American Leadership*, Walters and Smith note that many talented individuals and organizations concerned with fundamental systemic change have flourished in the Black community. They observe, "The leadership of a minority within a majority has implied the use of strategies of leverage and coalition rather than outright power."[1]

Martin Luther King Jr. moved civil rights forward by always nurturing a community of dedicated leaders, including both the seasoned organizers, such as Ralph Abernathy, Hosea Williams, and A. Phillip Randolph, and young activists like Andrew Young, later ambassador to the United Nations. Congressman John Lewis was only fifteen when he met King. The young and fiery Jesse Jackson served as a voice for the movement. King secured the legacy of African American leadership. Young recalls, "We were really and truly a very close band of brothers. When Martin died, we felt a responsibility to live up to the moral legacy he established and to carry his mantle."[2]

The civil rights movement was an example of a successful intergenerational model—students, young leaders, seasoned activists, and community leaders confronted the

*We were really and truly a very close band of brothers. When Martin died, we felt a responsibility to live up to the moral legacy he established and to carry his mantle.*

—Andrew Young

social inequities of the times. In Birmingham, Alabama, in 1963, youth from ages six to eighteen initiated a peaceful gathering at the Baptist Church. As they left for the protest downtown, they were arrested and placed in police vans. When those filled, police resorted to school buses. Three hours later, there were 959 children in jail. The next day, over a thousand more children stayed out of school. With the jails full, firefighters turned powerful hoses on the children. Television images of the confrontation shocked the nation, and the Birmingham business community agreed to integrate lunch counters and hire Black people. Known as the Children's Crusade, this civil rights victory was fueled by a young generation of activists following the path forged by King and his cohort of leaders.[3]

Native Americans have built a national network of leaders through a distinctive program designed around their cultural dynamics. Started in 1970 by LaDonna Harris and renowned Indian leaders, the American Indians for Opportunity Ambassadors Program has guided hundreds of emerging tribal leaders. Core cultural values shared across Native tribes are the bedrock of the Ambassadors Program. To ensure continuity, the founders have remained active for more than forty years. This continues the tradition of honoring elders and giving lifelong service to tribe and community. The program weaves traditional tribal values into contemporary reality—thus adapting to change while fostering a firm cultural identity.

Few have left a greater legacy of leaders than Dr. Antonia Pantoja, who in 1961 launched ASPIRA, which has now trained six generations of Puerto Rican leaders. *Aspirantes* (those who aspire) are the leadership force behind Puerto Rican advancement. Their leadership spirit challenges the obstacles limiting their community.

The enlightened leadership scholar and activist John Gardner believed that our highly volatile times would require "a whole army of leaders." He predicted that a very different model of leadership would emerge. "I can't emphasize strongly enough that we're at a historic moment. The next America is going to be forged at the grassroots. It is going to emerge from the communities of our great nation."[4] Leaders in communities of color have heeded Gardner's call. They are actively engaged in preparing "a whole army of leaders"—a multicultural, intergenerational force that will fulfill the promise of an equitable society that tends to the common good.

In Principle 7 we look at a new generation of leaders: the Millennials, a socially responsible activist generation that are defining a new human rights agenda. This is not surprising; they are the children of the progressive boomers, are diverse and multicultural, and stand on the legacy of civil rights. Yet they are inheriting a cauldron of almost insurmountable issues. *The Blueprint for the Millennial America*, a document developed by thousands of young people, states their concerns: "Our passage into adulthood has been marked by natural disasters, times of economic hardship, and the longest war fought in U.S. history." They are gearing up to address "looming federal debt, historically high wealth disparity, alarming environmental concerns, unstable foreign relations, years of endless war, suburban sprawl, and underperforming healthcare and education systems."[5] A closer look at the Millennial generation offers insights on how they are preparing to lead in this century and have a predilection for following the leadership principles of communities of color. They are an activist generation and by 2016 they will make up 33 percent of the electorate.[6]

## The Global Multicultural Millennials

WALK INTO ANY URBAN school today and you will see the future. Prince Williams County lies thirty miles from our nation's capitol. Rich in history and a Southern tradition, the county began the last century as a mainly White area, but times have changed. The majority of the students today are Hispanic, 20 percent are African American, 8 percent Asian, and 7 percent identify as mixed race. Schools across the nation— in Los Angeles, Dallas, Miami, Chicago, Cincinnati, and New York—are rich racial and ethnic medleys. These are the multicultural Millennials: by *2020 a majority of Americans eighteen and under will be non-White*.[7]

Forty percent of Millennials are already Black, Brown, Asian, and American Indian, and a growing percentage are beautiful mixed races. Millennial culture thrives on diversity. According to Jeff Rainer—a twenty-something who coauthored *The Millennials: Connecting to America's Largest Generation* with his boomer father Thom—"Diversity is simply our reality. It has always been a part of my life. Millennials have friends who look different, act different, and believe different. We *are* diverse."[8] Even when they say "I do," one in five marries someone from another race, and a whopping 87 percent said they would be willing to.

This generation has also grown up with a global mind-set. Half the people in the world are currently under thirty, and through technology have always been connected to other cultures, nations, and world events.[9] Since 20 percent of U.S. Millennials are children of immigrants, mainly Latino and Asian, they have friends from different countries in their own neighborhoods.[10] Millennials understand we live in an interdependent world; many believe they are called to work with their counterparts from other nations and continents.

We know that Black, Latino, and American Indian communities have ancient kinships with people from many countries. These were once based on geography, race, culture, and nationality. Today, young people have blasted these relationships wide open. A new international culture is emerging: they dress similarly; listen to world music, with its indigenous fusion flair; download the same shows, news, and movies; and use social media networking to build community. They share concerns for the future, and they stay connected.

A youth-led international political culture promoting democratic participation and social reform has also emerged. Fifty-four percent of U.S. Millennials believe their attitudes, beliefs, and priorities are more aligned with young adults of their generation *in other countries* than with older Americans in the United States.[11] The support, interchange, and use of similar strategies across countries are regularly reported and accessible on the Internet and on the nightly news.

Millennials not only see themselves as part of a world community but also are greatly concerned about global issues. Young People We Care headquarters in Ghana motivates young people to take action on issues that affect them, such as migration, the environment, and poverty. In 2011 young people in all 50 states and 102 countries participated in Global Youth Service Day.[12] Another organization, Young Ambassadors for Opportunity, a network of passionate, globally minded young professionals, educates and involves young people in eradicating world poverty through microfinancing. They support programs in

 *Fifty-four percent of U.S. Millennials believe their attitudes, beliefs, and priorities are more aligned with young adults of their generation* in other countries *than with older Americans in the United States.*

over 20 developing countries, such as raising funds to build a full-service bank for people living in poverty in Tanzania.[13]

## The 'We' Generation: Won't You Be My Neighbor?

MANY OF THE MULTICULTURAL MILLENNIALS were raised in traditional *We* cultures, which fostered a community focus and a collective identity. Other early influences cultivated this orientation. Mr. Rogers invited an entire generation to be his friends and neighbors. He taught them to get along; that there would be ups and downs; nobody's perfect; *oh yes*, friends fight; and sometimes sharing can be hard.[14] Millennials embraced his emphasis on relationships, communication, and collaboration—connecting points for collective cultures.

*Barney and Friends* taught children to be concerned for the welfare of everyone in the group, to find consensus and "win-win" solutions. The purple dinosaur invited a smorgasbord of characters to share their culture.[15] The younger Millennials were encouraged to speak a few Spanish words by the adorable and upbeat Dora the Explorer and her extended Latino family. Dora always helped people with the assistance of her plethora of diverse friends.[16]

Mr. Rogers, Barney, and Dora the Explorer expanded the concept of neighbors and friends beyond geographic boundaries; now it makes perfect sense to have hundreds of Facebook friends from many countries whom one has never met in person, and to be interested in their lives and concerned for their well-being.

Home video games, web-based learning, and wikis for creating collaborative websites have always been part of Millennials' lives, teaching them the interactive, participatory, and collaborative skills central to community stewardship. Wikipedia invites *everyone* to share their knowledge and insights. The Yelp website shares recommendations for food and other services. Millennials get information and advice from thousands of people. Yes, everyone's equal, and everyone's opinion counts! This resonates with the principle of leaders as equals.

Millennials have self-identified as Generation *We*. A Pew Research Center study, calling them *Generation Next*, finds they value group welfare over individual reward, and relationships and quality of life over high-paying jobs and personal ambition.[17] They like to travel and socialize in groups and get others' input on *every* decision. Their sense of caring about the well-being of others is the essence of collaborative cultures.

## Wired for Action

With an iPhone in one hand, a voter registration card in the other, and a computer in tow, the Millennials are getting ready to change the world! Seventy-one percent think political engagement is an effective way to address important issues.[18]

In the 1960s, when young people rallied for social change, a mainstay belief was the personal is political. People needed to understand how inequality and oppression affect individuals, not just society as a whole. Women held consciousness-raising groups to talk about female socialization and sexism. At university teach-ins, thousands learned about a costly and brutal war. Latinos, Blacks, and American Indians discussed the mental shackles of racism and reclaimed their history.[19] These activities built consensus, revealed the barriers that perpetuated inequity, and moved people to collective action.

Members of Generation *We* also discuss issues and learn from each other, but more expansively. Text messaging, Twitter, Facebook, MySpace, blogging, instant messaging, and YouTube spur online communities to learn about current issues, share opinions, and find good ideas. Social networking has actually created a movement in which the *personal becomes political.*

Recent studies found that nonpolitical online participation can instigate learning about important aspects of civic and political life—such as volunteering, community problem-solving, protest activities, and political voice—as well as developing personal responsibility and the desire to make a difference. Thus, as social networking expands, democratic engagement grows. Young people recognize the possibilities and rewards of collective undertakings.[20]

Technology also drives political engagement: in 2008, 37 percent of those aged eighteen to twenty-four got campaign information from social networking sites (more than did from newspapers) and watched the political debates online, versus 4 percent of people ages thirty to thirty-nine, and even fewer older citizens.[21]

 *Similar to Black, Latino, and American Indians, Millennials have achieved results through collective action, but they have drastically changed the* speed and scope *of social change. They are wired for action!*

Similar to Blacks, Latinos, and American Indians, Millennials have achieved results through collective action, but they have drastically changed the *speed and scope* through technology of social change. They are wired for action!

## Walking the Talk of Civil Rights

Like civil rights icons of the past, Millennials show a deep concern for social inequity. Eighty-four percent see the gap between the rich and the poor as too wide; 94 percent think this must be changed. And they are casting the civil rights net much wider to include gay, lesbian, transgender rights, and sexual orientation acceptance and rights. Eighty-two percent personally know or work with someone with these orientations; 56 percent support same-sex marriage. Raised by women who believed in gender equality, 88 percent believe women should have an equal role in society.[22]

This generation has good reason to pursue political activism. The national debt stands at $10 trillion, or $30,000 per person; one out of two adults are predicted to get cancer; the rivers are poisoned, the land polluted, the air gray; and Millennials will not live as long as their parents.[23] In addition, in 2009, 67 percent of college graduates had debt, averaging $24,000, up 6 percent from the previous year.[24]

The *Blueprint for the Millennial America* urges the younger generation to think long-term and imagine a more equal, accessible, empowered, and community-minded America in 2040. "We have the ability to experiment with new mediums to create change in the most effective way possible—by leaning heavily on the growing online community of activists and age-old neighborhood organizing." The expansive vision of Hilary Doe and Zachary Kolodin in "Blueprint for Millennial America" includes improving educational quality and accessibility, building a green infrastructure, promoting participatory democracy, creating a health care system emphasizing wellness, and reducing income inequality.[25]

*This generation has good reason to walk the road of political activism. The national debt stands at $10 trillion, or $30,000 per person; one out of two adults are predicted to get cancer; the rivers are poisoned, the land polluted, the air gray; and Millennials will not live as long as their parents.*

The emotional and powerful voices on the YouTube Video *Generation We: The Movement Begins* urge political power to bring about change: "Our birthright has been betrayed; we must restore and protect the earth, seek justice, and promote a sustainable world. We must change the perception of our nation as arrogant and greedy. We must vote in unprecedented numbers."[26] If the 2008 election was any indication, vote they will! For the first time, young people could have *more* voting clout than their elders.[27] Generation *We* is about to rock the vote—and even to elect people their age to office. Young Elected Officials (YEO) unites and supports leaders under the age of thirty-five (who constitute only 4.8 percent of current elected officials) who have a progressive agenda and want to be on the front lines of change. YEO is preparing a pipeline of young leaders to run for office.[28]

Similar to Black, Latino, and American Indian leaders who assume social responsibility, nine out of ten Millennials feel responsible to make a difference in the world. Seventy-eight percent are willing to make significant sacrifices, such as making less money to address the major environmental, economic, and security challenges facing our country. [29] Scott Beale, author of *The Millennial Manifesto*, urges his age group to do just that: "We will not be passive. We will participate in our national politics. It is time for us to make ourselves heard. A new generation is on the rise."[30] ASPIRA founder Antonia Pantoja would agree with Beale's analysis, as she believed: *"The young can change the world!"*

> *We will not be passive. We will participate in our national politics. It is time for us to make ourselves heard. A new generation is on the rise.*
>
> —Scott Beale,
> *The Millennial Manifesto*

## Community Stewardship

Young people are getting involved in their communities and volunteering at a higher rate than ever before. According to UCLA's American Freshman survey—conducted by the University of California for the past forty years—83 percent of entering freshman in 2005 volunteered at least occasionally during their high school senior year, the highest ever measured by this survey. Seventy-one percent said they volunteered on a weekly basis.[31]

Applications for AmeriCorps positions almost tripled from 2008 to 2010 and Teach for America applicants climbed 32 percent. This may reflect the sour economy, but according to a *New York Times* article it indicates that *young people want to serve a purpose.* "The Millennial Generation is just more interested in making a difference than making a dollar," remarks Max Stier, president and chief executive of the Partnership for Public Service. More are choosing public service; 2009 saw a 16 percent increase in young college graduates working for the federal government and 11 percent for nonprofits.[32]

The Young Nonprofit Professionals Network (YNPN), started in the late nineties, now numbers forty-seven chapters in every major American city. This volunteer-led virtual organization empowers a diverse cadre of nonprofit leaders. YNPN fosters synergy between generations so that future nonprofit leaders build on the previous success and good work of those who are retiring or moving on.[33]

 *The Millennial Generation is just more interested in making a difference than making a dollar.*
—Max Stier, President and Chief Executive of the Partnership for Public Service

YNPN is founded on the collective values and service orientation of Generation *We.* Three out of four believe it is their role in life to serve others.[34] This commitment to *service* and social responsibility gives YNPN the potential to spur a movement advancing public service and community stewardship.

## Sustaining and Healing the Earth

Generation *We* grew up seeing the beautiful blue sphere of planet Earth floating in the darkness of space, *right on their computers.* This powerful image reminds us we are all connected and interdependent. No wonder Millennials are the green generation concerned about climate change, global warming, and environmental disasters. Millennials believe "previous generations did great harm to the environment." Nearly nine in ten lament "*we have to clean this up.*" In the activist tradition of the leader as guardian of public values, 67 percent look at a political candidate's environmental views to determine whether they would vote for him. Fully 73 percent said they would like to use their skills in a job that benefits the environment.[35]

Doe and Kolodin in "Blueprint for the Millennial America" declare their deep respect for the environment and advocate the following actions: mitigating climate change, producing a green jobs sector, having fresh food available for all Americans, and developing renewable energy.[36] Pre-Columbian cultures understood that the environment sustains all life—and like those indigenous ancestors, Millennials believe we should be good stewards of the earth and live in harmony with nature.

*Like the indigenous ancestors of pre-Columbian cultures, Millennials believe that we should be good stewards of the earth and live in harmony with nature.*

Evidence of this is the Road to Rio+20, where youth organizations from fifteen countries are organizing to impact the 2012 United Nations Conference on Sustainable Development. Young people know the first Earth Summit took place twenty years ago, before many of them were born. Yet as the planet keeps getting warmer and more forests are destroyed, they are gathering to make their voices heard and to make sustainable development a world priority.[37]

## We Are the Ones: Intergenerational Leadership Now!

IN 2002, THE HOPI Indian elders prophesied that a universal tribe—a Rainbow Tribe—was coming that would reflect the iridescent beauty of humanity. This tribe would heal the earth, bring peace and understanding, and undo the damage done by the White civilization. Then the elders said, *"The time is now . . . We are the ones we have been waiting for."*[38]

I started connecting with the younger generation as I traveled to universities after this book was first published. I had little prior knowledge of the incredible impact Millennials were positioned to have, nor did I understand their deep-seated emotions about the future they were inheriting, or the rising activist sentiment that was brewing. I ended the first edition of my book with that Hopi prophesy. I believed the Rainbow Tribe was about to appear. After a few years on college campuses I knew: *it is this generation that will fulfill the promise of civil rights and heal our nation—and we must help them!*

But why should they be burdened like this—with college debt, national debt, and a future that for the first time will not better than their parents? I am saddened that my generation forgot the seventh-generation rule: the age-old promise to protect our young. How could we have abandoned our children's future? How could we leave them the chaos of climate change, diminishing resources, and a faltering world economy?

Young people today echo the voices of activists in communities of color, and we must join them—all four generations must work together to "heal the earth, bring peace and understanding, and undo the damage done by the White civilization." We owe it to our children and our grandchildren. It is time for intergenerational leadership—*¡Ahora!* Now!

Intergenerational leadership also requires changing the way Anglo society relates to "old people." The dominant culture needs both positive role models of aging—with beauty, strength, and grace—and real understanding of the potential contributions of older people. Fortunately, communities of color respect age and experience; historically, they have venerated older people for their wisdom and called them "elders."

 *In 2002, the elders of the Hopi Indian nation prophesied that a universal tribe—a Rainbow Tribe—was coming that would reflect the iridescent beauty of humanity. This tribe would heal the earth, bring peace and understanding, and undo the damage done by the White civilization.*

In this spirit, in 1977 thirty-seven American Indian elders came together and initiated the Traditional Circle of Indian Elders and Youth, which meets yearly and has grown to a coalition of hundreds of "wisdom keepers" across the country. A prototype for intergenerational leadership, the Circle passes on the culture's heritage to youth, supports the continued vibrancy of Indian communities, and addresses the important issues of the day—ensuring that the next generation is prepared to lead Indian people forward.[39]

Young leaders have plenty of knowledge and fresh, broad perspectives. The elders must listen, learn, and ask: "How do we stay relevant and reenergize our activism? How can we help you realize your dreams for a more equitable, peaceful, and sustainable world? What can we do to help clean up the mess we have left you?"

Traditional mentoring implied a hierarchy; established and usually older leaders handed down wisdom and knowledge. Thus, power was retained and passed on to select groups. In contrast, intergenerational leadership builds on the principle of leaders as equals, which fosters equitable relationships and develops each person's capacity. These relationships cultivate a deep sense of We, fostering mutual respect and partnerships. Antonia Pantoja would inspire her young leaders in this way: "What do you do about the future? I make the future. You make the future. We make the future together."

# Ten Essential Elements of Cultivating Intergenerational Leadership

INTERGENERATIONAL LEADERSHIP ALSO ENTAILS collective action, social accountability, and creating a circle of leadership focused on a better future. The following essential elements have proven successful in building relationships between generations.

1. **Listen:** Deep listening is an ancient tradition that enabled tribal people to reach consensus and craft a shared vision. We know the value of cross-cultural communication; today *cross-generational* communication challenges us to listen and learn from different age groups.

2. **Be real and walk the talk**: Authenticity is based on self-knowledge, honesty, sharing values, and insights. Answer the call to action and follow through on commitments.

3. **Embrace mutuality and equality**: Regardless of age, every person's talent and experiences are respected and there is shared learning and support. Responsibility is distributed equally.

4. **Stoke up the network**: Younger generations like to work in groups and be part of a network. Blacks, Latinos, and American Indians have relied on collective action and on building a community of leaders. Create a web of support between people of different ages. (See Next Steps for models of intergenerational networks.)

5. **Tap into your passion and common interests**: Social networking sparks community involvement and political action; use it also to find and connect with others through shared interests. Identify issues that spark your passion and spur you to action.

6. **Follow through with texting and social networking:** Use Facebook, Twitter, and the like to stay in touch and share information, as well as access information on current issues, social causes, and political and social events, and, of course, to build your network.

7. **Put relationships first**: Support and validation may be the most important thing people can offer one another. Be a stable factor in a rapidly changing world. Recognize that different age groups bring special gifts and complementary experiences.

8. **Think continuity**: Relationships take time to grow. Family, tribe, village, and geographic community are continuous, lifelong relationships. Communities of color are intact and see relationships as ongoing.

9. **Remember the power of *Sankofa***: A historical perspective that helps young people understand and integrate past experiences is one of the great gifts a more mature person offers. Elders can share successes and traditions; younger generations can transform this knowledge into innovative practices.

10. **Use the Seventh-Generation Rule**: Listen to the guidance of Chief Sitting Bull: "Let us put our minds together and see what kind of future we can build for our children."[40]

Principle 8, All My Relatives, acknowledges the shared human experience that connects us at a very deep level. This awareness, the wellspring of the We orientation, entails the responsibility to look after the well-being of others and to create a society that values and protects people's rights and dignity. When people see each other as relatives, the circle of leadership expands, generations come together and the community thrives.

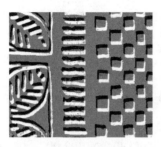

## NEXT STEPS

**Reflecting On
and Applying
Principle Seven**

# The Seventh-Generation Rule—
# Intergenerational Leadership

## Understanding the generations

Review the brief descriptions of the four generations living and working together today. Then complete the following exercise, which can help generate the understanding and respect needed for intergenerational leadership.

| TRADITIONALIST/ VETERANS | BABY BOOMERS | GENERATION X-ERS | MILLENNIALS |
|---|---|---|---|
| *1928–1945* | *1946–1964* | *1965–1979* | *1979+* |
| *Respect authority* | *Question authority* | *Technology savvy* | *Technology wired* |
| *Practical* | *Always learning* | *Self-reliant* | *Confident/ collaborative* |
| *Conservative with money* | *Job status/symbols* | *Flexible/informal workplace* | *Social responsibility* |
| *Loyal to workplace* | *Workaholic* | *Entrepreneurial* | *Rewrite the rules* |
| *Duty before fun* | *Heath and wellness* | *Life/work balance* | *Family and friends first* |

## Born in different times

In this exercise, people will form groups based on their generations and then discuss these questions:

- What are your values? What makes your generation unique?

- What major global or social events impacted your life? Favorite TV shows or trends?

- What significant contributions have you made, or do you hope to make?

Today it is rare for a group to include all four generations. Thus, people can volunteer to represent the views of their parents, grandparents, older or younger friends, and aunts and uncles, and discuss the characteristics of the generations these people came from.

Generational groups can then report back and learn from each other by discussing the following questions:

- What did you learn about the unique characteristics of the four generations?

- How has this broadened your understanding of how generations can work together?

- What are the challenges, connecting points, and learning opportunities between these groups?

## The seventh-generation rule

This ancient covenant of the seventh-generation rule defined the purpose of leadership, ensuring children's well-being and the future sustainability of the people or tribe.

- What are the indications that our leaders are not cognizant of this responsibility?

- How would our world be different if our leaders followed this rule?

- What steps can we take to make our leaders accountable?

 (NEXT STEPS 7 CONTINUED)

## Intergenerational leadership

As our multicultural age comes into full force, racial and ethnic diversity are becoming more accepted. Millennials report that diversity is part of their everyday lives. Today, overcoming intergenerational differences and ensuring the sustainability of future generations have become critical concerns.

- Have you cultivated friends and partners from other generations? How could you strengthen these relations or identify and cultivate new ones?

- Reviewing the following intergenerational models, are there opportunities for you to participate in or even start an intergenerational dialogue or group?

## Won't you be my neighbor?

Millennials have expanded the concept of a friend to include hundreds of Facebook friends and online acquaintances they have never met.

- Watch the YouTube video of Mister Rogers noted below. How do you feel about his invitation? How does this change the concept of neighbor?

- Today we are more interconnected and interdependent. How has the "global village" changed our concept of neighbor?

## How Millennial are you?

The Pew Research Center's 14-point survey (http://pewresearch.org/millennials/quiz/intro.php) is based on a scale from 0 to 100 and determines how "Millennial" a person is. The survey compares answers to a scientific nationwide survey alongside others of a similar age. My score was 42 even though I am a boomer. I thought it was because I am a cultural creative; they tend to be the more educated and leading-edge thinkers. My friends think it's because I "refuse to grow old, and have lots of young friends."

- What do the scores of people in your group, team, or class say about how different generations relate to one another?

- What makes the Millennial Generation such a critical force for this century? What parts of our discussion about this generation do you agree or disagree with?

## Recommended readings and resources

### Books

- *Blueprint for the Millennial America: A Report on the Findings from Think 2040* by Hilary Doe and Zachary Kolodin, eds. (The Roosevelt Campus Network, 2010), http://www.scribd.com/doc/44487427/Blueprint-for-Milennial-America. A vision composed by thousands of Millennials reflecting their shared values, priorities, and design for the future.

- *Generation We: How Millennial Youth Are Taking Over America and Changing the World* by Eric Greenberg and Karl Weber (Pachatusan, 2008).

### Videos

- "Children's March" by Lil Roman49 (YouTube). A rap video made by two young men for their government class accurately portrays the 1963 arrest of children in the Birmingham, Alabama, civil rights struggle.

- "Generation We: The Movement Begins," by Generation We (YouTube, http://www.youtube.com/watch?y=vknHKTyIMLY). This video presents the Millennial Generation's statement of their current challenge and how they are unique, diverse, and socially active.

- *Mister Rogers' Neighborhood,* "Introduction Theme Song" (YouTube, http://www.youtube.com/watch?v=FaYR5lwzomE).

 (NEXT STEPS 7 CONTINUED)

## Intergenerational leadership programs

**ASPIRA** is the only national organization dedicated exclusively to the education and leadership development of Latino youth. It offers ASPIRA Youth Leadership Development Clubs in schools and a myriad of after-school academic enrichment, dropout prevention, and college access programs. The ASPIRA Clubs are youth-directed leadership develop-ment clubs in which students grow their self-esteem, develop leadership skills and the motivation to go to college, take pride in their culture, and engage in community service. More information about ASPIRA can be found online at www.aspira.org.

**The National Urban League Young Professionals (NULYP)** inspires young pro-fessionals ages twenty-one to forty to empower their communities and change lives through the Urban League Movement. Over fifty chapters are led by young professionals and work on a five-point empowerment agenda to close the equality gaps for African Americans and other emerging ethnic communities in education, economic empower-ment, health and quality of life, civic engagement, civil rights, and racial justice. NULYP follows the legacy of the National Urban League founded in 1910 and is grooming the next tier of African American leaders. For more information, see http://www.nul.org/content/national-urban-league-young-professionals-nulyp.

**Circle of Latina Leadership (CLL)** is an intensive nine-month leadership program for Latinas in their twenties and thirties, mentored by established leaders. CLL includes leadership and self-development, cultural awareness, community action, and skill-building. Women complete a community action project and mentor junior high school youth. Elder leaders serve on a Leadership Council and guide the program as well as share their experiences. See more information at http://www.circleoflatinaleadership.org/.

**Global Kids** promotes global learning and youth development, ensuring that urban youth have the knowledge, skills, experience, and values they need to succeed in school, participate effectively in democracy, and achieve leadership in their communities and in the global stage. See http://www.globalkids.org/#/about-global-kids, and see the YouTube video on "Developing Youth Leadership for the Global Stage" at http://www.youtube.com/watch?v=3c_HCDIS4Uo&feature=related for more information.

**Traditional Circle of Indian Elders and Youth** is a spiritual circle open to all Indian people. Meeting annually since 1977, it brings the most respected leaders in Indian nations into council to nurture a grassroots renewal of traditional values and worldviews among Indian peoples, ensure the continuity of Native wisdom, and bring it to bear on important issues facing all peoples. The Circle gathers for six days each year at an encampment hosted by an Indian Nation. Every Circle gathering includes elders, runners (emerging leaders), young people, families, and children of all ages. The American Indian Institute acts as the Traditional Circle's sponsoring agent; see http://www.twocircles.org/.

## PRINCIPLE 8

# All My Relatives— *La Familia,* the Village, the Tribe

O N THE CARIBBEAN COAST of Nicaragua, where my family lived for generations, the Mosquito Indians greet each other by putting their hands to their chests and saying *"Kupia kumi"* ("We are one heart"). I was raised with this philosophy, an extensive and elastic concept of *familia,* which went way beyond blood or even distant kin. My Tío Cristobal lived on the banks of the Rio Coco, a dark chocolate-colored stream that flowed into the Caribbean. For the holidays, he would butcher the ceremonial pig and send the word out along the river: "Anyone who does not have a place for Christmas is welcome in my home." Thus, many a salty sailor, a neighbor who had fallen into disfavor with his wife, or a traveler who could not make it home gratefully shared the Christmas meal and family festivities.

This spirit of taking in strangers and treating them like kin was one of my mother's trademarks, particularly when it came to little children. When I was a teenager, my older sisters financed a small addition to our home, called Maria's Nursery after my mother. My mother, patiently and with her "don't try any funny business" love, cared for hundreds of children. Several *literally* became part of the family. They were *always* there and it seemed their mothers had abandoned them.

I found out later that in fact they had! One child, who had been nicknamed Peewee by my father, had a mother who just didn't come back. Perhaps my mother should have called the welfare department, but said instead, "They are like my children now. I can take good care of them." Peewee stayed the longest, but several other children also became part of the family. The funny part was that eventually the mothers would come back and be welcomed with open arms.

My mother's gift for caring for children who were not biologically her own was based on her expansive vision of *familia,* wide enough to include the *universal connection* people have to one another. When she was dying, she said, "I am not afraid, because the children will open the gates of heaven for me." Her concept of *familia* and responsibility was to those around her, but it was wide enough to include the *universal connection* people have to one another. My mother absolutely believed that Peewee and all those children she cared for were her children too.

This might seem strange, or like my mother was an exceptionally giving and spiritual woman (which she was). However, this is not that uncommon in collective cultures. Andrew Young said of his grandmother, "After informally adopting several children whom she raised along with her own, she was always taking in people throughout her life."[1] In communities of color, this willingness to take care of people who might be regarded as strangers in the mainstream culture is a natural evolution of the *We* identity at the heart of collective cultures. It reflects a spiritual understanding of the universal human connection and embodies the responsibility of leaders in communities of color to protect children and future generations.

 *In communities of color, this willingness to take care of people who might be regarded as strangers in the mainstream culture is a natural evolution of the We identity. It reflects a spiritual understanding of the universal human connection.*

## Universal Kinship

UNIVERSAL KINSHIP—THE CONCEPT THAT we belong to one human family—is the core of Christianity and the major world religions. When Jesus proclaimed "Our Father" at the beginning of the Lord's Prayer, he was affirming that people are spiritually one family. Dr. Lea Williams observed this same belief in Martin Luther King Jr.: "He had studied theology, philosophy and the comparative religions of the world. King understood our common humanity and spoke a universal message of brotherhood."

The Cherokee or Tsalagi tradition acknowledging people as "All my relatives" and the Lakota greeting *Mitakuye oyasin*—"We are all related"—mirror this belief. *Huayucaltia*, the greeting of the Nahuatl Indians of Mexico, translates as "We are all brothers and kin." The Zulu word for community—*umphakati*—means "We are all together on the inside."[2] Many greetings of indigenous people speak to a connection that is a priori—a relationship that already exists based on the unity and similarities of being human.

Today, religious and cultural beliefs that people come from one family are being verified by genetic anthropology, which combines DNA and physical evidence to reveal the history of human migration and our common ancestry. These studies conjecture that humans evolved in the last 100,000 years from a small number of tribes that migrated out of Africa. Furthermore racial differences account for only about 0.01 percent of genetic structure. The entire sequence of the human genome indicates that there is essentially one race—the human race.[3] Of course, the different races bring great beauty and diverse expressions to humanity, but our genetic commonalities as a human family are infinitely greater than those that separate us.

Quantum physics and system thinking also support the recognition that there is one human family. This replaces the Newtonian concept of the world as a machine with separate parts and segments. Margaret Wheatley, in *Leadership and the New Science*, describes this as a holistic view in which the universe is a dynamic living energy and reflects a vast network of patterns; nothing exists independent of its relationship to something else, and everything is related. Quantum physics is in fact affirming the early beliefs of indigenous cultures that saw people as interconnected and as related.[4] In many early cultures this was expressed as: "We are one planet and one people."

To understand the principle of *all my relatives*, let us first look at how this manifests in communities of color and then consider the different ways these relationships expand to embrace a much wider circle. We can then discern how treating people as relatives would transform leadership and create a society that is more compassionate, equitable, and socially responsible.

## The Kinship of Community

THROUGH THE PAST FIVE hundred years, communities of color have knitted strong and binding social nettings. Even among strangers, their common history and culture impart a deep feeling of togetherness. "*We* Shall Overcome" indicates the natural bonding that comes from the recognition that African Americans' ancestors survived the same trials and hardships.

There are nonverbal movements—lip movements, unique nods of the heads, *abrazos*, and handshakes—that Latinos, Blacks, and American Indians use to identify and bond with people of their ethnic group or race. The African American "high five" has now entered the mainstream—a great example of how easily people of color connect with one another. Latinos greet people with an *abrazo,* a full body embrace. Traditionally, they kissed one another on both cheeks. (In the Anglo culture, this type of intimacy is generally reserved for someone who is a close acquaintance or family member.) When American Indians first meet, they share their tribal backgrounds. Coming from cultures in which everything is related, this honors each other's ancestry and the historical ties between tribes.

The importance of acknowledging that *people are related* extends to leadership as well. Leaders are expected to treat all whom they lead as family members. This is easier to do when leadership is not a position or a passing stage, but a lifelong commitment. Dr. Lea Williams commends the longevity of the Black leaders she studied in the 1960s, whose average tenure was twenty-six years.[5] John Echohawk has led the Native American Rights Fund since 1977. Raul Yzaguirre spent over thirty years building the National Council of La Raza into the largest and most influential Hispanic organization in America. Andrew Young has walked the road of community service for more than fifty years. Ada Deer is an elder who served as the first chairwoman

*Somehow I learned that I belonged with my people and that I had a responsibility to contribute to them. I will participate in changing the situations of injustice and inequality that I encounter because they deny people their rights and destroy their potential.*

—Dr. Antonia Pantoja

of the Menominee Nation and is still actively involved with her tribe in northern Wisconsin.

The enduring commitment of these leaders is held together by lifelong relationships fashioned on a family or tribal model. Until Dr. Pantoja died at the age of eighty, her devotion to her community was clothed in her deep sense of justice. "Somehow I learned that I belonged with my people and that I had a responsibility to contribute to them. I will participate in changing the situations of injustice and inequality that I encounter because they deny people their rights and destroy their potential."[6]

## Relationships Carry Responsibility

IN THE MAINSTREAM SOCIETY, leaders may espouse Christian brotherhood and have good intentions regarding others. However, this does not mean that they see themselves as *responsible* for other people's well-being. The emphasis on individualism may even lead to blaming people for their own plight. As Dr. Joseph points out, this posture allows leaders to be concerned with private virtues and individual behavior, but not with social accountability. They can ignore the underlying social structures and institutions that perpetuate economic disparity and leave some people without basic necessities. In fact, much of the emphasis in U.S. politics today concerns itself with people's individual lifestyles and choices, not with overarching social responsibility.

Central to American Indian culture, on the other hand, is the belief that *relationship always carries responsibility*. Based on their circular, dynamic, and holistic view of the universe, they believe everything is related through the One Great Spirit. The respect shown to the four-legged animals, the winged animals, things that crawl, trees, stones, and all living things flows from this belief. Connected by this Spirit, human beings are one family, with the Earth as their mother and the Sun as their father. Because these relationships imply responsibility, native people must take care of the Earth, live in harmony with nature, and treat each other as esteemed family members. Even the term *Great White Father*, used by native people to describe the top Anglo leader, was a relationship term—a form of respect that also implied a reciprocal obligation, although not necessarily the kind that exists between parent and child. There were some responsibilities Indians would assume and others that the Great White Father was expected to carry.

Seeing people as relatives, as members of one big family, as one's community or village presents a different model of how leaders relate to their followers. "American Indian leaders," reflects Ada Deer, "are entrusted to look out for and improve people's welfare. They have a sense of obligation and responsibility to the tribe. Responsibility and obligation have a different connotation to Indian people. In Anglo society, it means *have to*, but to Indians it means *want to*. Contributing to the welfare of others is an honor and part of our nature."

*Responsibility and obligation have a different connotation to Indian people. In Anglo society, it means* have to, *but to Indians it means* want to. *Contributing to the welfare of others is an honor and part of our nature.*

—Ada Deer

Benny Shendo describes the Jemez Pueblo as "a community of mutual care where people see themselves as an extended tribal family. On the reservation, there are no homeless people. People always have a home. In our language we treat each other as brothers and sisters because spiritually we are all related." When relationships include responsibility, leaders become accountable for safeguarding the common welfare and treating everyone fairly and with respect.

## You Are a Person Because of Other People

Dr. Joseph describes the kinship among people in the African American community as the *cosmology of connectedness* inherited from their African roots. It reflects the traditional belief in *ubuntu* (literally "you are a person only because of other people"), which signifies that interactions with others define a person's humanity. *Ubuntu* manifests as people doing good through kindness and compassion to one another and to the entire community. Practicing *ubuntu* means people recognize their inner connections and acknowledge that humanity is one.[7] It is the basis for leaders being one among equals.

*Like a tribal drumbeat,* ubuntu *resonates across African cultures and wraps people together—my humanity is tied to your humanity.* It is not an ethereal spiritual concept of oneness, but a real day-to-day obligation to be sharing, open, and welcoming toward others. Since *Ubuntu* signifies that one's identity and well-being depends on other people, it underscores the collective and the tribe.[8] The familiar saying "It takes a *village* to raise a child" reflects this and emphasizes people's communal responsibility to all children.

*Ubuntu* nourished the unity of African slaves. When biological parents and children were ripped apart and sold to different owners, the community shared the role of mother and father. Dr. Joseph describes these relationships: "The [slave] quarter community addressed each other with familial titles and behaved towards one another as brothers and sisters with quasi-familial reciprocal obligations." He notes that this sense of responsibility for others extended to the *greater community* as well.[9] Dr. Lea Williams describes how this has continued to advance African Americans: "Our communities take care of one another. That has been our vision and salvation. It is what we must hold onto for our future well-being." Seeing each other as related or as family remains a fundamental characteristic of Black leadership today.

 *Our communities take care of one another. That has been our vision and salvation. It is what we must hold onto for our future well-being.*

—Dr. Lea Williams

## La Raza Is Inclusive

A crucial difference between Latinos and both Blacks and American Indians is that there is no legal definition of what it means to be Latino. To be eligible for Bureau of Indian Affairs services, an Indian must be an enrolled member of a tribe recognized by the federal government. LaDonna explains, "Native Americans have blood *quantism* that was imposed by the treaties and Anglo colonialists, which means that a person must have legal proof of their bloodline in order to be enrolled in a tribe." Many Indians, however, recognize that a person's identity and sacred regard for the Indian way of life are the defining characteristics. LaDonna relates to a more mystical definition: "Blood runs the heart. The heart knows what it is."

African Americans have a more legally evasive identity. According to Dr. F. James Davis, author of *Who Is Black? One Nation's Definition,* the answer has been anyone with any known African Black ancestry. One of the mechanisms that made this a de facto proposition was what anthropologists refer to as the *hypo-descent rule*, which assigns racially mixed persons the status of the subordinate group. In the racist South, this was effectively the basis for the *one-drop rule*, which came to mean that anyone with any Black blood was considered Negro.[10]

Although the racial division in U.S. society imposed great burdens on Black people and American Indians and resulted in centuries of segregation, it also allowed for their cultures and communities to stay intact. Racial isolation nourished their identities and values and permitted their spiritual foundation to flourish.

Latinos, on the other hand, have only been recognized as a group since the 1980 U.S. Census and there is still no set legal definition. In fact, Latinos are hybrids that come in many colors—black, brown, yellow, white, and red, as well as latté, mocha, chocolate, and many mixtures in between. It is paradoxical, then, that Latinos have a collective identity known as La Raza—"the race." *Que viva la raza* (long live the race) was a frequent slogan during the 1960s when César Chávez and Dolores Huerta were organizing the United Farm Workers, and it remains a rallying cry today. La Raza has a somewhat different connotation than race in English. La Raza is more of a *cultural identity magnet* springing from a shared history, worldview, and common values.

As a blend of European and many indigenous cultures, Latinos embody a rich multicultural heritage. La Raza, therefore, does not signify racial exclusivity nor propose that one race is better than another. Inclusion is a historical reality and a heartfelt cultural value. Yzaguirre believes this inclusiveness opens the door and welcomes people to partake in *Latinizmo* (the Latino cultural experience). "America needs a different paradigm of what it means to be Latino. The prototype of Native or African Americans, where your blood content defines who you are, does not work. Latinos are a culture, not a race. Inclusiveness and sharing are cherished values. My definition of Latino is anybody who wants to be a Latino: *bienvenido—welcome to the family*. This concept would revolutionize America's race consciousness."

 *My definition of Latino is anybody who wants to be a Latino:* Bienvenido— welcome to the family. *This concept would revolutionize America's race consciousness.*

—Raul Yzaguirre

To explore Yzaguirre's concept in more depth, we could say that Latinos are a culture and culture is learned. There are many opportunities for people to become fluent in Spanish, live in a Latin country or *barrio*, adapt core cultural values, marry into the family, and even be taught to salsa with the best of them. Add to this Latino generosity, the spirit of *bienvenidos,* and the desire to be *simpatico,* and people who are of like mind are welcomed into the culture. Sometimes it is difficult to discern whether people are born Latino or are simply "born-again Latinos!" With the growing demographics, influence, and emphasis on the international aspects of *Latinizmo,* many more people will be finding and enjoying their Latino affinity.

Yzaguirre is actually referring to an old tradition in communities of color. As mentioned earlier, Latinos designate people who become "like family" as *compadres* or *comadres, padrinos* or *padrinas.* American Indian, African tribes, and other indigenous communities across the planet have ceremoniously initiated people into their tribes. Although these people were not born members, they exhibited—through their lives, special feats, loyalty, or marriage—their bond to the tribe. Today, people who have a special affinity with the Native American culture are referred to as having an "Indian heart." Black families often adopt people who are not of their racial background but have strong and loyal ties to their family and race, and they may even refer to them as *brothers, sisters, my other mother, or auntie.*

 *Because culture is learned, the important thing to realize is that people can develop affinities and sensitivities for a number of different cultures. Leaders can acquire multicultural competencies, and expand their abilities to reach and connect with people from an increasing diversity of cultures.*

Because culture is learned, the important thing to realize is that people can develop affinities and sensitivities for a number of different cultures. Leaders can acquire multicultural competencies, and expand their abilities to reach and connect with people from an increasing diversity of cultures.

## A Society in Which People Are Relatives

**A**S EMPHASIZED PREVIOUSLY, IN collective cultures, *relationship always implies responsibility.* When leaders see people as relatives, as members of the universal human family, they accept the social responsibility to address the social and economic structures perpetuating inequities. We are our brothers' and sisters' keepers. Dr. Joseph believes that when leaders tend to public values and social institutions" they personally model the behaviors they aspire to see in society. "*Ubuntu,* where people are supposed to act with humaneness, compassion, and care, is an example of how *a private value can be reflected as a public value.* The private aspect is how individuals act towards each other, and the public values are ensuring that the society is structured in such a way that people are cared for and treated humanely. Condoning and sanctioning the values of *ubuntu* would engender this type of society.

As Ada Deer surmises, "Indian people see themselves as connected, as one community, and as relatives. If you don't see the human race that way, then you can take more than your share. You can be selfish. It is okay to take advantage of people. You see, it is a completely different way of looking at the world."

Ubuntu, *where people are supposed to act* with humaneness, compassion, and care, is an example of how a private value can be reflected as a public value. *The private aspect is how individuals act towards each other and the public values are ensuring that the society is structured in such a way that people are cared for and treated humanely.*

—Dr. Jim Joseph

When Andrew Young served as U.S. ambassador to the UN, he found in South Africa a model based on spiritual connectedness and the power of speaking the truth. "When the truth is spoken without judgment, but rather to point to the possibilities of a 'more excellent way of living' together as brothers and sisters, in spite of the differences of race, class or creed, there is the potential of everyone accepting a new start. This is the way God deals with us as his children, and it is also the way we must learn to deal with each other."[11] Young believes this way of thinking brought reconciliation and understanding to South Africa and has the potential to heal the world.

*When the truth is spoken without judgment, but rather to point to the possibilities of a "more excellent way of living" together as brothers and sisters, in spite of the differences of race, class, or creed, there is the potential of everyone accepting a new start.*

—Andrew Young

César Chávez followed in this tradition. He not only embraced Latino and Filipino immigrants and farm workers, but also spoke to neglected and marginalized people everywhere. He attracted people from across the country, including an ecumenical religious following, labor union support, and the respect of government officials. Finally, he led a national boycott against grape growers, inviting people everywhere to participate. Chávez cast his net very wide, reminding people that the same insecticides that were killing farm workers and their children presented a threat to all Americans, as the toxic residues persisted on produce. Like King, who described a dream for all God's children, leaders in communities of color must ensure that the table is wide enough to include all people of goodwill who are ready to build a society that will benefit the human family.

## Living Simply So Others Can Simply Live

BECAUSE LEADERS IN COMMUNITIES of color are expected to set an example, many purposely live in a way that does not create social and economic disparities. I recall the first time I picked up my mentor, Bernie Valdez, at his home for our monthly lunch, where we just talked and ate. (In oral tradition cultures, knowledge is passed on through conversation and stories—food is also crucial.) Because he was a highly respected leader, I had unconsciously expected his house to reflect his stature in the community. Yet the man who later would have the Colorado Hispanic Heritage Center and a public library named after him lived in a little house where he and his wife Dora had raised their children. Just visiting his home reminded me why I was bothered by the contradictions I had seen in leaders in Washington and in corporations. Leadership as exemplified by Bernie was not having a big house or the trappings of wealth and influence. It was a lifelong commitment to live in your community, to serve your people, and to remain an ordinary person while accomplishing great things.

Andrew Young remembers a similar commitment: "Martin and Coretta King lived in an old wooden framed house near Ebenezer Baptist Church. There was nothing fashionable about his neighborhood, it was all but a slum. But Martin viewed living modestly as part of his commitment to social justice."[12] Likewise, César Chávez, who grew up in the migrant camps of California, continued to live humbly throughout his life, never making more than $6,000 a year.[13] King and Chávez studied deeply the philosophy of Mahatma Gandhi, who set the standard for living as modestly as one's followers did.

Although these examples may seem absurd in our materialistic and status-conscious society, there are ethical and practical ways to accomplish a more equitable economic balance. They underscore a great economic disparity that develops when some people gobble up more than their share while others scarcely have enough to survive. Multicultural leadership implies a sense of generosity based on making a commitment to the collective *We* and accepting the responsibility for community stewardship. Part Four, Leading in a Multicultural World, examines how multicultural leadership principles can help individuals, organizations, and our society reach a new equilibrium that tempers the growing materialism with a renewed sense of sharing and generosity.

## Generosity Flows Naturally to One's Relatives

THERE IS A GROWING understanding today that we are intricately connected and interdependent, moving us closer to seeing all people as relatives. This is crucial if we are to restore the circle of life for each other and for future generations. Leaders are challenged to bring together splintering groups who spar over resources, conflicting political and religious ideologies, and class and racial distinctions. In the competitive atmosphere of our country, resources are divided up and parceled out inequitably, so that many do not partake of the American harvest. Evidence of this is the growing poverty rate: in 2010 over 46.3 million—one in seven Americans—lived below the poverty line,[14] and the number of people who lacked consistent access to adequate food soared to 49 million.[15] While the number of homeless is difficult to calculate, it is estimated that there are up to 3.5 million every year.[16] If society viewed all people as relatives, all would have at least the basic necessities, such as enough food and a roof over their heads.

LaDonna Harris believes that rekindling the sense of kinship is crucial: "If people on earth had this sense of family and responsibility toward one another, it would lay the foundation for world peace and human understanding." General Bob Neighbors, a truly warm and compassionate military leader who was one of my students at the Center for Creative Leadership, echoed this urgency. He was genuinely concerned about the escalating conflicts that were tearing apart prospects for a more peaceful world. "At any time on thc planet some thirty conflicts are raging that are fueled by what people perceive as religious, political, or ethnic differences. Humanity is at a crossroads; we must find peaceful ways to assuage our perceived disagreements."

*If people on earth had this sense of family and responsibility toward one another, it would lay the foundation for world peace and human understanding.*

—LaDonna Harris

Over sixty years ago, President Kennedy voiced similar sentiments: "We can make the world safe for diversity. For in the final analysis, our most basic common link is that we all inhabit this small planet. We all breathe the same air. We all cherish our children's future and we are all mortal."[17] A visionary leader, Kennedy sensed that continuing global friction threatened our planet and our very existence. He recognized that our individual safety and well-being is linked to our ability to tap into the shared human experience—the common ground that unites us all.

Like the sun that radiates warmth and light to all, the deep spiritual traditions of communities of color embrace the oneness, unity, and equality of all people. These traditions, in which people are seen as relatives, offer tried and true ways to create the world King envisioned in which all people have three meals a day, education, dignity, and freedom and there is a real chance for world peace and human understanding.

## Spirituality, Leadership, and Social Responsibility

BECAUSE SPIRITUALITY IS A unifying and all-encompassing stream in communities of color, references are interspersed throughout this book. It is further explored in the discussion of Principle 9, *Gracias*: Gratitude, Hope, and Forgiveness, which looks at the enduring faith that ensured the survival of communities of color. These vibrant forms of spirituality nurture a sense of our common humanity and a commitment to creating a society that cares for all its people.

Many leaders in communities of color have sought not just to liberate the human spirit, but to alleviate the harsh conditions many people encounter here on earth. In Young's book, *An Easy Burden*, the chapter "The Lord Is with This Movement" confirms the integration of spirituality and social action. During the early civil rights protests, all demonstrators were required to sign a pledge for nonviolence that included these principles:

 *The vibrant forms of spirituality nurture a sense of our common humanity and a commitment to creating a society that cares for all its people.*

- Meditate daily on the life and teachings of Jesus

- Walk and talk in the manner of love—for God is love

- Pray daily to be used by God in order that all men may be free

- Strive to be in good spiritual and bodily health[18]

Dr. Lea Williams described Black civil rights leaders as *servants of the people*, "sustained by and drawing strength from, an abiding faith—faith in God, faith in self and in others, faith in the vision and in the integrity of the cause." There were practical implications of this conviction: "Faith plays a defining role because it assures the servant leader that even in the midst of fear and confusion, amid turmoil and uncertainty, appropriate actions and responses will somehow be revealed because they walk by faith and not sight."[19] The faith traditions in communities of color are the foundation for leadership that integrates spirituality with social responsibility.

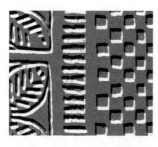

**NEXT STEPS**

**Reflecting On
and Applying
Principle Eight**

# Universal kinship

Reflect on the meaning and implications of the many sayings that express the belief in human connectedness and the universal human family:

- *Kupia Kumi*—We are one heart

- *Mitakuye oyasin*—We are all related

- *Huayucaltia*—We are all brothers and kin

- *Umphakati*—We are all together on the inside

- *Ubuntu*—I am a person only because of other people

In pairs or small groups, stand and repeat these sayings to one another several times. (English is fine.) The goal is to *experience* human connectedness and to glimpse the ancient belief that human beings are one family.

Explore the emotional or heart aspects of this exercise—how did it make you feel? Describe the power that comes from understanding that you are part of the *We*—the collective—and are supported by this. Discuss what our society might look like if people truly embraced this ancient and pervasive belief.

# Relationships always carry responsibility

Relating to people as family and kin is not just a feel-good theoretical concept. In fact, the leaders profiled in this book have dedicated their lives to serving people because *relationships always carry responsibility.*

- Which of the examples of leaders acting on this sense of responsibility have stuck with you?

- What benefits would our society reap if we followed their example?

## The mechanism of exclusion

The blood quantism imposed on the America Indian community and the "one-drop rule" imposed on African Americans were mechanisms of exclusion and discrimination. Discuss the effects of such legal definitions on people's lives.

- What distinguishes the Latino community? How does the basis of their identity differ from that of American Indians and African Americans? Why does Yzaguirre believe this could "revolutionize America's race consciousness"?

- There are many stories of people who leave their culture of origin to live in other cultures, adopt the customs, and become accepted as kin. Think of some experiences you have had in which you felt connected to other cultures. Discuss concrete steps people can take to develop sensitivities to and affinities with different cultures.

## Living as relatives

The Jemez Pueblo people believe "spiritually we are related."

- What does this imply for how people should treat one another?

- What are the implications for multicultural leadership?

## Recommended readings

- *An Easy Burden: The Civil Rights Movement and the Transformation of America* by Andrew Young (HarperCollins, 1996).

- *Latinos: A Biography of the People* by Earl Shorris (Norton, 1992).

- *Mankiller: A Chief and Her People* by Wilma Mankiller and Michael Wallis (St. Martin's Press, 1993).

**PRINCIPLE 9**

# Gracias—Gratitude, Hope, and Forgiveness

A FEW YEARS AGO, I trudged through the Nicaraguan jungle to the mining town of Bonanza where I was born. The green canopies are lush with banana trees and brazen tropical flowers hanging from vines. Even today, many decades later, there are only three streets. The stark isolation is apparent the moment the cargo plane touches the dirt runway carved in the sea of jungle trees. *How did it happen?* I asked myself. *How did this miracle that is my life ever occur?* My mother and grandmothers would have *no problema* answering. To them it was always *gracias a Dios*—their faith never failed them.

Since serving as a Peace Corps volunteer in Chile over forty-five years ago, I have listened to thousands of people share their journeys, and I know this reliance on God's providence is not unique. Our collective journeys reflect the unflappable faith and hope that wrap around communities of color like serapes on cold nights. Practicing *Sankofa*—reflecting on our past—reveals the bones of our common journeys and honors the Herculean obstacles our parents and *antepasados* overcame for us to become who we are today.

Migrant workers, sharecroppers, garbage collectors, growing up in shacks with no running water or electricity, immigrants who couldn't speak English—an unlikely gene pool for the next generation of distinguished American leaders. Yet this was the fertile ground that cultivated the strength of character, hope, and belief in God's grace (or life's goodness) that in turn brought the substance of leadership to communities of color—a past that is reflected in our ninth and final principle—*Gracias:* Gratitude, Hope, and Forgiveness.

## Unos Cuentitos: *A Few Little Stories*

ROSSING THE RIO GRANDE, Maria Guajardo's parents became migrant workers in the California fields under the searing sun. Her mother only finished the second grade; her father never attended school. They sacrificed so that their children could go to school. Guajardo made their dream come true: she attended Harvard University, obtained a doctorate from the University of Denver, and served as Denver's Director of the Mayor's Office for Education and Children. Education, which her parents only dreamed of, has become Maria's passion and life's work.

Ada Deer grew up in a one-room log cabin on the banks of the Wolf River in the Menominee Indian reservation, in the cold windy forests of northern Wisconsin. There was no indoor plumbing, electricity, or running water. She loved to read, and her keen intelligence was noticed by the elders. After the Tribal Council awarded her a scholarship to go to the university, she felt compelled to help her brothers and sisters. Four out of five received college degrees. She later directed the American Indian Studies program at the University of Wisconsin, helping many students, Indian and non-Indian alike, to attain a college degree.

David Wilson remembers his father, a sharecropper in the Mississippi Delta, learning to read by looking at the newspapers they had tacked to the wall to keep the wind out of their wobbly shack. Theirs was a deeply spiritual family, and Wilson's father believed God's grace would look after them. With great determination, David became the first of his nine siblings to go to college, earning a doctorate. He has dedicated himself to education, distinguishing himself as vice president of Auburn University, extension chancellor at the University of Wisconsin, and now president of Morgan State University in Baltimore.

Her signature appears on U.S. dollar bills. Anna Escobedo Cabral, who served as the U.S. treasurer, remembers changing elementary schools over twenty times as her family migrated with the ripening of the crops. Eventually, her father became a laborer because he wanted his children to stay in one school. However, he was injured and suffered spinal disabilities. Lacking worker's compensation, he bought an old truck and became a junkman. He would pick up metal trash and creatively fix old appliances and other things he found. Anna, the oldest, helped him sort through the trash. She accepted a scholarship only when her counselor convinced her that she could help her family more if she went to college.

More than four hundred years ago, Ken Salazar's family cofounded the city of Santa Fe. Since the 1800s they have lived in the majestic, but economically depressed San Luis Valley in Colorado. Salazar grew up in a remote rural area with no electricity or phone lines. His parents were humble poor farmers, but, as he likes to say, "We were rich in values." Stressing hard work, community, and faith, his parents urged their eight children to study hard and pursue their education. They all completed college. Ken served as a U.S. senator and Secretary of the Interior under the Obama administration. His brother John served as congressman from the third district in Colorado.

These childhood stories are not uncommon. They reveal a foundation of faith, sacrifice, service to others, and hope for the future. Without these, our parents would have constantly griped about their unfair situations, become bitter, and simply given up. They might have grown to hate people who did not give them a fair shake or held resentment because the doors of opportunity were tightly guarded.

For Black, Latino, and Indian leaders, *gracias* (gratitude), hope, and forgiveness are three attributes that transformed oppression and need into an enduring faith in life's

 *For Black, Latino, and Indian leaders,* gracias *(gratitude), hope, and forgiveness are three attributes that transformed oppression and need into an enduring faith in life's goodness.*

goodness. Jesse Jackson advised, "Suffering breeds character. Character breeds faith. In the end, faith will not disappoint."[1] Faith and spirituality together have been the collective and unifying force sustaining communities of color during centuries of toil and discrimination and continue to provide the strength for leadership and social action.

# Spirituality: A Collective and Unifying Force

I N MAINSTREAM LEADERSHIP, SPIRITUALITY usually connotes self-development. For instance, Peter Block, in *Stewardship: Choosing Service over Self-Interest*, defines leadership as a commitment to "working on yourself first."[2] Stephen Covey focuses on individual character development and follows in the same vein.[3] But when Andrew Young searched for his own spiritual calling, he looked through a different lens: "Western Christian theology conceives of liberation primarily in personal terms. I needed to see the relationship among ethics, theology, and *socio-economic liberation*."[4]

The term *spiritual responsibility* reflects the integration of leadership, spirituality, and social activism. Dr. Lea Williams recalls, "The Church was the platform from which Black leadership sprang. It was a natural progression from *spiritual responsibility* to social and political involvement." Walters and Smith note the continuing importance of religion and the church in Black politics and leadership as "incubators of political activism, race-group identity and solidarity, as well as a major institution of political leadership and resource mobilization."[5]

In Hispanic cultures, *fé* (faith) permeates everyday life; it can be seen in home altars, the wearing of holy medals, *estaturas de santos* (statues of saints) and sacred items in visible places—even in cars. God's providence is acknowledged on a daily basis. The saying "*Esta en los manos de Dios*" (it's in the hands of God) reflects this assurance. Before something happened, my Tía Anita would proclaim, "*Este va a pasar si Dios quiere*" (this will occur if God wills it). Afterward she would say, "*Este paso, gracias a Dios*" (thank God for making it happen). As a child, I surmised that coming or going, before or after, Tía Anita had it covered.

Leaders tap into this spiritual stream to inspire hope and bolster people's faith that by working together they can uplift the community and their lives. César Chávez said, "I don't think I could base my will to struggle on cold economics or on some political doctrine. I don't think there would be enough to sustain me. For the basis must be faith."[6]

> *The Church was the platform from which* Black leadership sprang. It was a natural progression from spiritual *responsibility to social and political involvement.*
>
> —Dr. Lea Williams

Chavez expressed the integration of faith and social action succinctly when asked how the striking farm workers would achieve their goals: "We're going to pray a lot and picket a lot."[7]

## Spirituality Is Responsibility Toward Others

THE "BACKSEAT DRIVER" BRAND of religion tells people how to live, what life decisions to make, and what kind of lifestyle they should pursue. However, too often such religions are *not* equally concerned with ensuring that people have the economic means, resources, or education they need to meet their basic needs and to live with dignity. Not to imply a direct cause and effect, but the intrusion of religious and morality platforms into politics has coincided with burgeoning poverty, homelessness, lack of medical insurance, failing education, and a rise in single-parent households.

When relationships imply responsibility, *spirituality is a moral obligation to ensure others' well-being and the collective good.* The concept of the leader as community steward and guardian of public values grows out of this conviction.

 *When relationships imply responsibility, spirituality is a moral obligation to ensure others' well-being and the collective good. The concept of the leader as community steward and guardian of public values grows out of this conviction.*

Andrew Young's family had a biblical creed that guided their lives: "From those to whom much has been given, much will be required." His family had a *living* faith—to serve God and their community and to help others who were not as fortunate. Young grew up in a middle-class family in New Orleans. "In my family, faith and a good education were intertwined with the commission to serve others." Hungry strangers who heard of his grandmother's goodness always showed up at her house to get something to eat.[8]

Federico Peña's family settled in Texas over 250 years ago. His great-great-great-grandfather was a founder of Laredo, and his grandfather had a seat on the City Council; other ancestors served in the first territorial legislature, as mayor of Laredo, as school board president. In some cultures, this might be the perfect setup to think of oneself as privileged. Not Peña. Like his ancestors, he chose the path of public service. "I saw my life as one of helping people who were being discriminated against and had no voice."

His life shows this commitment. On May 1, 2006—designated as a nationwide "day without immigrants"—he asked the organizers of the Denver March if he could address the group. As a businessperson he certainly would not profit from standing up on such a divisive issue, but he urges people to speak out for what is right: "For those of us who attended religious worship this

*I saw my life as one of helping people who were being discriminated against and had no voice.*

—Federico Peña

past weekend, we should conduct a full moral gut check as we watch immigrant workers wither in our deserts, drown in our rivers, and die on our highways . . . I believe that a nation earns respect when it shows compassion and decency."[9]

## Leadership as Spiritual Activism

LADONNA HARRIS OBSERVES, "In American society, churches are one place, work is somewhere else, education is over there, and none of them relate to each other. For Indian people, *spirituality is the integrating force of their lives and the essence of leadership.*" The separation of spirituality from other aspects of life in the U.S. contributes to a moral schism: leaders can act unethically and irresponsibly, yet claim to be religious and churchgoing people.

A closer look at U.S. history reveals the historical antecedents of isolating religion from public life. In past centuries many European immigrants were fleeing religious persecution and oppressive state religions. The founding fathers purposely protected the nation from this type of government through the First Amendment, which states there will not be an official religion and guarantees people freedom of religious expression. President Jefferson further expanded this into the concept of separation of church and state.

While this concept preoccupies our leaders, the idea of having a discussion about morality, ethics, and spiritual responsibility falls by the wayside. Congressional leaders are taken away in handcuffs, a president breaks moral codes—all still proclaiming they are churchgoers and good Christians. Perhaps the failing morality in political and in corporate leaders is due not to whether they attend church but to the lack of a moral and ethical code that integrates *social responsibility* and *spiritual responsibility*.

President Obama advises a deeper conversation about religion: "It's wrong to ask believers to leave their religion at the door before entering the public square. Abraham Lincoln, William Jennings Bryan, Martin Luther King Jr.—indeed, the majority of great reformers in American history—were not only motivated by faith, they also used religious language to argue for their cause. To say men and women should not inject their 'personal morality' into policy debates is a practical absurdity; our law is by definition a codification of morality."[10]

In this Obama emulates leaders in communities of color. Historically, leadership, responsibility, and spiritual activism have always been intertwined. Archbishop Romero of El Salvador was part of the liberation theology movement that interlaced social justice and responsibility, particularly for the poor in Latin American countries. In the 1960s, when California farm workers organized a union to advocate for decent wages and working conditions, they marched in a procession with a statue of Our Lady of Guadalupe leading the way. Chávez uplifted them with such traditional religious practices as pilgrimages, fasting, retreats, public prayers, and worship services.

Andrew Young recounts how the civil rights movement was infused with new spirituality after the use of fire hoses, billy clubs, and police dogs in Birmingham, Alabama and the arrests of their children. "The marchers were praying and crying to no avail. Then someone shouted, 'God is with this movement.' Over five thousand people marched past the dogs and police singing the old spiritual, 'I want Jesus to walk with me. All along my pilgrim journey, Lord. I want Jesus to walk with me.' Bull Conner, the Birmingham police chief, was shouting, 'Stop them, stop them,' but nobody responded."[11]

According to Young, the paralysis of those onlookers who earlier had used violence to stop the demonstrators was evidence of the spiritual transformation and healing that was taking place. As Martin Luther King Jr. expressed it, "The religious aspect of our quest for justice is a struggle to make our society whole."[12]

Spirituality is integral to every aspect of the American Indians for Opportunity Ambassadors Program. For example, the identity discussion "Who are you?" and the reflection on personal power "Where do we get our medicine or strength?" concern spirituality. This is the personal power or "medicine" a leader carries that allows her to contribute to the community and obtain greater consciousness, awareness, and balance. A person's spirit will lift that person out of oppression, social inferiority, and self-doubt. Part of a leader's sacred duty is to ensure that spirituality is acknowledged in every aspect of the community's endeavors.

Bennie Shendo concurs: "There are a lot of folks who are searching for who they are, for meaning in life. They have lost that spiritual connection. In my community, I could not even fathom the thought of separating the *spirituality* of who we are as a people from who I am. It is how we carry ourselves every day." The Jemez songs and ceremonial way of life are as circular and as constant as the seasons, reminding people of their relatedness and responsibility to each other and the tribe.

In communities of color, spirituality centers on relationships. The traditional African philosophy of *seriti* is the spirit and power of all life—the vital life force of each individual in the context of *interaction with others and the community*. The more good deeds a person does, the more he shares with humanity, the greater his *seriti* grows. If he does bad deeds, his *seriti* diminishes. *Seriti* is a reflection of a person's moral substance, influence, goodness, power, and humanity.[13]

 *There are a lot of folks who are searching for who they are, for meaning in life. They have lost that spiritual connection. In my community, I could not even fathom the thought of separating the* spirituality *of who we are as a people from who I am.*

—Benny Shendo

*Seriti* explains why Nelson Mandela, after nearly three decades in jail, did not seek revenge on his persecutors. If he had, he would have lessened the goodness that comes from forgiveness and reduced his *seriti*. Through his forgiving and seeking reconciliation and by doing good, his life force—his *seriti*—grew, and so did that of his family, clan, and even his nation.

Communities of color have always seen spiritual responsibility as doing good for others. This resonates with *seriti* and drives a collective and spiritually responsible form of leadership that uplifts the whole community. Through practicing gratitude and forgiveness communities of color have emerged as a spiritual force for healing and reconciliation.

## Gratitude and Thanksgiving

Gratitude was deeply ingrained in early *We* cultures, in which just surviving was a blessing indeed. Most indigenous cultures had celebrations to give thanks for the cycles of nature, such as the change in seasons, the glorious full moon, and the rain that quenched the earth. The harvest celebration gave thanks for the first crops that would ensure survival through the cold winter. *Gracias*, being grateful, is a key quality that cultivates hope because people concentrate on *what they have*, not *what they lack*.

From before the European conquest of this hemisphere, the seeds of gratitude planted by their indigenous ancestors nourished Latino people. The two meanings of *gracias*— *grace* as well as *thank you*—imply that to be happy and to live in what Christians refer to as "a state of grace," one must be *grateful. Gracias a Dios*, a cherished philosophy of life, is also a common refrain in conversation, often spoken after someone acknowledges something good that has happened. Gratitude encompasses an appreciation for parents, family, the community, the *antepasados*, and the blessing of children.

"*Gracias a la Vida*" ("Thanks to Life"), a treasured song by Chilean artist Violeta Parra, is steeped in this spirit of thankfulness. The song thanks life for our ability to see and to hear, and to have feet to walk with; for cities, puddles, beaches, deserts, mountains, plains, the stars in the heavens, for the alphabet and words so we can communicate, and for our mothers, friends, brothers, and sisters. We are grateful for both smiles and weeping because they allow us to distinguish happiness from sorrow. The ending confirms that it is *your song and everyone's song*: "Thanks to life, that has given me so much."

African American spirituality has been fashioned in this tradition. "Praise the Lord" and being thankful for life's blessings are as central as the hymnal in Black churches. Historically, this was simply to make it through another day and have enough to eat. Many White people do not have the same awareness of being thankful for *daily survival*. White churches do not emphasize prevailing over pain and hardship in the same way Black churches do. African Americans agree that God guided them out of the land of Egypt. This sentiment is in their national anthem. "Lift Every Voice and Sing"—"God of our weary years, God of our silent tears. Thou who has brought us thus far on the way."

Gratitude and thanksgiving reflect the reverence for life inherent in Indian culture. In *Voices of Our Ancestors*, Dhyani Ywahoo of the Eastern Tsalagi (Cherokee) Nation speaks to this connection: "What is praying? To rise in the morning and to thank the sun, and then at midday, when the sun is overhead, thank all of those who have come before. And as the sun descends over the western horizon, say thank you. Oh, a day has passed and another day shall come. I am thankful."[14] In this spirit, Native American gatherings, community celebrations, and meetings always begin with a prayer of thanksgiving.

Expressing *gracias* is a great gift that communities of color bring to America—an antidote to the raging materialism that is dividing our nation into a land of haves and have-nots. It is the opposite of taking more than one's share. Like a spiritual salve, *gracias* can soothe the cultural angst that comes from always wanting more "stuff" than one has.

## Hope and Optimism

In his book *Emotional Intelligence*, Daniel Goleman defines optimism as the greatest motivator, because it expresses a strong expectation that things will turn out all right, despite setbacks and frustrations. He cites research that optimistic people tend to be more successful.[15] Optimism can also be described as hope—an essential trait in communities of color. Hope and optimism was my mother getting on a banana boat with five of her eight children to cross *El Golfo de Mexico*. Optimism is coming to a strange land, struggling to learn English, working two jobs, and seeking education for your children.

A *New York Times/CBS News* poll validated optimism as a Latino cultural trait, noting that 75 percent of Latinos believed their opportunity to succeed was better than that of their parents. Only 56 percent of non-Hispanics thought this was true. Additionally, 64 percent of Latinos thought life would be better for their children. This jumped to 83 percent for Hispanic immigrants who have come here seeking opportunity, but was only 39 percent for non-Hispanics. Hope is what drives Latino immigrants to make the perilous Rio Grande crossing.[16] In 2011 a *Washington Post* article reported that although African-Americans and Hispanics were more likely to be left broke, jobless, and concerned that they lack the skills needed to shape their economic futures, *they also remained the most hopeful that the economy would soon right itself and allow them to prosper.*[17]

A belief in God's mercy and an enduring hope that they would overcome is the very substance of African American culture, allowing them to thrive in adversity. Dr. Joseph, whose father was a minister, identifies optimism as central to their religious experience: "Every sermon always ended with something about hope. It never stopped with 'things are so bad.' It stopped with 'things may be bad; *however,* there is always the possibility of a better life.' Without the gift of hope, the Black community couldn't have held on and had the courage to overcome. African American leaders have to dispense hope. If people are not hopeful, they won't act to change things. It's not naïve optimism, it is a hopeful realism."

Hope builds on the perennial belief in the Promised Land—the assurance that one day Black people will be free. Hope was kept alive by hymns such as "Hear That Freedom Train A-Coming, Coming, Coming" and "Woke Up This Morning with My Mind Stayed on Freedom." The hope of justice, noted Martin Luther King Jr., springs from the unrealized promise of America—the promissory note that our country's founders gave to all people that they would enjoy life, liberty, and the pursuit of happiness. This hope has sustained the Black community in their search for equality and freedom.

Just as gravity holds everything to the earth, spirituality is the magnetic force of America Indian culture, binding people together. There is no separation between the spiritual and material worlds like that found in Eurocentric cultures. The Indian worldview is one of wholeness, relatedness, and responsibility. Hope is anchored in dreams, visions, prophecy, and the good counsel of the wise elders and shamans. This hope kept tribes together even when they were removed from their lands and the Bureau of Indian Affairs relocated them to urban areas. Without hope, tribes would have blown away like tumbleweeds in a sandstorm.

Each tribe has its own prophecies and medicine men, but since the loss of their land the emphasis has been on survival, hope for the future, and the dream of peace. When Black Elk, a medicine man from the Lakota Nation, was only nine, he had a vision that devastation was coming and he should urge people to find new strength to survive. Today, Leon Shenandoah is the Tadodaho (Firekeeper, Speaker, or Chief of Chiefs) of the Iroquois Confederacy. In his address to the United Nations in 1985, he spoke of the hope that "the four sacred colors of humans would stand together in the interest of peace." He continued, "We must unite the religions of the world as a spiritual force strong enough to prevail in peace."[18] This is similar to the Hopi prophesy about the rainbow people who would heal the earth, bring peace and understanding, and undo the damage of the White civilization.

## Forgiveness and Reconciliation

Although in this book I have not lingered on the travails endured by communities of color, we can learn critical leadership lessons by reflecting on these. As Dr. Joseph says, "African Americans had to come out of desegregation and the pain of racism and work hand in hand with the communities that oppressed them." This could happen only through the practice of forgiveness: "When Martin Luther King Jr. talked about loving the enemy, he was talking about reconciliation. He used the word *love,* not *reconciliation,* but it was the same notion that there had to be forgiveness."

Dr. Joseph connects this to the African philosophy of *ubuntu.* "*Ubuntu* expresses that one's humanity can only be defined through how one interacts with others. If you damage the humanity of another person, then the whole of humanity is damaged in the process. The African American community has always taught this value. You forgive not only because it is ordained by the creator, but you live in this kind of relationship with other people because it is also in your self-interest."

Reconciliation, according to Dr. Joseph, is one of the *public values* leaders need to create a diverse society. "African Americans have been schooled on how to tolerate unacceptable behavior and continue working with the people who inflicted these wounds. *So one of the key contributions African Americans make to the world is reconciliation.* The challenge of resolving conflict through reconciliation and bringing people together may be as important in the twenty-first century as freedom was at the dawn of the nation states. In an interdependent world, one of the primary public values must be reconciliation based on tolerance and respect for others."

For Latinos, forgiveness has entailed healing the psychological trauma of the Spanish conquest. Genetically, Latinos are mestizos (of both indigenous and European, but predominately Spanish, parentage). Although that designation

 So one of the key contributions African Americans make to the world is reconciliation. *The challenge of resolving conflict through reconciliation and bringing people together may be as important in the twenty-first century as freedom was at the dawn of the nation states.*

—Dr. Jim Joseph

is infrequently used in the northern hemisphere, it is commonly used in Central and South America. Octavio Paz, the Mexican writer and Nobel Prize winner, described the pain and stigma of being a mestizo as an indelible inferiority complex. He believed that mestizos were made to feel ashamed of their Indian roots. At the same time, they were rejected by their arrogant Spanish fathers, who often did not recognize them as legitimate offspring. This denial negated the very talents and attributes inherited from their European ancestors and denigrated their indigenous roots as well.[19]

Many Latinos credit the marriage of indigenous spirituality and the Catholic faith as the wellspring for the ensuing forgiveness and cultural integration. A symbol of this cohesion is Our Lady of Guadalupe, who appeared as a mestiza with many indigenous symbols surrounding her. At a time when the native people were being extinguished, she spoke in the Nahuatl language, bringing a message of hope that they would survive. She promised to hear their lamentations and to remedy their suffering.

As a mestiza she represents the fusion of the two cultures that are today's Latinos. Guadalupe was the vision and promise of the future, a healing force that planted seeds of forgiveness and compassion.[20] Today, Latinos recognize that the blood of the Spanish conquistadores runs through our veins and is present in the language we speak, and that many positive aspects of our fusion culture come from Spanish roots. We have forgiven the transgressions of our Spanish ancestors and now consider them part of our heritage and *familia*.

Forgiveness also allows people to begin anew. At the start of each year, Cherokee tribal members make a procession to the stream and gather together. People then swirl water above their heads seven times, washing away any thoughts or actions that are not beneficial for their future well-being. Particularly important is forgiving anyone who had offended or hurt them. This allows them to replenish relationships, strengthen the collective, and start with a clean slate each year.[21] This is similar to the Jewish Day of Atonement—Yom Kippur—on which people ask forgiveness for transgressions of the previous year. Knowing that intentions are good but that for many reasons people may falter, they request forgiveness in advance for any mistakes in the coming year.

*Sankofa*—looking at history in the bright light of truth—is easier when the process includes forgiveness and reconciliation. Then the truth really can set us free! We can birth new understandings and new pathways. Jesus identified forgiveness as the crux of Christian living. It is also a wise and magnanimous leadership trait. Reconciling the *past,* having gratitude for what one has *today,* and being optimistic for the *future* all nourish continuity and community integration—the foundation for the circle of leadership.

To achieve our vision of multicultural leadership requires nurturing the qualities of *gratitude, hope, and forgiveness.* These strengthen a leader's ability to validate people for their contributions as well as to acknowledge their gifts. As reflected in the stories of leaders in communities of color, *gracias* and hope seed a positive and inspirational tactic, a unifying force, integrating social responsibility with spiritual activism.

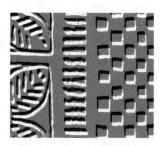

## NEXT STEPS

**Reflecting on and Applying Principle Nine**

# Gracias—Gratitude, Hope, and Forgiveness

## Practicing *gracias*

Gratitude focuses attention on what one has rather than what one wants. Practicing gratitude brings a sense of contentment with one's life.

- This week, take five minutes each day and write down ten things for which you are grateful. I like to include ordinary things like a good cup of coffee, a warm bath, or a savory meal. You will notice as the week goes by that you have a greater appreciation for yourself, the people in your life, and the many cherished possessions you have.

- Continue this practice by ending each day with a reflection on things for which you are grateful. If you try this for a week, you will find it makes for a positive ending to the day and may even help ensure a good night's sleep.

- In your organization or group, agree on a regular time (such as just before the weekly meeting) for expressing gratitude and appreciation. Start with organizational benefits, then share the talents, and contributions of each individual. If members have difficulty expressing this, use a nice piece of paper with room for everyone to write positive comments. Develop an *attitude of gratitude* and see people's motivation rise!

- Develop a gratitude habit. Commit to a weekly "gratitude day" on which you make a point of thanking people for their help, ideas, good work, and commitment. An easy way to develop this habit is to name a gratitude day: this could be Marvelous Mondays (to get each week started in a constructive way), or Thankful Thursdays, or Fortunate Fridays (to end the week on a positive note). On this day, send out emails or notes, or make a quick call and thank folks for their contributions during the past week. Mark your gratitude days on your calendar so you develop a habit of thanking folks on a regular basis!

## Cherokee cleansing ceremony

Forgiveness is starting over, letting go of old transgressions, and making room for the new. Forgiveness can be an act of community affirmation. "Letting go and cleansing" ceremonies are useful after a contested election or difficult organizational change, to release old baggage, to start on a new track or strategic direction, and with individuals or groups who want to let go of past grievances.

- The group gathers in a circle (outside, if possible) around a crystal bowl filled with water, symbolizing the Cherokee walk to the river. People step up individually, scoop a handful of water and swirl it above, stating what they want to release or whom they would like to forgive—obstacles, situations, or past experiences that stand in the way of growth and power.

- Another process is having people write about grievances or things they would like to get rid of. They can then reflect individually, share with the group, or both. People stand in a circle and either wad up the paper and throw it into a wastebasket, burn it in an urn, or bury it in the earth. It is important that each person make a statement about what he or she is releasing so that the group can support them in this.

## Spirituality and social responsibility

- How is spirituality defined in communities of color and what role has it played in their ability to survive and thrive under adverse conditions? How does this spirituality anchor leadership?

- *Seriti* integrates one's spiritual integrity with right action toward one's fellow humans. Why is this a critical need in our world today? Who are some leaders whose *seriti* reflects a strong moral force and goodness toward humanity? Think of people you know and have observed, not necessarily the more prominent leaders.

## Recommended readings

- *Long Walk to Freedom: The Autobiography of Nelson Mandela* by Nelson Mandela (Little, Brown, 1995).

- *Our Lady of Guadalupe: Faith and Empowerment Among Mexican-American Women* by Jeannette Rodriguez (University of Texas Press, 1994).

# Leadership for a Multicultural Age—

## Making the Commitment:
## Personal, Organizational, and Political

W E BEGIN THIS final part: *Making the commitment: personal, organizational, and political* with an invitation to become part of our global community and actively work to build a diverse society. This means we must fashion inclusive organizations and promote active participation in our democracy.

We will explore a concept known as *destino* in the Latino community, similar to an African American's *calling* and the American Indian's *vision quest*. Becoming a multicultural leader is a *calling*—and once you say *Yes*, you embark on an ambitious journey that starts with embracing such qualities as generosity, service to one's community, and understanding the dynamics of exclusion—such as the difference between *assimilation* and *acculturation*.

The American melting pot required immigrants to assimilate and shed their ethnic and national backgrounds. This created cultural uniformity and discounted the contributions of diverse groups. Today, effective leadership requires the ability to *acculturate*. Such leaders allow people to be receptive, skillful, and adaptable to other cultures while staying centered in their own. Acculturation is the portal to our multicultural world.

Most organizations have traditionally operated from a monocultural reference point and an individualist focus. People of color and those who are not part of the dominant culture have to "fit in" to be successful. This is known as *hierarchical pluralism*. However, cultural integration requires *egalitarian pluralism,* whereby the unique traditions and contributions of diverse people become part of the organizational framework. We will clarify the distinctions between *hierarchical* and *egalitarian pluralism* (a table contrasting their key differences appears in the Next Steps section).

On a national level, building a diverse nation requires the transformation of our society into one in which *life, liberty, and the pursuit of happiness* are equally accessible to everyone. Multicultural principles provide a blueprint that can invigorate our democracy, enlarge our vision of what it means to be American, and ensure the full inclusion of many cultural traditions.

# Making the Commitment:
# Personal, Organizational, and Political

IN MY LAST YEAR of college, I struggled in an intellectually and culturally alien terrain. During those four years, I had never met another Latino student. The University of Florida admitted only two African Americans during my senior year. I finished college before affirmative action, before Latinos became a recognized ethnic group, and before women started forming a greater proportion of students on college campuses. For a Nicaraguan female immigrant from a low-income family to obtain a college education in the early 1960s was as rare as the glorious quetzal bird that floats in the tropical rainforests. Why was *I* given the prize of a higher education?

Latinos have an intriguing concept—*destino* (destiny)—that suggests that outside forces and a greater power guide one's life. *Destino* relates to one's purpose—the exact content or nature of one's life. One can gain a deeper understanding of one's *destino* by reflecting on family history, significant events, talents and inherent gifts or positive attributes, the circumstances of one's birth, early experiences, and so on. As one embraces one's life journey, one's *destino* becomes clearer and more encompassing.

*Destino* is in sharp contrast to the Euro-American belief in individual effort and self-determination. Latinos believe it is impossible to control chance, serendipity, fate, or unplanned events. Life, they feel, is a dance between individual efforts and the lessons, gifts, and experiences life brings. Like an acorn that must be nurtured to grow into the great oak, the seeds of one's *destino* can only flourish with care and effort. *Destino* is the existential core, the "overarching purpose" that Robert Greenleaf believed anchors servant leaders. When Stephen Covey urges leaders to examine their values and principles and develop a personal mission statement to guide their lives, he is asking them to explore their *destino*. This type of reflection provides firm footing when making tough life decisions.

When I was twenty-one and about to graduate from college, I was wading in some very turbulent waters—*what should I do with my life?* I was given many unique opportunities, for which I was deeply grateful. In keeping with *mi cultura y familia* and in the spirit of *We* cultures, I wanted to give back. During my soul searching, President Kennedy was assassinated. Kennedy was not only an inspiration to my generation; he was revered by Latinos as a charismatic and socially responsible leader who resonated with our cultural values. Recalling his earlier call to public service, I told my parents, "I'm joining the Peace Corps and going to South America."

"*Aye Dios mío!*" If going 120 miles away to college was a cultural taboo, going to the other side of the world was a category-five hurricane. What could they do? I was twenty-one and as stubborn as the mahogany that grows in the Nicaraguan jungle. Telling me over and over that I could always come home, my family watched as their petrified, yet excited, youngest daughter boarded a plane for Santiago, Chile. I was following my *destino*! I was too young to understand it then, but I had answered the call to service, to following the path of leadership, and to becoming a world citizen.

### *Destino:* A Calling and Personal Vision

IN HIS BRILLIANT EXPLORATION of mystical and mythological journeys, Joseph Campbell identifies answering the *call* or invitation as the first step in personal transformation, beckoning a person to a new level of awareness, skill, and increased freedom. It is a challenge to grow, to engage in an adventure, and to seek greater fulfillment.[1] The leaders whose voices speak to us in this book answered the call to serve their communities, to work for the advancement of humankind, and to don the mantle of leadership.

In many Indian tribes, answering one's life's calling was done through a solitary vision quest to learn, "Who am I? What is my vision and what was I born to do?" Young people spent time alone in nature pondering these questions until a special sense of direction surfaced from their inner self. One's vision is power, unique purpose, or medicine.

A *calling* in the African American community refers to one's life work and connotes a spiritual force that magnetizes a person. When one accepts one's calling, through reflection, prayer, and intuitive insight, the way unfolds. In the Black community, there is a strong connection between one's calling and the uplifting of one's people. Andrew Young recalls the leaders of the civil rights movement: "Everyone had a calling. Most were religious and spiritual leaders who understood that the gospel could be applied to political and economic situations. We were committed to confronting segregation and focused on a specific moral agenda."[2]

At his commencement speech at Connecticut College in 1998, Young counseled students to heed their personal calling. "I want you to look at the world and realize it calls you to leadership. You needn't know where you are going. You only need to take one step at a time. History will lead you down the paths of excellence and creativity."[3] Mayor Michael Hancock followed this tradition. As a teenager serving as the president of the Denver youth council he was asked about his future: "I want to go first for city council and then I really see myself as the first Black mayor of Denver." Elected in 2011 at forty-one years old, he was not Denver's first Black mayor, but one of the youngest ever elected.

 *Everyone had a calling. Most were religious and spiritual leaders who understood that the gospel could be applied to political and economic situations. We were committed to confronting segregation and focused on a specific moral agenda.*

—Andrew Young

The time in history in which one lives influences one's calling; indeed, movements and social changes can shape and define a whole generation. For example, my calling was affected by civil rights, the women's movement, and integration. We have explored the social forces sculpting the character of the Millennial Generation. To be relevant and effective, leaders must be in sync with their times and understand the long-term implications of social movements. Given the powerful influence of diversity in defining the twenty-first century, those who aspire to lead today must also answer the call to multicultural leadership.

## Making a Personal Commitment

The first step in making a decision is to establish your intention—the ideal you are committed to, the result you would like to achieve. Intention is willpower, unerring focus, and an unrelenting belief that you will achieve the desired end. When you answer the call to become a multicultural leader, you commit to honoring the unique experiences and background of each person you encounter while connecting with the core human essence we all share.

You'll need to assess your background, experiences, exposure to different cultures, and any negative images you may have about certain groups. If you are a person of color, your experience with people outside of your community may be just as limited as that of a White person who lives in the suburbs. It's a helpful barometer to understand where you fall on the *assimilation–acculturation continuum* (see Next Steps at the end of this part). Let us first look at the process of assimilation and its role in forging U.S. identity, and then explore acculturation as a pathway to multicultural leadership.

## Assimilation: The *Entrada* to the American Dream

*Assimilation* melded one people out of the myriad nationalities that came to our shores, facilitated our national cohesion and character development, and unified our young country. Eager to belong, many White immigrants cut ties to their homelands and relinquished the customs and language of their grandparents. Assimilation set the tone for a country where conformity, homogeneity, and valuing sameness were the *entrada* to the American dream. *E pluribus unum*—to make one out of many—was the crucible of the American experiment.

Cutting one's roots and losing touch with one's grandparents can be painful and leave a sense of disorientation. People who make such sacrifices often demand that others do likewise. "If I gave up my ancestry and language, why do you insist on holding on to yours? What I am gaining must be worth my sacrifice." The country and way of life people were embracing had to be superior. Assimilation fed ethnocentricity, which in turn bred cultural insensitivity and a predisposition to impose our values on others. Recognition that all cultures are unique expressions of the human experience became as rare as the languages our grandparents had spoken.

Many assimilated people believe others should fit in too. Today, the English Only movement

 *Assimilation set the tone for a country where conformity, homogeneity, and valuing sameness were the* entrada *to the American dream. E pluribus unum—to make one out of many—was the crucible of the American experiment.*

indicates that some people still see assimilation as necessary to cultural cohesion. (Contrast this with Chile, where a national initiative aims to have all people bilingual in Spanish and English by 2020.) People of color are also pushed to assimilate and fit into the dominant U.S. culture in order to succeed. In communities of color, this is called *whitewashing*. Raul Yzaguirre notes on how difficult this is for Latinos: "The road to success that has been offered is to assimilate, change your name, and lose your accent. All those things hold an empty promise that will result in a hollowing out. '*Te quita el corazon*'—it rips out your heart."

Although assimilation crafted one nation out of the potpourri that came to America, as we evolve into a multicultural nation, assimilation is no longer an adaptive advantage. But can a person shed the skin of assimilation and learn to acculturate?

## It's Never Too Late to Acculturate

**A**S IT WAS FOR other students in that era, America's ethnocentric tenor was part of my education. I joined the Peace Corps to help *those countries* south of the border, which I had learned were backward and desperately needed the help of powerful Uncle Sam. Imagine my culture shock to find that Santiago had an old European flavor, with flower-lined *avenidas*, stately museums, and ornate buildings. Chile was the second oldest democracy in our hemisphere, with educated, informed people. President Frei was Hispanic, as were the senators, the cabinet members, the mayors of all the cities, the presidents of Chilean universities, the directors of television stations, and the heads of its army, navy and every major business. Growing up in the good old USA, I had no idea that anyone of my race could achieve such high-level leadership. Successful people in my childhood were, without exception, White—which is still true for most U.S. leaders in top positions.

Although the land of opportunity had given me many gifts, I had been stripped of my cultural pride and history. The knowledge, contributions, and exquisite histories of the inhabitants before Columbus were buried like the lost city of the Incas. Thus began the redemption of my Hispanic soul. I embraced my multicultural heritage. *I am Latina and American.* I chose the path of acculturation. Latinos call acculturation *crossing over*—it means a person has learned to go back and forth between cultures and functions successfully in both.

# An Invitation to Acculturate

U NLIKE ASSIMILATION, whereby one's culture, language, and background are discarded, acculturation is an *adding on*, expanding process, which begins with listening and being open to learning. One must be willing to step out of one's cultural conditioning, actively engage in cross-cultural experiences, and learn and adapt to diverse perspectives. Acculturation increases one's cultural repertoire, creativity, adaptability, and flexibility, and promotes cross-cultural competency. When people learn to acculturate, they can thrive in different cultural environments.

You can learn to acculturate by reading or taking courses about other cultures; joining international clubs or organizations that serve communities different from one's own; hosting foreign exchange students; and championing diversity practices at work. You can also attend churches of different denominations, learn another language or key words to indicate respect, live in an integrated neighborhood, or travel to different countries. Most cities today have cultural celebrations such as Chinese New Year, Oktoberfest, Juneteenth (commemorating the end of slavery in the U.S.), and Cinco de Mayo, where you can sample the delectable food, music, dance, and customs of a variety of ethnicities and nationalities. By seeking these out, leaders learn practices and approaches that resonate with many types of people, and they develop *cultural adaptability*.

*Acculturation increases one's cultural repertoire, creativity, adaptability, and flexibility, and promotes cross-cultural competency. When people learn to acculturate, they can thrive in different cultural environments.*

Yzaguirre explains how acculturation is beneficial for Hispanics and society as a whole: "Hispanic success for both practical and quality of life reasons needs to be, 'I treasure who I am, I treasure my parents, my culture, my language, and I don't have to give up any of that in order to succeed. Indeed, if I keep all those things, it will make me more successful in pragmatic as well as self-fulfilling terms.' Latinos have a unique contribution to make to America, and we can't do that if we give up our cultural core that makes us who we are."

*Keep in mind that assimilation–acculturation is a continuum.* Since culture is learned, people can constantly upgrade their skills and understanding. The important thing is to continue being inquisitive and open-minded, to keep learning about our multicultural world. Fortunately, our expanding diversity, emerging world community, technology, and the globally oriented younger generations have replaced the historical tendency to assimilate with a growing appreciation that the path to multicultural competency and understanding is not assimilation, but acculturation.

## Connect with Diversity Partners

There are some ideal guides in the exciting adventure of acculturation: returned Peace Corps volunteers, people who have worked in other countries, our neighbors who are naturalized citizens, recent immigrants, and aficionados of languages and cultures. They can become *diversity partners* and help you boost your cultural savvy!

Working with community leaders in Richmond, Indiana, I was urging people to seek out diversity partners when the Anglo editor of the local paper stood up and approached the owner of *El Rodeo* Mexican restaurant. By doing this, they expanded their circle of friends and learned to maneuver across communities, as well as shared some very tasty meals.

It's normal to gravitate toward similar people with whom we are more comfortable. In *Why Are All the Black Kids Sitting Together in the School Lunchroom?* Beverly Daniel Tatum describes this natural inclination as the result of racial identity formation, historical segregation, and the internalization of dominant culture perceptions about race. She urges us to educate ourselves, find the courage to change, and make a concerted effort to reach out to people from different backgrounds.[4]

### Diversity Partners

Diversity partners come from different backgrounds, communities, or cultural groups. Like good ambassadors, they introduce each other to new vistas and terrains. Through their relationships and social interaction, diversity partners adapt and change to support each other.

Leadership requires taking risks and getting out of our comfort zone. Although many of us have diverse friends, social segregation is still all too common. Diversity partners can get you onto the *acculturation fast track*, so seek them out. (Additional suggestions can be found in the Next Steps section). Of course, many young people today already have friends from many backgrounds. Through intergenerational partnerships, they can model cultural inclusiveness and include different ages as well.

# Creating Multicultural Organizations

**A**NSWERING THE CALL to multicultural leadership also implies changing organizational structures. Most U.S. organizations today are fashioned around Euro-American culture and hierarchical structures. Although diverse people are included, they must assimilate, adhere to dominant cultural values, and follow prescribed behavior. This hierarchical pluralism prevents organizations from genuinely benefiting from cultural diversity.

Dr. Joseph explains the limitations of hierarchical pluralism: "Dominant cultural values are at the top and are impermeable. Everyone has to conform to them. People who are different can come in and be included, but they must understand their traditions don't mean anything. Their values are subservient and they must adapt." The underlying message of hierarchical pluralism is *We who are in control don't have to change, because our way is better!* People of color and others who are not from the dominant culture must fit in—read the script, wear the uniform, talk and think like their White counterparts. Many recognize this as window dressing and tokenism, not inclusion.

## Dismantling Hierarchical Pluralism

To "fit in," people of color must identify White cultural norms, which is difficult because the dominant culture is ubiquitous; its unspoken rules are just that—a covert code. Because Whites are often blind to their own existence as a group, as well as their advantages and privileges, they don't understand that *business as usual* is really *doing business our way.* In their creative book on diversity in the workplace, *Leading in Black and White*, Ancella Livers and Lewis Clark coined an interesting term, *miasma*, to describe how elusive White culture is for Black managers. *Miasma* is defined as a diaphanous fog—a state of unease, difficult to grasp, but ever-present—a confusing murky environment of misperception and distortion in which Black managers work.

This use of *miasma* is based on the assumption that everyone is the same and includes a low tolerance for differences. Livers and Clark further observe, "Blacks often feel that Whites are sizing up their professional potential and suitability by how closely they fit or emulate White middle-class norms." Since miasma is elusive, but real, the actual reason Black managers don't fit in or succeed is never recognized or addressed. Livers and Clark believe this has created a racial divide in corporate America, whereby Black managers become isolated and assume a defensive stance.[5]

People of color who do succeed often stifle their cultural identity, leading to additional segmentation in communities of color, as their best and brightest become distant from their communities. Ultimately, organizations dissipate the vitality and assets of the increasingly multicultural workforce and miss out on the talents, unique perspectives, knowledge, creativity, innovation, and energy that diversity offers. At the very least, those stymied by hierarchical pluralism tend to "check out" and are less participatory and motivated.

Until organizations change, minority professionals can learn the ropes from people like Keith R. Wyche, president of U.S. operations for Pitney Bowes Management Services.

 *Ultimately, organizations dissipate the vitality and assets of the increasingly multicultural workforce and miss out on the talents, unique perspectives, knowledge, creativity, innovation, and energy that diversity offers.*

In his book *Good Is Not Enough,* Wyche suggests seeking a high-level mentor to teach the unwritten rules of the game, being *overly prepared and twice as good,* constantly learning and improving, never giving up regardless of obstacles, and remembering that the people who will help you don't always look like you do.[6]

As more people master these abilities and move up in organizations, they will reach a critical mass that transforms organizations into *egalitarian pluralism,* which opens the door to the values and perspectives of many cultures.

## Egalitarian Pluralism

Egalitarian pluralism is representative of all people in an organization, not just those who have traditionally held power. Organizations must be willing to reinvent themselves by altering their language, structure, and methods of operations and by welcoming diverse leaders to the table to share their perspectives and experiences. This requires deep listening and open dialogue. *Changing structures, norms, and values is the key to egalitarian pluralism and the foundation for multicultural leadership.*

Operating from an egalitarian framework takes organizations into new territory. This is the challenging and exciting work facing multicultural leaders. It begins with discussing and integrating practices such as the leader as equal, collective and shared responsibility, and generosity and reciprocity. (A comparison of *egalitarian* and *hierarchical pluralism* is included in the Next Steps section.)

The values and principles of multicultural leadership we've talked about can guide organizations in transforming leadership to truly reflect diversity at all levels, especially the higher echelons. These principles also offer people of color, who have *mainstreamed* into dominant-culture organizations, alternative ways of leading and tools they can use to create inclusive work environments. These principles validate their abilities as multicultural people and strategically position them for leadership.

## Political Engagement: Fulfilling the Promise of Pluralism

THE LEADERSHIP PRINCIPLES in communities of color grew out of historical exclusion; the need for political influence called for concerted community organizing: voter registration campaigns, mass demonstrations, community education, legal battles, and political rallies. In a democratic society, groups who have been historically excluded have a great equalizer—*the vote!*

Martin Luther King Jr. reminded people that the most important walk they would ever take was the short walk to the ballot box.[7] The power of the vote can ensure that our elected representatives mirror our diverse nation and follow the principles of community stewardship.

However, we have a long way to go. In 2011 only 17 percent of congressional representatives were Black, Latino, American Indian, and Asian American Pacific Islanders.[8] Women are only 16 percent of Congress.[9] Moreover, even though the 2010 Census revealed that almost 30 percent of the population was a racial or ethnic minority, *96 percent of senators are White.*[10] And most are quite wealthy. Ordinary citizens with average incomes rarely win elections. Representative government has been hijacked by special interest groups funding hefty campaign chests.

*The leadership principles in communities of color grew out of historical exclusion; the need for political influence called for concerted community organizing: voter registration campaigns, mass demonstrations, community education, legal battles, and political rallies.*

According to The Center for Responsive Politics the 2008 election confirmed one truism about American democracy. "Money wins elections." The cost for a U.S. House of Representatives campaign rose to an average of $1 million; for Senate races it was a staggering $5.6 million. Even more disconcerting, in nine out of ten congressional races, the candidate that spent the most money won![11] The Obama presidential campaign's $750 million shattered all fundraising records. He did rely on smaller donors nearly as much as larger donors, pulling successive donations mostly over the Internet.[12] *Still he spent the most dough of any candidate in history. Many people lament the United States has the best government that money can buy!*

There is a stark disparity between the means of ordinary Americans and their elected officials. In 2009, 44 percent of congressional representatives were millionaires, while fewer than 1 percent of Americans are that wealthy. And congressional members keep getting richer; their personal wealth increased more than 16 percent between 2008 and 2009.[13] The halls of Congress are also filled with lawyers: 34 percent of representatives and 52 percent of senators.[14] Not that lawyers and millionaires cannot be exemplary public servants and guardians of the public good. However, the mandate of our democracy is government *of, by and, for the people*. Rising poverty rates, lack of health care coverage, high employment, and low wages are only a few indicators suggesting that today's congressional leaders are not actively constructing a society that takes care of its people—the essence of leadership in communities of color.

*Sankofa* advises us to remember the lessons of the past. Making good on the promise of justice and equality has required the long-term involvement of a critical mass of people who demanded social responsibility and social reform. The right to vote was won only through centuries of organizing, massive demonstrations, and at the cost of many lives. Leadership principles in communities of color offer a blueprint for the regeneration of American democracy, but *there are no shortcuts*. Active citizenship will always be the lifeblood of a healthy democracy. Ensuring that elected officials reflect our growing diversity is perhaps the most critical challenge of our democracy today.

Understanding this urgency, leaders in communities of color organized a political revival for the 2008 presidential campaign. By following community stewardship principles that encourage participation and shared leadership and by integrating technology to expand their reach, initiatives such as Voto Latino, Native Vote, Operation Black Vote and the National Black Churches Initiative, and Asian and Pacific Islander's American

Vote pushed for voter turnout.[15] And it worked! *Five million additional voters went to the polls.* African American, Hispanic, and Asian participation each increased by 4 percent.[16] A motivating factor was the identification with Barack Obama's candidacy that reflected America's diversity, promoted change, and represented a new generation.

Young voters (ages eighteen to twenty-nine) increased their voting by a phenomenal 11

 *Active citizenship will always be the lifeblood of a healthy democracy. Ensuring that elected officials reflect our growing diversity is perhaps the most critical challenge of our democracy today.*

percent over their 2000 vote. "Rock the Vote" brought over twenty-two million young people under thirty to the ballot box. "That," says Tanene Allison, a self-proclaimed new media and social justice activist, "is a testament to our engagement in changing democracy." Allison, a Millennial blogger for *HuffPost Politics*, is convinced that a tidal wave of young activists will broaden the scope of civil rights, give it a twenty-first-century makeover, and take the movement digital.[17]

It is my hope that this book will inspire people from an array of cultural backgrounds to join communities of color, the millennial generation, and people of goodwill everywhere in fulfilling the promise of democracy and in creating our multicultural future.

## *Sankofa*—Shaping Our Global Future

WE ARE LIVING IN a fluid moment in history. Great cultural and generational shifts are redefining our global landscape. A colorful multicultural bazaar where many cultures intersect and many generations interact is replacing the Euro-American dominance that shaped the past five centuries. The emergence of a global culture containing the jewels of many traditions is the defining characteristic of the twenty-first century. The principles in this book invite us to incorporate new ways of leading more effectively in this increasingly diverse world:

- *Sankofa* integrates the past as we create a more inspiring future.

- *I* to *We* embraces a collective sense of community.

- *Mi casa es su casa* invites generosity and advises "never take more than your share."

- *A leader among equals* reminds us to treat every person with respect.

- *Leaders as guardians of public values* urges activism and social responsibility.

- *Leaders as community stewards* beckons us to work for the common good.

- *The seventh-generation rule* protects the young and cultivates a sustainable future.

- *All my relatives* encompasses the oneness of humanity, the *familia*, village, and tribe.

- Gracias—*gratitude, hope, and forgiveness*—inspires the spiritual qualities that nourish us.

Multicultural leadership principles reflect humanistic values that promote justice and equality and integrate *spiritual responsibility* and *social accountability*. The strife and poverty in our world would not exist if leaders followed these values and became the sculptors of an equitable and caring world. Multicultural leadership also implies global stewardship and the sustainability of future generations. This honors the diversity *and* universality of the one human family and fulfills the promise of the seventh-generation rule.

Like the radiant and multicolored flowers in a garden or the prolific rainforest, diversity represents life's vigor, variety, and unending beauty. To craft our global future, this must be our vision. Multicultural leaders must anchor our future in our most noble aspirations. This shared and inspiring vision will foster a sense of our collective human destiny— one that transcends cultural differences and builds an intergenerational circle. Like an American Indian prayer arrow, this vision will lodge goodwill in people's hearts, bringing creative power and energy, courage and hope. Based on the understanding that *we are all relatives*, this vision of our multicultural future embraces our universal humanity.

As we embark on the good work of creating this future, we are confident that one day the children of the seventh generation will look back at our time in history and say that we fulfilled the Hopi prophesies. We became the universal tribe—the rainbow warriors who reflected the iridescent beauty of humankind, restored the earth, brought peace and understanding, and healed the damage caused by previous generations. Today, we rejoice in the words of the Hopi elders:

> All that we do now must be done in a sacred
> manner and in celebration. We are the ones we
> have been waiting for.
>
> —The Hopi Elders, Oraibi, Arizona.[18]

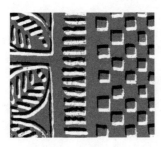

## NEXT STEPS

**Reflecting On
and Applying
Part Four**

# Leadership in a Multicultural World

## Assimilation and acculturation

Assimilation in America has long ushered people into a monocultural way of life, but it is not an adaptive advantage in our multicultural age. Fortunately, people can learn to *cross over*—to acculturate, developing cross-cultural competencies.

Where would you rate yourself on this continuum?

| Associations center on White culture ◄●► | Many diverse cultural associations |
|---|---|

ASSIMILATION_____ACCULTURATION

        −5   −4   −3   −2   −1   0   +1   +2   +3   +4   +5

| Minimal experience with other cultures ◄●► | Seeks out diverse cultural experiences |
|---|---|

ASSIMILATION_____ACCULTURATION

        −5   −4   −3   −2   −1   0   +1   +2   +3   +4   +5

| Desire to fit in, conform ◄●► | Has learned how to "fit in" |
|---|---|

ASSIMILATION_____ACCULTURATION

        −5   −4   −3   −2   −1   0   +1   +2   +3   +4   +5

| Belief that the White way is superior | ◄ ● ► | Cultural flexibility—many ways |
|---|---|---|

ASSIMILATION _____ ACCULTURATION

−5  −4  −3  −2  −1  0  +1  +2  +3  +4  +5

| English only | ◄ ● ► | Supports language and cultural exposure |
|---|---|---|

ASSIMILATION _____ ACCULTURATION

−5  −4  −3  −2  −1  0  +1  +2  +3  +4  +5

This part of the book described a variety of cross-cultural experiences that could increase your ability to acculturate—to add more *Salsa, Soul, and Spirit* to your life. Having considered your own assimilation or acculturation experience, which of these resonate with you? Discuss them with others; brainstorm further possibilities and how to make them happen.

## Addressing hierarchical pluralism

Review the table on the next page, *Two Organizational Paradigms*.

Do you have experience with any organizations that embody hierarchical pluralism? How did the status quo block inclusive leadership and discouraged or impede the potential contributions of people of color?

Select one or two areas from the table and use them to analyze the organization. Come up with two or three concrete actions that could help this organization encourage acculturation to bring it closer to egalitarian pluralism. How might this benefit the organization?

## Identifying and cultivating diversity partners

Diversity partners offer a one-on-one way to form relationships with folks who are very different from us. The following steps promote deeper intercultural relationships and can be used by individuals or in classes, conferences, and organizations:

**Step One**: Set your intention: "I am a person who reaches out and wants to expand my cultural relationships." Then seek out opportunities. The next class, church, community, or social event you attend, sit by a person who is "different" and start up a conversation. (Note: If you are a teacher or are facilitating a meeting, ask people to do this right now.)

**TWO ORGANIZATIONAL PARADIGMS**

## Hierarchical Pluralism

- History is seen from the dominant cultural perspective—and believed to be "the truth" or "reality."

- Everyone must conform to dominant cultural values and perspectives. There is only one worldview. Ethnocentric.

- Diverse people must conform to dominant-culture behavior, dress, norms, thinking, and communication patterns. Homogenous and homogenized.

- Operating rules, structures, and systems are in alignment with dominant-culture values and orientation. Business as usual.

- Intelligence is measured by reading comprehension, critical thinking, and problem-solving—I.Q. standardization. Rational.

- Primary learning is through information, reading and the scientific method, and the use of experts. Analysis.

- Tokenism—one can speak for the many.

- Traditional thinking is sequential and linear. Action- and task-oriented thinking.

- The long-term end is to retain and expand power and to control resources and people.

- Few at the top, generally White males. Privilege, advantage, and entitlement. Inner circle. Clubby.

- Collaboration as a decision-making and team-building tool. Competition-based.

- Scope: pervasive, institutionalized, covert discrimination, normative, dominance unrecognized.

- Cultural patriarchy and dominance.

## Egalitarian Pluralism

- History and tradition reflect the experiences and backgrounds of diverse cultures that make up the whole.

- The values, perspectives, and worldviews of all subgroups are respected and integrated. Multicultural.

- Diversity is infused at all levels of the culture, organization, and society—"differences add value." Heterogeneous.

- Operating rules, structures, and systems are dynamic, flexible, and responsive to people's needs.

- Intelligence and ability are assessed by a variety of measures (emotional, kinetic, and spiritual). Emotional, spiritual, and cultural I.Q.

- Different styles of learning and processing information are validated: "We can all learn from one another."

- *Bienvenidos,* inclusiveness is a cherished trait—welcome to the table.

- Multidimensional thinking—there are many paths to the same goal or ends.

- The long-term end is to include equitable representation at all levels of the organization and society.

- Many share power and responsibility. Competency, education, and hard work are the avenues to success. Empowerment.

- Collaboration as a tool for advancing authentic representation: all voices are heard.

- Scope: interactive, fluid, change-oriented, synergistic, adaptive, encouraging diverse approaches.

- Multicultural: circular, shared leadership.

 (NEXT STEPS PART 4 CONTINUED)

**Step Two**: Practice a short introduction to put the other person at ease. Share why you are attending this event or taking this class. Talk about what you do, an interest you have, or the situation you are participating in.

**Step Three**: Ask each other's names and what they mean; describe the communities where you were raised and what you like about them; share your favorite holidays and cultural traditions.

**Step Four:** Discuss how you could learn more about each other's community, lifestyles, traditions, and so on. Agree to be diversity partners.

**Step Five:** Make a plan for cultivating more diversity partners. Commit to meeting two "diverse" people at each event you attend. Join a group, club, or organization that is different from your usual circle.

## Revitalizing our democracy

Pluralism holds the promise of authentic democracy, yet our democracy is faltering. Our government seems to be sold to the highest bidder, and civic engagement needs to be rekindled.

- What have you learned about multicultural leadership as reflected in communities of color that can revitalize democracy?

- Review the voting initiatives launched by communities of color in the 2008 presidential initiative. Discuss how these reflect leadership principles in communities of color. How has technology furthered the reach of the civil rights movement (e.g., YouTube, social networking, text messaging to promote voting)?

- Discuss strategies on building partnerships and diverse alliances to create the critical mass needed to change our society so it reflects the democratic values on which it was founded.

## Recommended readings and resources

### Books

- *Good Is Not Enough: And Other Unwritten Rules for Minority Professionals* by Keith R. Wyche with Sonia Alleyne, (Portfolio: The Penguin Group, 2008).

- *Leading in Black and White: Working Across the Racial Divide in Corporate America* by Ancella B. Livers and Keith A. Carver (Jossey-Bass, 2003).

- *Translation Nation: Defining a New American Identity in the Spanish-Speaking United States* by Hector Tobar (Riverhead Books, 2005).

- *Why Are All the Black Kids Sitting Together in the School Cafeteria? A Psychologist Explains the Development of Racial Identity* by Beverly Daniel Tatum (Basic Books, 1999).

### *Film*

- *A Class Apart: A Mexican American Civil Rights Story* (PBS: —American Experience, 2009).

  The film depicts the history of an underdog band of Mexican American lawyers who argued Hernandez v. Texas in front of the Supreme Court. Before this case was won, Texans claimed there could be no discrimination against Hispanics because Mexican Americans were classified as Caucasian. The story is a good understanding of Mexican American identity and why assimilation has not been the chosen course.

### Video

- "United We Win" (Voto Latino), http://www.youtube.com/watch?v=McdaptPy5uw

- "Black Voting Rights" (Kern County League of Women Voters), http://www.youtube.com/watch?v=PzSwZzEYPzo.

# Notes

### Preface

1. Armas, Genardo C. "America's Face Is changing," *CBS News*, February 11, 2009. from http://www.cbsnews.com/stories/2004/03/17/national/main607022.shtml.www.cbsnews.com/stories/2004/02/17/national/main607022.shtml (accessed October 20, 2010).

2. Gayanashagowa, The Constitution of the Iroquois Nations, compiled by Glenn Welker, prepared by Gerald Murphy (Cleveland: National Public Telecomputing Network, 1996), http://www.indigenouspeople.net/iroqcon.htm (accessed July 27, 2011).

3. Ira S. Wolfe, *Geeks, Geezers, and Googlization: How to Manage the Unprecedented Convergence of the Wired, the Tired, and Technology in the Workplace* (Lancaster: Ira S Wolf and Poised for the Future Company, 2009).

4. Eric Greenberg and Karl Weber: *Generation We: How Millennial Youth Are Taking Over America and Changing the World* (Mustang: Pachatusan, 2008).

5. Pew Research Center, "Millennials: A Portrait of Generation Next—The Millennials: Confident, Connected, Open to Change," Pew Research Center, released February 24, 2010, http://pewresearch.org/millennials.

6. Barack H. Obama, *Dreams from My Father: A Story of Race and Inheritance* (New York: Three Rivers Press, 2004), 457.

### Introduction

1. U.S. Census Bureau, "State & Country Quick Facts," last modified June 3, 2011, http://quickfacts.census.gov/qfd/states/00000.html.

2. Article 1, Section 2, Clause 3 of the U.S. Constitution.

3. Jeffrey M. Humphreys, "The Multicultural Economy 2005: Minority Buying Power in the New Century" (Athens: Simn S. Selig, Jr. Center for Economic Growth, University of Georgia, 2005).

4. Louis E.V. Nevaer, *Managing Hispanic and Latino Employees: A Guide to Hiring, Training, Motivating, Supervising, and Supporting the Fastest Growing Workforce Group* (San Francisco: Berrett-Koehler, 2010), 1–4.

5. Algernon Austin and Marie T. Mora, "Hispanics and the Economy: Economic Stagnation for Hispanic American Workers, Throughout the 2000s" (Washington, DC: Economic Policy Institute, 2008), http://www.epi.org/publications/entry/bp225 (accessed July 20, 2011).

6. Frances Hesselbein, "Managing in a World that is Round," *Leader to Leader Journal No.2,* Fall 1996. New York: Leader to Leader Institute, http://www.pfdf.org/knowledgecenter/journal.aspx?ArticleID=136

7. Carlos Fuentes, "The Reconquest of Spain," chap. 3 in *The Buried Mirror: Reflections on Spain and the New World* (New York: Houghton Mifflin, 1992). For an in-depth understanding of the history of Spain see this book.

8. Ronald Segal, *The Black Diaspora* (New York: Farrar, Straus & Giroux, 1995).

9. "World Factbook: Brazil," Central Intelligence Agency, https://www.cia.gov/library/publications/the-world-factbook/geos/br.html (accessed July 20, 2011).

10. "World Factbook: Mexico," Central Intelligence Agency, http://www.theodora.com/wfbcurrent/mexico/mexico_people.html (accessed July 20, 2011).

11. Donna Lee Van Cott, "Latin America's Indigenous Peoples," *Journal of Democracy,* 18 no. 4 (October 2007): 127.

12. David Madland and Ruy Teixeira, *Progressive America: Millennial Generation* (Washington: Center for American Progress, 2009), http://www.americanprogress.org/issues/2009/05/pdf/millennial_generation.pdf (accessed July 20, 2011).

13. Kristina J. Bartsch, "The Employment Projections for 2008–18," *Monthly Labor Review* (November 2009), http://www.bls.gov/opub/mlr/2009/11/ (accessed July 20, 2011).

14. Unless otherwise noted, all quotations from leaders in communities of color who were special contributors for this book come from personal interviews conducted with them, which were transcribed verbatim and then coded for common themes and patterns.

15. Thomas L. Friedman, *The World Is Flat: A Brief History of the Twenty-First Century* (New York: Farrar, Straus and Giroux, 2005), 11.

16. "Most Widely Spoken Languages in the World," Nations Online, last modified May 27, 2011, http://www.nationsonline.org/oneworld/most_spoken_languages.htm.

Determining the world's second most commonly spoken language is complicated. There is agreement that Mandarin Chinese is first. English, Spanish, and Hindi vie for second, depending on whether the designation includes only native speakers. The United States, for instance, has the second highest number of Spanish speakers in the world, many of whom are not native speakers.

17. U.S. Census Bureau News. Facts for Features: Hispanic Heritage Month 2010: CN 10-FF 17. July 15, 2010. http://www.census.gov/newsroom/releases/archives/facts_for_features_special_editions/cb10-ff17.html (accessed November 14, 2011).

18. Mark Hugo Lopez and Gabriel Velasco, "A Demographic Portrait of Puerto Ricans," Pew Hispanic Center, June 13, 2011, http://pewhispanic.org/reports/report.php?ReportID=143.

19. Article 1, Section 2, Clause 3 of the U.S. Constitution, http://law2.umkc.edu/faculty/projects/ftrials/conlaw/thirteenthamendment.html.

20. W. E. B. Du Bois, *The Souls of Black Folk* (New York: Modern Library Edition, 2003). The original work was penned in 1903.

21. Coretta Scott King, *The Words of Martin Luther King, Jr.* (New York: Newmarket Press, 1983), 21.

22. Dhyani Ywahoo, *Voices of Our Ancestors* (Boston: Shambala, 1987), 111, 225. Ywahoo is a Cherokee teacher from the Etowah Band of the Eastern Tsalagi.

23. Paula Gunn Allen, *The Sacred Hoop: Recovering the Feminine in American Indian Traditions* (Boston: Beacon Press, 1986), 60–61.

24. Burt Nanus, "What Is Vision—And Why It Matters," chap. 1, in *Visionary Leadership* (San Francisco: Jossey-Bass, 1992).

25. *Sankofa* is an Akan word that means "one must return to the past in order to move forward." A film entitled *Sankofa* was made by Haile Gerima in 1993 (Mypheduh Films, Inc., P.O. Box 10035, Washington, DC 20018). For additional information, see http://www.duboislc.net/SankofaMeaning.html.

26. Greenberg and Weber, *Generation We*.

**Part One: A New Social Covenant**

1. Lance Secretan, *One: The Art and Practice of Conscious Leadership* (Caledon, Ontario: The Secretan Center, 2006), 14.

2. King, *The Words of Martin Luther King, Jr.*, 25.

**Principle 1: *Sankofa*—Learn from the Past**

1. "Lift Ev'ry Voice and Sing," (NAACP, Louisville, KY Branch), http://www.lounaacp.org/lifthistory.html (accessed December 12, 2011). In 1919, the NAACP adopted this song as "The Negro National Anthem."

2. "Dropout Rates in the United States: 2000," National Center for Educational Statistics, Institute of Education Sciences, http://nces.ed.gov/pubs2002/droppub_2001 (accessed August 26, 2006).

3. "Hispanics Gaining Jobs but Suffering Worse Wage Losses in U.S. Labor Force," Pew Hispanic Center, http://www. pewtrusts.org/news_room_detail.aspx?id=23184 (accessed December 15, 2011).

4. Robert Stillwell, "Public School Graduates and Dropouts from the Common Core of Data: School Year 2007–08," National Center for Education Statistics, Institute of Education Sciences, 2010, http://nces.ed.gov/pubs2010/2010341.pdf (accessed December 15, 2011).

5. A groundbreaking study on the Americas before colonization is Charles C. Mann's *1491: New Revelations of the Americas before Columbus* (New York: Knopf, 2005). Mann documents that given the death rate of Indians who died from European diseases, the estimates of the pre-Columbian population range from twelve and a half to twenty-five million (see p. 100).

6. Adam Smith, *An Inquiry into the Nature and Causes of the Wealth of Nations*, 5th ed., ed. Edwin Cannon (London: Methuen and Co., 1904), first published 1776.

7. Thomas Hobbes, *Leviathan, or the Matter, Forme, & Power of a Common-Wealth, Ecclesiasticall and Civil*, ed. J.C.A. Gaskin (London: Andrew Crooke, 1651; Oxford, UK: Oxford Press, 1988).

8. Max Weber, The *Protestant Ethic and the Spirit of Capitalism* (New York: Scribner, 1958).

9. Myron P. Gutmann, *Toward the Modern Economy: Early Industry in Europe 1500–1800* (New York: Knopf, 1988).

10. Mann, in *1491: New Revelations of the Americas before Columbus*, states "Cortez believed the military conquest of the [Aztec] Alliance had to be accomplished and justified by an equivalent spiritual conquest. 'The Indians must be led to salvation'" (p. 31).

11. Barry Lopez, *The Rediscovery of North America* (New York: First Vintage Books Edition, 1992).

12. As noted in Carlos Fuentes, *The Buried Mirror*.

13. Alexis de Tocqueville, *De la démocratie en Amerique*. This book was published in two volumes, the first in 1835, the second in 1840. English-language version is *Democracy in America*, trans. and ed. Harvey C. Mansfield (Chicago: University of Chicago Press, 1985).

14. Robert Bellah with Richard Madsen, William M. Sullivan, Ann Swidler, and Steven M. Tipton, *Habits of the Heart: Individualism and Commitment in American Life*, updated ed., with new introduction, "The House Divided" (Berkeley, CA: University of California Press, 1996).

15. Robert Putnam, *Bowling Alone*: The Collapse and Revival of American Community (New York: Simon & Schuster, 2000).

16. Scott Allen, "Web of Friendships Unravel, Study Says," *Boston Globe*, June 23, 2006, http://www.boston.com/news/nation/articles/2006/06/23/its_lonely_out_there/ (accessed December 15, 2011).

17. "Gross National Income Per Capita 2010, Atlas Method and PPP," World Bank, last modified July 1, 2011, http://siteresources.worldbank.org/DATASTATISTICS/Resources/GNIPC.pdf (accessed July 27, 2011).

18. Anna Bleker, "How Does America's Credit Card Debt Stack Up?" last modified May 18, 2009, http://www.creditcards.com/credit-card-news/credit-card-debt-stacking-up-1264.php (accessed July 27, 2011).

19. Courtney E. Martin, "Time Off for the Overworked American: Our National Work Ethic Should Make Us Consider Passing Legislation to Ensure We're All Taking Enough Vacation," *The American Prospect,* May 18, 2007, http://prospect.org/cs/articles?article=time_off_for_the_overworked_american (accessed July 27, 2011).

20. Craig Kielburger and Marc Kielburger, *From Me to We: Turning Self-Help on Its Head* (Canada: Wiley, 2004), 34.

21. New Economics Foundation, "The Happy Planet Index 2.0," http://www.happyplanetindex.org/public-data/files/happy-planet-index-2-0.pdf (accessed July 27, 2011).

22. Kielburger and Kielburger, *From Me to We,* citing "Affluenza," a PBS program on overconsumption, first broadcast in 1997 by PBS and produced by John de Graaf.

23. Annie Leonard, *The Story of Stuff: How Our Obsession with Stuff Is Trashing the Planet, Our Communities, and Our Health—And a Vision for Change* (New York: Free Press, 2010).

24. M. Scott Peck, *The Different Drum: Community Making and Peace* (New York: Simon & Schuster, 1988).

25. De Tocqueville, *Democracy in America.*

## Principle 2: I to We—
## From Individualism to Collective Identity

1. Norma Carr-Ruffino, *Managing Diversity: People Skills for a Multicultural Workplace* (Andover, UK: International Thomson Publishing, 1996).

2. Michael Boon, *The African Way: The Power of Interactive Leadership* (Cape Town, South Africa: Zebra Press, 1996), 18.

3. Kate Prendergast, "Updating Our Origins; Biology, Genetics and Evolution: An Interview with Steve Jones," *Science and Spirit* 10, no. 5 (2000): 24.

4. Christina Baldwin, *Calling the Circle* (Newberg, OR: Swan Raven, 1994).

5. Riane Eisler, *The Chalice and the Blade* (San Francisco: Harper and Row, 1987).

6. "Modern Forms of *Homo sapiens* First Appear about 195,000 Years Ago," http://www.talkorigins.org/faqs/homs/species.html (accessed December 1, 2006).

7. "Mastering the Change Curve," HRDQ, Training Tools for Developing Great People Skills, http://www.hrdqstore.com (accessed December 15, 2011)

8. For information on the American Indian Ambassadors program, see Americans for Indian Opportunity, http://www.aio.org/ (accessed December 15, 2011).

9. James A. Joseph, *Remaking America: How the Benevolent Traditions of Many Cultures Are Transforming Our National Life* (San Francisco: Jossey-Bass, 1995), 74.

10. Ibid.

11. Barbara Walters, "The 10 Most Fascinating People of 2005," *ABC News Special*, November 29, 2005.

12. For Albert Einstein quotes, see http://www.heartquotes.net/Einstein.html (accessed July 31, 2011).

## Principle 3: Mi Casa Es Su Casa—
## A Spirit of Generosity

1. Boon, *The African Way*, 32 and 33.

2. Joseph, *Remaking America*, 27.

3. Ibid., 76.

4. Ancella B. Livers and Keith A. Carver, *Leading in Black and White: Working Across the Racial Divide in Corporate America* (San Francisco: Jossey-Bass, 2003).

5. Northern Trust Wealth, "Wealth in Black America," Winter Issue, January 2011. http://www.northerntrust.com/wealth/11-winter/wealth-in-black-america.html. (accessed November 4, 2011).

6. Lauren Gard, "African American Giving Comes of Age," Special Report—Philanthropy 2004, *Business Week,* November 29, 2004, http://www.businessweek.com/magazine/content/04_48/b3910417.htm (accessed August 26, 2006).

7. Joseph, *Remaking America,* 73.

8. Nelson Mandela, *Long Walk to Freedom: The Autobiography of Nelson Mandela* (London: Little, Brown and Company, 1994).

9. The Shelby Report, "Hispanic Buying Power," July 1, 2011, found that Latinos spent a greater percent of their income on dining out than non-Hispanic consumers. http://www.theshelbyreport.com/2011/07/01/hispanic-buying-power/ (accessed December 15, 2011)

10. César Chávez, "Farm Workers Prayer," César Chávez Foundation, www.chavezfoundation.org (accessed July 15, 2011).

11. The theory of survival of the fittest, often mistakenly attributed to Darwin, is in fact the work of economist Herbert Spencer who based his work on Darwin's theory of natural selection. See Jonathan H. Turner, Leonard Beeghley, and Charles H. Powers, *The Emergence of Sociological Theory*, 5th ed. (Belmont, CA: Wadsworth Thomson Learning, 2002), 43–55.

12. David Loye, *Darwin's Lost Theory of Love: A Healthy Vision for the New Century* (San Jose, CA: toExcel/iUniverse, 2000).

13. Marc Ian Barasch, *Field Notes on the Compassionate Life* (New York: Rodale Press, 2005).

14. Annalyn Censky, "Poverty rises in America," CNN Money: September 13, 2011. http://money.cnn.com/2011/09/13/news/economy/poverty_rate_income/index.htm

15. Friedman, Howard Steven, "5 Countries with the highest poverty rate (OECD)," Huff Post World. June 15, 2011. http://www.huffingtonpost.com/howard-steven-friedman/5-oecd-countries-with-the_b_877368.html#s290783&title=4_Highest_Poverty (accessed November 14, 2011).

16. What the 2010 Census tells us about poverty in the U.S. Current Population Reports: August 13, 2011. http://www.census.gov/prod/2011pubs/p60-239.pdf (accessed November 14, 2011).

17. Jared Bernstein and Isaac Shapiro, "Nine Years of Neglect: Federal Minimum Wage Remains Unchanged for Ninth Straight Year, Falls to Lowest Level in More than Half a Century," Center on Budget and Policy Priorities, August 31, 2006, http://www.cbpp.org/cms/index.cfm?fa=view&id=635 (accessed July 27, 2011).

18. Jennifer Liberto, "CEOs earn 343 times more than typical workers," CNN Money, April 20, 2011, http://money.cnn.com/2011/04/19/news/economy/ceo_pay/index.htm (accessed July 27, 2011).

19. Institute for Policy Studies: Executive Excess 2011: The massive CEO rewards for tax dodging. http://www.ips-dc.org/reports/executive_excess_2011_the_massive_ceo_rewards_for_tax_dodging (accessed November 14, 2011).

20. Ibid.

21. Mark Whitehouse, "Number of the Week: Class of 2011, Most Indebted Ever," Wall Street Journal, May, 7, 2011, http://blogs.wsj.com/economics/2011/05/07/number-of-the-week-class-of-2011-most-indebted-ever/ (accessed July 27, 2011).

22. Richard Wolf, "Number of uninsured Americans rises to 50.7 million," USA Today, last modified September 17, 2010, http://www.usatoday.com/news/nation/2010-09-17-uninsured17_ST_N.htm (accessed July 27, 2011).

23. Christie, Les, "Foreclosures up a record of 81% in 2008," CNN Money: January 15, 2009. http://money.cnn.com/2009/01/15/real_estate/millions_in_foreclosure/index.htm (accessed November 14, 2010).

24. J. M. Burns, Leadership (New York: Harper Torch Books, 1978).

## Part Two: Leadership Styles in Communities of Color

1. Ronald W. Walters and Robert C. Smith, African American Leadership (New York: State University of New York Press, 1999), 216.

2. Peter Block, Stewardship: Choosing Service over Self-interest (San Francisco: Berrett-Koehler, 1993).

3. Walters and Smith, African American Leadership, 107.

4. For a more comprehensive description of the collaborative leadership process, see Hickman, Robinson, Bordas, et al., "Leadership in the 21st Century" in Leading Organizations: Perspectives for a New Era (Thousand Oaks, CA: Sage, 1998), 572–580.

5. Paulo Friere, The Pedagogy of the Oppressed, trans. Myra Bergman Ramos, special anniversary edition (New York: Continuum, 2000).

6. Peggy McIntosh, White Privilege and Male Privilege: A Personal Account of Coming to See Correspondences through Work in Women's Studies (Wellesley, MA: Wellesley College, 1988).

7. R. K. Greenleaf, The Servant as Leader (Newton Center, MA: The Robert Greenleaf Center, 1970).

## Principle 4: A Leader Among Equals— Community-Conferred Leadership

1. Norma Carr-Ruffino, Managing Diversity, 232.

2. See Océano Dicconario Inglés: Español (Barcelona: Oceano Grupo Editorial, S.A., 2002). The Jemez Pueblo use the term cacique for their traditional governing body, a group that represents the various clans and religious leaders. This usage is an artifact of the Spanish conquest dating back to 1540 and is indicative of the blending of indigenous and Spanish cultures. In Spanish cacique means chief or can also connote a political boss.

3. National Community for Latino Leadership, Inc. (NCLL), Reflecting an American Vista: The Character and Impact of Latino Leadership 1, no. 1, January 2001. NCLL is a national organization founded in 1989 whose mission is to develop ethical, responsible, and accountable leaders on behalf of the U.S. Latino population. See http://www.latino-leadership.org/.

4. As cited in Joseph, Remaking America, 209.

5. Lea Williams, Servants of the People: The 1960s Legacy of African American Leadership (New York: St. Martin's Press, 1998), 28.

6. Antonia Pantoja, Memoir of a Visionary (Houston, TX: Arte Público Press, 2002), 61.

7. Pantoja, National Hispana Leadership Institute (presentation, Washington, DC, September 1989).

8. Walters and Smith, *African American Leadership*, 117.

9. Pantoja, *Memoir of a Visionary*, 84.

**Principle 5: Leaders as Guardians of Public Values—A Tradition of Activism**

1. Pantoja, National Hispana Leadership Institute

2. Williams, *Servants of the People*, 46.

3. For additional information and references to race, ethnicity, and culture, see Vincent Sarich and Frank Miele, *Race: The Reality of Human Differences* (Boulder, CO: Westview Press, 2004), and I. Hannaford, *Race: The History of an Idea in the West* (Baltimore: Johns Hopkins University Press, 1996).

4. Paulo Freire, *The Pedagogy of the Oppressed*, trans. Myra Bergman Ramos, special anniversary edition (New York: Continuum, 2000).

5. McIntosh, *White Privilege and Male Privilege: A Personal Account of Coming to See Correspondences through Work in Women's Studies*.

6. Ibid.

7. Andrew Young, *An Easy Burden: The Civil Rights Movement and the Transformation of America* (New York: HarperCollins, 1996), 252.

8. Andrew Young, "Pilgrimage of Jesse Jackson," interview on *Frontline*, July 21, 1995, http://www.pbs.org/wgbh/pages/frontline/jesse/interviews/young.html (accessed May 10, 2006).

9. Federico Peña, "We Are America" march speech, Denver, Colorado, May 1, 2006), shared during personal interview and not posted for public access.

10. Martin Luther King Jr., "Letter from a Birmingham Jail," April 16, 1963, http://www.africa.upenn.edu/Articles_Gen/Letter_Birmingham.html.

11. Martin Luther King Jr., http://www.brainyquote.com/quotes/authors/m/martin_luther_king_jr.html (accessed December 7, 2006).

**Principle 6: Leaders as Community Stewards—Working for the Common Goal**

1. Peter Block, *Community: The Structure of Belonging* (San Francisco: Berrett-Koehler, 2008).

2. Greenleaf, *The Servant as Leader*, 7.

3. Antonia Pantoja, interview by Lillian Jimenez (Latino Educational Media Center, New York, January 18, 2002).

4. National Community for Latino Leadership, *Reflecting an American Vista*.

5. Pantoja, *Memoir of a Visionary*, 84.

6. John White, *Black Leadership in America* (New York: Longman, 1994), 191.

7. Williams, *Servants of the People*.

8. Ibid., 17.

9. Thom S. Rainer and Jess W. Rainer, *The Millennials: Connecting to America's Largest Generation* (Nashville, TN: B & H Publishing Group), 61.

10. Mandela, *Long Walk to Freedom*, 24–25.

11. National Community for Latino Leadership, *Reflecting an American Vista*.

12. James M. Kouzes and Barry Z. Posner, *The Leadership Challenge*, rev. ed. (San Francisco: Jossey-Bass, 2003).

14. Carr-Ruffino, *Managing Diversity*, 332.

16. Pantoja, quoted in "Puerto Rico Profile: Dr. Antonia Pantoja," *Puerto Rico Herald*, November 17, 2000.

15. Walters and Smith, *African American Leadership*, 123.

16. Ibid., 211.

**Part Three: Creating the Circle of Leadership**

1. Gayanashagowa, The Constitution of the Iroquois Nations.

2. Ira S. Wolfe, *Geeks, Geezers, and Googlization* (Lancaster, Penn: Ira S. Wolfe and Poised for the Future Company, 2009).

3. "In 2011 the Baby Boomers Start to Turn 65: 16 Statistics About the Coming Retirement Crisis That Will Drop Your Jaw." End of the American Dream, http://endoftheamericandream.com/archives/in-2011-the-baby-boomers-start-to-turn-65-16-statistics-about-the-coming-retirement-crisis-that-will-drop-your-jaw (accessed August 2, 2011).

4. Report of the United Nations World Commission on the Environment and Development, December 11, 1987, http://www.un.org/documents/ga/res/42/ares42-187.htm (accessed July 27, 2011).

5. See "Child Poverty Rates by Country," NationMaster.com, http://www.nationmaster.com/graph/eco_chi_pov-economy-child-poverty (accessed August 2, 2011).

**Principle 7: The Seventh-Generation Rule: Intergenerational Leadership**

1. Walters and Smith, *African American Leadership,* 17.

2. Andrew Young, *Frontline* interview, July 1995.

3. Organization of American Historians, "The Children's Crusade and the Role of Youth in the African American Freedom Struggle," Oxford Journals. *OAH Magazine of History* 19, no. 1 (2005): 31–36, http://maghis.oxfordjournals.org/content/19/1/31.full

4. From a speech delivered by John Gardner to Leadership USA (November 18, 1995, Pomona, California), listed in Direct Quotes: Contemporary Consultants (1966; a printed workbook available from Mary Jo Clark and Pat Heiny, P.O. Box 52, Richmond, Indiana 47375).

5. Hilary Doe and Zachary Kolodin, eds., "Blueprint for Millennial America," (The Roosevelt Institute Campus Network, 2010), http://www.rooseveltcampusnetwork.org/chapter/1875/blueprint-millennial-america.

6. Peter Leyden, Ruy Teixeira, in partnership with Eric Greenberg, "The Progressive Politics of the Millennial Generation," New Politics Institute

7. Sam Roberts "Births to Minorities Are Approaching Majority in U.S.," *New York Times,* March 11, 2010, www.nytimes.com/2010/03/12/us/12census.html, (accessed October 20, 2010).

8. Rainer and Rainer, 61.

9. Greenberg Eric and Karl Weber: *Generation We: How Millennial Youth are Taking on America and Changing Our World Forever,* 23

10. Rainer and Rainer, 81.

11. Greenberg and Weber, 12.

12. For more information on Young People We Care, see http://www.ypwc.org/home/what-is-ypwc.html.

13. Young Ambassadors for Opportunity is a network of globally minded young professionals dedicated to providing economic opportunities for people living in chronic poverty. For more information, see http://www.opportunity.org/young-ambassadors-for-opportunity.

14. Fred Rogers Center, Mission Statement, http://www.fredrogerscenter.org/mission/about-fred-rogers/legacy-of-fred-rogers (accessed August 1, 2010).

15. Lynne Heffley, "Barney Is Far from Extinct," *Los Angeles Times,* March 23, 2008, http://articles.latimes.com/2008/mar/28/entertainment/et-barney28.

16. Arrieta, Rolando, "Me llamo Dora: An Explorer in Modern America," NPR: April 14. 2008. http://www.npr.org/templates/story/story.php?storyId=89531478

17. Pew Research Center, "Millennials: A Portrait of Generation Next."

18. Ibid.

19. "A Decade of Dissent: Student Protests at the University of Michigan in the 1960s" (Bentley History Library, University of Michigan, http://bentley.umich.edu/exhibits/dissent/teachins.php (accessed December 15, 2011).

20. Joseph Kahne, Nam-Jin Lee, and Jessica Timpany Feezell, "The Civic and Political Significance of Online Participatory Cultures among Youth Transitioning to Adulthood," DML Central Working Papers, Youth & Participatory Politics, February 5, 2011, http://ypp.dmlcentral.net/sites/all/files/publications/OnlineParticipatoryCultures.WORKINGPAPERS.pdf.

21. Ibid.

22. Leyden, Teixeira, and Eric Greenberg.

23. See Greenberg and Weber, *Generation We.*

24. For information on student loan debt, see Scott Cohn, "The Debt That Won't Go Away," CNBC, December 20, 2010 http://www.cnbc.com/id/4068090527.

25. Rainer and Rainer, 7.

26. Doe and Kolodin, eds., "Blueprint for Millennial America."

27. YouTube Video: "Generation We: The Movement Begins," http://www.youtube.com/watch?v=vknHKTy1MLY (December 15, 2011).

28. Leyden, Teixeira, and Greenberg. For information on Young Elected Officials Network, see www.yeonetwork.org (accessed December 15, 2011)

29. Young Nonprofit Professional Network: promotes an efficient, viable, and inclusive nonprofit sector that supports the growth, learning, and development of young professionals. http://ynpn.org/

30. Rainer and Rainer, 36–37.

31. Scott Beale, *Millennial Manifesto*, (Self-published, 2003), 9. (available on Amazon.com).

32. Cooperative Institutional Research Program, Freshman Survey, December 2005 http://www.heri.ucla.edu/pdfs/06cirpfs_norms_narrative.pdf.

33. Catherine Rampell, "More College Graduates Take Public Sector Jobs, *New York Times,* March 1, 2011, http://www.nytimes.com/2011/03/02/business/02graduates.html (article uses data from the American Community Survey of the United States Census Bureau).

34. The Young Nonprofit Professionals Network promotes an efficient, viable, and inclusive nonprofit sector that supports the growth, learning, and development of young professionals: http://ynpn.org.

35. Rainer and Rainer, 7.

36. Wendy Koch, "Millennials Say Environmental Cleanup Is Left to Them," *USA Today: Greenhouse,* last modified September 23, 2010, http://content.usatoday .com/communities/greenhouse/post/2010/09/millenials-see -environment-their-responsibility/1.

37. Doe and Kolodin, eds., "Blueprint for Millennial America."

38. For more information on the Road to Rio+20, see http://www.roadtorioplus20.org/take-action.

39. The Rainbow Tribe is based on a Hopi Cree prophecy about people of all cultures coming together to restore the earth through action and deed. They will be known as the Warriors of the Rainbow. See the Manataka American Indian Council, a nonprofit society promoting American Indian history and culture, http://www.manataka.org/page235.html (accessed August 2, 2011).

40. See the Access Foundation, American Indian Institute, Traditional Circle of Indian Elders and Youth, February 2011, http://access.foundationsource.com/nonprofit/american-indian-institute.

41. Great Quotes: Sitting Bull. http://www.great-quotes.com/quotes/author/Sitting/Bull (accessed November 14, 2011).

**Principle 8: All My Relatives—
*La Familia,* the Village, the Tribe**

1. Young, *An Easy Burden*, 14.

2. Boon, *The African Way*, 74.

3. "DNA Shows Humans Are All One Race," *New York Times*, August 22, 2000. Updated information supports the 2000 studies: DNA studies indicate that all modern humans share a common female ancestor who lived in Africa about 140,000 years ago, and all men share a common male ancestor who lived in Africa about 60,000 years ago. "Genetic Anthropology, Ancestry, and Ancient Human Migration," Human Genome Project Information. http://www.ornl.gov/sci/techresources/Human_Genome/elsi/humanmigration.shtml (accessed December 15, 2011).

4. M. J. Wheatley, *Leadership and the New Science* (San Francisco: Berrett-Koehler, 1993).

5. Williams, *Servants of the People*, 185–186.

6. Pantoja interview, January 2002.

7. Joseph, *Remaking of America*, 73.

8. Boon, *The African Way,* 31–32.

9. Joseph, *Remaking of America*, 79.

10. Dr. F. James Davis, *Who Is Black? One Nation's Definition* (University Park, PA: Penn State Press, 2001).

11. Andrew Young, *A Way Out of No Way* (Nashville, TN: Nelson, 1994), 131.

12. Ibid.

13. "César E. Chávez: Middle School Biography," California Department of Education, http://chavez.cde.ca.gov/ModelCurriculum/Teachers/Lessons/Resources/Biographies/Middle_Level_Biography.aspx (accessed December 4, 2006).

14. Annalyn Censky, "Poverty rises in America," CNN Money: September 13, 2011. http://money.cnn.com/2011/09/13/news/economy/poverty_rate_income/index.htm.

15. Jason DeParle, "Hunger in the U.S, at a 14-Year High," *New York Times*, November 16, 2009, www.nytimes.com/2009/11/17/us/17hunger.html.

16. "How Many People Experience Homelessness?" National Coalition for the Homeless, Factsheet, July 2009, http://www.nationalhomeless.org/factsheets/.

17. John F. Kennedy, Brainy Quote, http://www.brainyquote.com/quotes/authors/j/john_f_kennedy.html (accessed October 17, 2006).

18. Young, *An Easy Burden*, 163.

19. Williams, *Servants of the People*, 144.

**Principle 9: Gracias—Gratitude, Hope, and Forgiveness**

1. Jesse Jackson, "1988 Democratic National Convention Address," (speech, Atlanta Georgia, July 19, 1988).

2. Block, *Stewardship: Choosing Service over Self-interest.*

3. Stephen Covey, *The Seven Habits of Highly Effective People* (New York: Simon & Schuster, 1989).

4. Young, *A Way Out of No Way*, 31.

5. Jacques E. Levy, *Cesar Chavez: Autobiography of La Causa* (Minneapolis: First University of Minnesota Press edition, 2007), 27.

6. Walters and Smith, *African American Leadership*, 77.

7. Cesar E. Chavez Foundation, "Education of the Heart—Quotes by Cesar Chavez," United Farm Workers, http://www.ufw.org/_page.php?menu=research&inc=history/09.html (accessed July 27, 2011).

8. Young, *An Easy Burden*, 15, 23.

9. Federico Peña, "We Are America," (speech, Denver Colorado, May 1, 2006).

10. Barack Obama, "On Religion: Politicians Need Not Abandon Religion," *USA Today*, July 10, 2006.

11. Young, *A Way Out of No Way*, 83.

12. Ibid., 299.

13. Boon, *The African Way*, 35–38.

14. Ywahoo, *Voices of Our Ancestors*, 133

15. Daniel Goleman, *Emotional Intelligence: Why It Can Matter More than IQ* (New York: Bantam Books, 1995).

16. *New York Times/CBS News* poll based on telephone interviews conducted July 13 to 27, 2003, with 3,092 adults throughout the United States, www.nytimes.com/packages/html/politics/20030806_poll/20030806poll-results.html (accessed July 27, 2011).

17. Michael A. Fletcher and Jon Cohen, "Economy Poll: African Americans, Hispanics Were Hit Hardest but Are Most Optimistic," *Washington Post,* February 20, 2011, http://www.washingtonpost.com/wp-dyn/content/article/2011/02/19/AR2011021904126.html (accessed July 27, 2011).

18. Shenandoah, chief of Onondaga Nation and Tadodaho ("Firekeeper") of the Haudenosaunee, address to the General Assembly of the United Nations, October 25, 1985, http://nativenewsonline.org/history/hist0722.html (accessed July 27, 2011). The Tadodaho can be described as president, spiritual elder, and principal chief of the Grand Council, the eldest democracy in North America. For a historical perspective, see http://www.ratical.org/many_worlds/6Nations/EoL/chp2.html (accessed July 27, 2011).

19. Octavio Paz, *The Labyrinth of Solitude*, 2d ed. (New York: Penguin USA, 1977). First published in Spanish in 1950, *The Labyrinth of Solitude* is considered one of the most enduring and powerful works ever created about Mexico and its people, character, and culture. Paz won the Nobel Prize for literature in 1990.

20. According to the Catholic Church, Our Lady of Guadalupe is the Patroness of the Western Hemisphere. Her influence as a cultural icon, if not as a religious figure, is evident in the myriad images and writing about her in many other countries. To understand her apparition at the time of the conquest, read Jeannette Rodriguez, *Our Lady of Guadalupe: Faith and Empowerment Among Mexican-American Women* (Austin, TX: University of Texas Press, 1994).

21. Ywahoo, *Voices of our Ancestors*, 41.

**Part Four: Leadership for a Multicultural Age—Making the commitment personal, organizational, and political**

1. Joseph Campbell, *The Hero's Journey: Joseph Campbell on His Life and Work*, 3rd (centennial) ed., ed. and introduction Phil Cousineau, producer/foreword author Stuart Brown (Novato, CA: New World Library, 2003).

2. Young, *Frontline* interview, July 1995.

3. Andrew Young, Commencement Speech at Connecticut College, 1998, last modified May 12, 2003, http://www.conncoll.edu/events/speeches/young.html (accessed July 27, 2011).

4. Beverly Daniel Tatum, *Why Are All the Black Kids Sitting Together in the School Cafeteria? A Psychologist Explains the Development of Racial Identity* (New York: Basic Books, 1999).

5. Livers and Caver, *Leading in Black and White.*

6. Keith R. Wyche with Sonia Alleyne, *Good Is Not Enough: And Other Unwritten Rules for Minority Professionals* (Portfolio: The Penguin Group, 2008).

7. Martin Luther King Jr., "Our God Is Marching On," (speech, Montgomery, Alabama, March 25, 1965), http://www.mlkonline.net/ourgod.html.

8. Jennifer E. Manning, "Membership of the 112th Congress: A Profile," CRS Report for Congress (2011): 6–7, http://www.fas.org/sgp/crs/misc/R41647.pdf (accessed July 27, 2011).

9. "Facts on Women in Congress 2011," Center for American Women and Politics, Rutgers University, http://www.cawp.rutgers.edu/fast_facts/levels_of_office/Congress-CurrentFacts.php (accessed December 15, 2011).

10. Manning, "Membership of the 112th Congress," 6.

11. "Money Wins 9 Out of 10 Congressional Races: Priciest U.S. Election Ever," Open Secrets: Center for Responsive Politics, November 5, 2008, http://www.opensecrets.org/news/2008/11/money-wins-white-house-and.html (accessed July 27, 2011).

12. "Barack Obama 2008 Fundraising Totals" Open Secrets: Center for Responsive Politics, http://www.opensecrets.org/pres08/summary.php?id=n00009638.

13. "Congressional Members' Personal Wealth Expands Despite Sour National Economy," Open Secrets: Center for Responsive Politics, November 17, 2010, http://www.opensecrets.org/news/2010/11/congressional-members-personal-weal.html (accessed July 27, 2011).

14. Caroline May, "The More Things Change: Few Demographic Distinctions Will Change in the 112th Congress," *The Daily Caller,* November 6, 2010, http://dailycaller.com/2010/11/06/the-more-things-change-few-demographic-distinctions-in-112th-congress/ (accessed July 27, 2011).

15. For more information on voting initiatives in communities of color, see Voto Latino: It's Your Country, Represent! http://www.votolatino.org/; Operation Black Vote: http://operationblackvote.wordpress.com/; Native Vote: Every Vote Counts! http://www.nativevote.org/; and Asian and Pacific Islanders American Vote: http://www.apiavote.org/.

16. U.S. Census Bureau, "Voter Turnout Increases by 5 Million in 2008 Presidential Election, U.S. Census Bureau Reports: Data Show Significant Increases Among Hispanic, Black and Young Voters," July 20, 2009, http://www.census.gov/newsroom/releases/archives/voting/cb09-110.html (accessed July 27, 2011).

17. Tanene Allison, "Online and Off, Millennials Redefine Civil Rights Activism," *HuffPost Politics*, July 15, 2008, http://www.huffingtonpost.com/tanene-allison/online-and-off-millennial_b_112873.html (accessed July 27, 2011).

18. "Statement from the Hopi Elders, Oraibi, Arizona, Hopi Nation" The Boggs Blog, released May 28, 2009, http://boggsblog.org/2009/05/28/statement-from-the-elders-oraibi-arizona-hopi-nation/; see also "Hopi Elders' Prophecy, released March 2002, also at http://www.matrixmasters.com/takecharge/hopi-prophecy.html.

# Index

# About the Author

Juana Bordas learned leadership from her hardworking immigrant parents, especially her mother, Maria, who cooked food and scrubbed floors in the school lunchroom so that Juana could get a scholarship to a Catholic school. "Their vision for the future, determination, and sacrifice taught me the very essence of Servant Leadership."

The first in her family to go to college, she joined the Peace Corps and worked in the barrios of Santiago, Chile. Juana later received the U.S. Peace Corps' Franklin Williams Award for her lifelong commitment to advancing communities of color.

A former faculty member at the Center for Creative Leadership, Juana taught in the Leadership Development Program—the most highly utilized executive program in the world. She served as advisor to Harvard's Hispanic Journal on Public Policy, the Kellogg National Fellows Program, and the board of the Greenleaf Center for Servant Leadership. She is trustee of the International Leadership Association and received an honorary doctorate from Union Institute and University.

Juana was a founder and executive director of Denver's Mi Casa Women's Center, recognized today as a national empowerment model. She was founding president of the National Hispana Leadership Institute, the only program in America that prepares Latinas for national leadership. In 2001, she launched the Circle of Latina Leadership "to prepare the next generation of Latina leaders." For her extensive work with Latinas, she was commended by Latina Style Magazine for creating "a nation of Latina leaders."

Juana received Denver's 2008 Martin Luther King Jr. Award for Social Responsibility and the Wise Woman Award from the National Center for Women's Policy Studies. She is in the Colorado Women's Hall of Fame, and in 2009 the Denver Post and the Colorado Women's Foundation named her the Colorado Unique Woman of the Year. Today, Juana is President of Mestiza Leadership International (MLI), a company that focuses on leadership, diversity, and organizational change. MLI'S mission is to prepare collaborative and inclusive leaders for our multicultural and global age. She received an honorary doctorate from Union Insitute—a university noted for their commitment to social change, justice, and diversity.

To learn more and to exchange ideas with Juana, see the following online resources:

- www.JuanaBordas.com
- Friend me on Facebook: http://www.facebook.com/JuanaBordas
- Follow me on Twitter: http://twitter.com/#!/JuanaBordas

232

## Berrett–Koehler
Publishers

**Berrett-Koehler** is an independent publisher dedicated to an ambitious mission: *Creating a World That Works for All*.

We believe that to truly create a better world, action is needed at all levels—individual, organizational, and societal. At the individual level, our publications help people align their lives with their values and with their aspirations for a better world. At the organizational level, our publications promote progressive leadership and management practices, socially responsible approaches to business, and humane and effective organizations. At the societal level, our publications advance social and economic justice, shared prosperity, sustainability, and new solutions to national and global issues.

A major theme of our publications is "Opening Up New Space." Berrett-Koehler titles challenge conventional thinking, introduce new ideas, and foster positive change. Their common quest is changing the underlying beliefs, mindsets, institutions, and structures that keep generating the same cycles of problems, no matter who our leaders are or what improvement programs we adopt.

We strive to practice what we preach—to operate our publishing company in line with the ideas in our books. At the core of our approach is stewardship, which we define as a deep sense of responsibility to administer the company for the benefit of all of our "stakeholder" groups: authors, customers, employees, investors, service providers, and the communities and environment around us.

We are grateful to the thousands of readers, authors, and other friends of the company who consider themselves to be part of the "BK Community." We hope that you, too, will join us in our mission.

### A BK Currents Book

This book is part of our BK Currents series. BK Currents books advance social and economic justice by exploring the critical intersections between business and society. Offering a unique combination of thoughtful analysis and progressive alternatives, BK Currents books promote positive change at the national and global levels. To find out more, visit **www.bkconnection.com**.

# Berrett–Koehler
# Publishers

A community dedicated to creating
a world that works for all

**Visit Our Website:** www.bkconnection.com

Read book excerpts, see author videos and Internet movies, read our authors' blogs, join discussion groups, download book apps, find out about the BK Affiliate Network, browse subject-area libraries of books, get special discounts, and more!

**Subscribe to Our Free E-Newsletter, the *BK Communiqué***

Be the first to hear about new publications, special discount offers, exclusive articles, news about bestsellers, and more! Get on the list for our free e-newsletter by going to **www.bkconnection.com**.

**Get Quantity Discounts**

Berrett-Koehler books are available at quantity discounts for orders of ten or more copies. Please call us toll-free at (800) 929-2929 or email us at **bkp.orders@aidcvt.com**.

**Join the BK Community**

**BKcommunity.com** is a virtual meeting place where people from around the world can engage with kindred spirits to create a world that works for all. **BKcommunity.com** members may create their own profiles, blog, start and participate in forums and discussion groups, post photos and videos, answer surveys, announce and register for upcoming events, and chat with others online in real time. Please join the conversation!